OIL AND WATER

OIL AND WATER

Media Lessons from Hurricane Katrina and the Deepwater Horizon Disaster

Andrea Miller, Shearon Roberts, and Victoria LaPoe

University Press of Mississippi / Jackson

www.upress.state.ms.us

The University Press of Mississippi is a member
of the Association of American University Presses.

First printing 2014

∞

Library of Congress Cataloging-in-Publication Data

Miller, Andrea, 1967–
Oil and water : media lessons from Hurricane Katrina and the Deepwater
Horizon disaster / Andrea Miller, Shearon Roberts, and Victoria LaPoe.
pages cm
Includes bibliographical references and index.
ISBN 978-1-61703-972-0 (hardback) — ISBN 978-1-61703-973-7 (ebook)
1. Disasters—Press coverage—United States. 2. Hurricane Katrina,
2005—Press coverage. 3. BP Deepwater Horizon Explosion and Oil
Spill, 2010—Press coverage. 4. Mass media—Objectivity—United
States. I. Roberts, Shearon, 1984– II. LaPoe, Victoria, 1977– III. Title.
PN4784.D57M55 2014
070.4'4936334—dc23   2013039750

British Library Cataloging-in-Publication Data available

CONTENTS

Acknowledgments   vii

Hurricane Katrina Timeline   ix

Deepwater Horizon Oil Disaster Timeline   xiii

Introduction   3

1. Seeking Information in Disaster   15

2. Journalists Live Their Disaster Stories   36

3. National versus Local Disaster News   65

4. Who Runs This Disaster? The Media and the Blame Game   82

5. Sources and Accuracy in Disaster   100

6. Visuals of Disaster   125

Conclusion   145

Appendix 1. Studying the News of Two Disasters: A Timeline   157

Appendix 2. Annotated Bibliography of Studies Contributing to This Book   159

Appendix 3. Additional Disaster-Related Research by the Authors   163

Notes   165

Index   185

ACKNOWLEDGMENTS

This has been a labor of love born out of two tragedies, seven years in the making, and a true team effort. As professionals turned academics, we truly understand the different parts of the stakeholder equation—the social scientist, the audience member, the news creator. We study disaster with an eye on making journalism better and we hope this book is a contribution to that effort.

We would like to thank our professional contacts for their invaluable contributions, including Lynn Cunningham of the New Orleans *Times-Picayune*, Monica Pierre of Entercom, and Chris Slaughter of WWL-TV for providing access to their outlets, journalists, and archives. To the journalists who wanted to remain anonymous, we recognize your efforts as well. We would also like to thank the hard-working scientists of the Gulf Coast who gave us their time during the oil disaster and, a year later, our editor, Craig Gill, and the "HIPIP" crew: Renee Edwards, David Brown, Stephanie Houston Grey, Michael Rold, and Chris Mapp.

Funding for the HIPIP projects came from a grant from the Mississippi-Alabama Sea Grant Consortium Coastal Storms Program. Funding for some travel came from W. Lawrence and Susan K. Patrick through a Broadcast Education Association Scholarship.

We would also like to thank our families, including Grace and Zachary Miller, Zachary Ramjattan, and Bernadette Roberts. Finally, deep appreciation to our wonderful spouses, Doug Miller, Nicholas Ramjattan, and Ben LaPoe (who was also our fabulous copy editor), for their support, sacrifice, and encouragement.

HURRICANE KATRINA TIMELINE

8/24/2005   Tropical Storm Katrina Forms
Warning Issued for Florida

8/25/2005   Katrina Hits Florida (Category 1)

8/26/2005   Katrina Makes Way to Gulf of Mexico

8/27/2005   New Orleans Voluntary Evacuation Order
Weather Service Predicts High Possibility Katrina Will
    Directly Hit New Orleans

8/28/2005   Mandatory Evacuation Order Given as Katrina Strengthens
    to Category 5

8/29/2005   Katrina Makes Landfall at 6:10 a.m./Ninth Ward Levee
    Breached
FEMA Sends 1,000 Employees at 11:00 a.m./Given Two
    Days to Reach New Orleans

8/30/2005   Second Levee Is Breached/80 Percent of New Orleans Under
    Water

8/31/2005   At 12:30 p.m., Water Levels Stop Rising
Superdome—25,000 People/Red Cross Shelters—
    52,000
Blanco Asks for More National Guard/Estimated 50,000–
    100,000 People on Rooftops

9/1/2005   National Guard—30,000; Media Reports Mass Looting and
    Violence
Superdome—45,000; on *Paula Zahn Now*, at 8:00 p.m.,
    FEMA Director Michael Brown Says He Had Just Been

Informed About the Severity of Katrina and Evacuees at Superdome

Bush Says Levee Breach Was Entirely Unanticipated

9/2/2005   Bush Says "Brownie" Is "Doing a Heck of a Job"

9/3/2005   National Media Report that Scientists Had Warned of Levee Breach Many Times

9/4/2005   Danziger Bridge Shootings; *Times-Picayune* Open Letter to Bush

Officials Said Two Officers Committed Suicide

9/5/2005   Officials Tell Remaining People in New Orleans to Evacuate; Bush Makes Second Visit

9/6/2005   Bush Announces Plans to Investigate Hurricane Relief Failures

Nagin Orders Police to Move Everyone Not Involved in Recovery Efforts

9/7/2005   CDC and EPA Tell People Not to Have Contact with Contaminated Flood Water

34 Bodies Found in Nursing Home

9/8/2005   Congress Approves $51.8 Billion Spending Bill for Relief Effort

Warning of Fraud Websites Claiming to Help Katrina Victims

9/9/2005   100 Louisiana National Guard Return from Iraq to Help

Thad Allen Becomes Relief Leader in Gulf; FEMA Director Michael Brown Returns to DC

9/10/2005 FEMA Abandons Plan of Not Letting Media in to Report on Storm Victims' Recovery

9/11/2005 NOPD Says Will Not Forcibly Remove Citizens

Bush's Third Visit to Gulf

9/12/2005   FEMA Director Michael Brown Resigns

9/13/2005   Nursing Home Charged with Negligent Homicide
               Nagin Says Will Reopen Parts of City, Including French
                    Quarter
               Nagin Announces a Phased Repopulation Plan

9/14/2005   NOAA Says Katrina Most Destructive Hurricane in History

9/17/2005   Nagin Tells Businesses to Come Back to French Quarter;
                    Allen Says Use Extreme Caution

9/19/2005   Hurricane Rita Strengthens; Mayor Nagin Rescinds Encour-
                    agement to Return

9/24/2005   Hurricane Rita Breaches Levees; Ninth Ward Flooded Even
                    More

9/27/2005   NOPD Chief Eddie Compass Announces Resignation
               Michael Brown Blames Slow Response on State and Local
                    Officials
               Nagin Welcomes Algiers Residents; Curfew from 6:00 p.m.
                    to 8 a.m.

10/1/2005   Official Death Toll: 1,135

10/4/2005   Reported 1.5 Million Evacuated from Louisiana During
                    Disaster; 1 Million Applied for Federal Aid
               Official Death Toll Changed to 1,836; 2,500 Still Missing

10/9/2005   Ninth Ward No Longer Under Water

DEEPWATER HORIZON
OIL DISASTER TIMELINE

4/20/2010   7:00 a.m. BP Officials Celebrate Seven Years without Injury on Rig
9:45 p.m. Rig Explodes—Kills 11 and Injures 17

4/21/2010   Coast Guard Arrives
Oil Leak Estimates at 8,000 Barrels a Day
100,000 US Barrels of Dispersants Approved by EPA for Use

4/24/2010   BP Reports 1,000 Barrels Leaking a Day

4/25/2010   Oil Covers 580 Square Miles

4/26/2010   Oil Spotted 36 Miles Southeast of Louisiana/Booms Set Up

4/27/2010   Slick Grows to 100 Miles Across and 20 Miles from Louisiana Coast

4/28/2010   NOAA Estimates Leak at 5,000 Barrels a Day

4/29/2010   BP Announces Control Test to Burn Off Oil

4/29/2010   Jindal Declares a State of Emergency
100,000 Feet of Boom Set Up
300,000 Feet Extra Boom Prepared for Use

4/30/2010   Oil Found on Shore in Venice, Louisiana
Obama Stops New Offshore Drilling

5/2/2010   Obama Meets with Fishers and Coast Guard in Venice
First Relief Well Drilling Begins

5/5/2010   BP Announces Smallest of Three Leaks Capped

5/7/2010   Dome Placed Over Largest Leak
                  Pipes Oil to Storage Vessel

5/9/2010   Tar Balls Reported on Alabama's Dauphin Island

5/10/2010   Containment Dome Fails
                  BP Tries "Junk Shot" Strategy

5/12/2010   BP Releases First Public Video of Leak

5/13/2010   BP's Tony Hayward Calls Leak Tiny

5/14/2010   BP Riser Attempt Fails When Underwater Camera Bumps It

5/15/2010   Coast Guard and EPA Authorize Underwater Dispersants

5/16/2010   Second Relief Well Drilled

5/19/2010   Oil Contacts Louisiana Coastline

5/21/2010   BP Begins Live Underwater Video Feeds
                  New Estimates Are 84,000 Barrels Per Day

5/22/2010   Obama Establishes Bipartisan Committee to Investigate
                  Offshore Drilling

5/23/2010   BP Rebuffs EPA to Change Dispersants
                  Says Oil Onshore More Harmful Than Dispersants

5/27/2010   Obama Announces 6-Month Moratorium on New
                  Deepwater Drilling Permits

5/29/2010   BP Says Top Kill Fails and Moves to Cap Containment

5/30/2010   BP's Hayward Says He'd Like His Life Back

5/31/2010   Hayward Says No Evidence of Oil Underwater
                  Oiled Pelican Image First Appears

6/1/2010   Oil Washes onto Gulf Islands National Seashore

6/4/2010   Tar Balls Found at Pensacola, Florida

6/6/2010   BP Abandons Plan to Cap Three Remaining Vents

6/15/2010   Obama Meets with BP

6/16/2010   BP Agrees to Fund a $20 Billion Account

6/17/2010   Hayward Addresses US House Energy Subcommittee on
                    Oversight and Investigations
                BP Announces Hayward No Longer Involved with Deep-
                    water Horizon
                Officials Warn Public Not to Swim East of Alabama Line

6/25/2010   Hurricane Alex Causes Relief Rigs to Disconnect

7/15/2010   Leak Stopped

8/4/2010   BP Says Well in "Static Condition"

1/6/2011   White House Commission Investigating Oil Spill Concludes
                    the Spill Was a BP "Systematic Management Failure"

OIL AND WATER

INTRODUCTION

I think you can compare to Katrina in the sense that people who live here are
smacked in the face again. It is disastrous. There is a lot of uncertainty. It is a
national disaster. It is not going away. This region has taken it on the chin again.
—Sheldon Fox, local television reporter[1]

Residents along the Gulf Coast know that to speak of their cities, neighborhoods, and landmarks, they have to clarify, "Are we talking pre-Katrina
or post-Katrina?" Even newcomers are stigmatized as belonging to a post-
Katrina reality, devoid of the context and deep-rooted traditions of the
people of this region. To date, Katrina remains the most expensive hurricane the United States has ever seen and one of the deadliest.[2] In less than
five years, the region was to add to the superlatives, suffering the greatest
environmental and maritime accident of all time—the Deepwater Horizon
oil disaster. The headlines here have screamed "Oil and Water," and for a
region whose livelihood and way of life are these two natural elements,
for the Gulf Coast this blessing, in recent times, has been its curse. From
elementary school science lab we know that oil and water do not mix. The
former settles on top of the latter, clumping in pockets, trapping any water
from seeping through. The Deepwater Horizon oil disaster placed a seal on
the region's problems that the Katrina floodwaters exacerbated five years
earlier: poverty, crime, unemployment, inadequate public schools, and the
worse health indicators in the nation. Yet, despite the overarching downers,
this region, known for its southern hospitality, colorful politicians, outdoor
lifestyle, and diversity of people has begun a push back against the stigma
that it is down on its luck indefinitely. Springtime British Petroleum (BP)
ads beckon viewers across the nation to come spend their summer in the
French Quarter, on the beaches of Pensacola or Gulf Shores, or at a Mississippi casino. The region's folks are finding new ways to use new media
formats to let the nation and the world know, for better or worse, that the
Gulf Coast is open for business.

In the future, climatologists, environmentalists, and historians will
have their say on the scope of these two disasters, but this is a book about

journalism. The work of journalists unavoidably ends up at the core of the works of others who later dissect major events for fiction or scholarly endeavors. In this book, however, we aspire to go behind the scenes and capture the world of these two crises from the point of view of the tenets of journalism, and the experiences of the journalists who were thrust into these disasters, both as professionals and victims. The journalism of Katrina and the BP oil spill is crucial to the account of these disasters because of the pervasive role it played in saving lives. The stories also helped preserve the solidarity in a region as diverse as the Gulf states, but one connected by the waters that define it. To understand the events and journalism of these two crises, one must first appreciate the characteristics of the region.

For many around the globe, their first exposure to the region was the news coverage of Hurricane Katrina. One of the authors of this book is from Trinidad. Years later, she continues to hesitantly agree when countrymen say: "Oh, you live in the place that flooded." But the Gulf region is not a homogenous area. Comprising border cities on the Texas side, like Galveston to the extreme west, and then north Florida cities like Pensacola to the extreme east, the area has traditionally conservative politics. Southwest Louisiana stands out along the Interstate 10 stretch as an anomaly, with French-speaking Acadiana cities and the infamous and historic New Orleans. The city has been the epicenter of not only culture but controversy because it tends to swallow up most narratives of the diversity of the region and the state of Louisiana. To outsiders, Louisiana is a victim of its own vices. A documented pattern of colorful and corrupt (and/or racist) politicians in Louisiana had voters once, with heads spinning, trying to decide whether to vote for the "crook or the Klan" in the 1991 gubernatorial elections between former KKK Grand Wizard David Duke and corrupt Governor Edwin Edwards.

Just as the history of the region can no longer be told without Hurricane Katrina or the oil spill, Louisiana's history is hopelessly intertwined with the flamboyant and ruthless Huey P. Long. His election as governor in 1928 began a decades-long hold on the structure of Louisiana politics that remains today. Long commanded gubernatorial powers in Louisiana, much like the nation's presidents in recent times have been critiqued for expanding federal executive power. "From the days of Huey Long to the present, the Louisiana Legislature has, in many ways, been an extension of the governor," explains Bob Mann, political historian who has worked with several Louisiana politicians. Thanks to Long's precedence, Louisiana's governor still selects who heads up both chambers, and members are reluctant to act until the governor sets the agenda. "More than eighty years later," Mann points out, "there is still no independent legislative body in this state."[3]

The body of work by some of the governors is unsavory. Richard Leche and Edwin Edwards both went to prison. "And Long, while not convicted of a crime, exerted ruthless and near-dictatorial powers over Louisiana government," said Mann. "Recent governors like Foster, Blanco, and Jindal have done quite a bit to mitigate that image, but I'm afraid the taint on our political system still exists."

Current popular culture has taken the rich history of the region and highlighted only problematic stereotypes. Guns, critters, and gators—that's the current popular perception of Louisiana with the rise of five very popular television cable reality series. *Sons of Guns* documents a family gun business in Baton Rouge; *Swamp People* takes us gator hunting, often with subtitles, due to thick Cajun accents; and *Billy the Exterminator* does little to quash the stereotype, but much to squash bugs and other southern Louisiana pests. *Pawn Stars* has added an adjective, making it *Cajun Pawn Stars*. And the latest to enter the crowded landscape of Louisiana reality shows is *Duck Dynasty*, about a family who got their millions making duck hunting calls.

But these cliché depictions of Louisiana are not new. For the past eighty-five years, filmmakers have taken advantage of the state's unique social and physical environment to emphasize hedonism, mystery, ugliness, and romance. "If the viewing public was to believe each film's depiction of Louisiana, her culture, and her people, the state would be the repository of mental illness," said Assistant Professor Danny Shipka, who studies pop culture stereotypes at Oklahoma State University. The progression began with crime in 1950's *Panic in the Streets*, then overt racism in 1976's *Mandingo*, child prostitution in 1978's *Pretty Baby*, murder in 1983's *Southern Comfort*, necrophilia in 1980's *Macabre*, and a flare for sexual aberration in 1991's *Zandalee*.[4] The buffet of mayhem depicted by Hollywood scripts feeds into the typecasting of the state's people and culture.

Then came 1994's *The Waterboy*—a film that probably should have had its own language option due to the thick, artificial accents of Adam Sandler and Kathy Bates. "Few of these films present anything positive in regards to Louisiana," Shipka said, "a fact which, consequently, consolidates the socially constructed negative stereotype of the state."[5]

These were the portrayals sold across the nation, and indeed the world, of Louisiana and the Gulf South. In fact the state has exploited this cinematic interest, turning Louisiana, and by extension the region, into the new Hollywood South, thanks to big studio tax incentives dating back as far as *Tarzan and the Apes* shot in 1918.[6] Now, Katrina has offered new story lines for filmmakers. A major storm hitting New Orleans was written into the plot of *The Curious Case of Benjamin Button* and Denzel Washington's feature film *Déjà Vu*. Locals finally have a depiction they can call their own in HBO's *Treme* series, which won a 2011 Peabody Award and which *Times-Picayune* TV columnist Dave Walker states finally "gets New Orleans right."[7] The French architecture, mixed with a hot, humid climate, are the ingredients of "the state's mystifying landscape and unique culture [that] create an innate background for dramatic and exploitative narratives," said OSU's Danny Shipka. The uniqueness of the culture allows filmmakers to develop features that focus on the idea of the "other." "Louisiana is an entirely separate world outside of the cultural hegemony," Shipka said, "therefore, artistic portrayals commonly posit the culture as strange, provincial, dangerous, sexy, and/or illiterate."

Life in Louisiana is a free-for-all—"Laissez le bons temps rouler" as they say around the state. Mardi Gras is a destination for partygoers and not an event that leads up to a religious holiday. Some feel it is a constant Carnival mentality: everyone makes a mess and sweeps it up later, or sometimes never. These perceptions are the roots of victimization—the feeling that victims are not worthy of help because they live in an undisciplined manner. The image is what Mann calls "looser politics" that are less upright and where rules don't apply. One nationally syndicated columnist, after the oil disaster, suggested in her column that the federal government "take over" the state of Louisiana, because the politicians were incapable of taking care of local affairs.[8] And she was not alone; national public opinion was divided over rebuilding New Orleans.[9] Yet what was not pointed out is that the region, without New Orleans, would not be the same, not just culturally, but economically. For much of the nation and perhaps the world, the perceptions of the South are guided by popular culture and our unfortunate affinity for disaster, of all sorts. Louisiana is the black sheep of the Gulf Coast family who always gets into trouble and other family members have to keep bailing out. Not only is this feeling held on a national level, but within the Gulf Coast, as we found. Mississippi set its own recovery path as the anti-Louisiana model, with a do-it-ourselves approach.

While Katrina put Gulf states into competition with each other for federal relief, the oil spill was a unifying denominator. When the underwater gusher was finally capped on July 15, 2010, between 170 and 200 million gallons of oil had leaked. Sixteen thousand miles of Gulf Coast had been affected—Texas, Louisiana, Mississippi, Alabama, and Florida. Two million gallons of chemical dispersants that were released into the waters added another layer of uncertainty to the long-term consequences. As the oil seeped out across the waters that these states shared in common, so too the region banded together for the first time since those first few days after Katrina in a strong force of humanity and solidarity. However, the BP oil spill reinforced the notion of a region in disaster perpetuity with victims so neglected, why should the rest of the nation care? "The greatest negative reaction," according to Bob Mann, "may have been that we tested the public's capacity for sympathy for our state and region and may have inadvertently cemented in the public's mind that we are a hapless state in a perpetual state of disaster and crisis" brought on by a history of incompetence and ignoring existing problems. Hurricane Katrina picked the scab off a long-neglected injury, and the region bled out.

While Americans may feel taxed on sympathy for the Gulf, the region's residents remained shell-shocked, many still coming to grips with the new realities of the people and places they called home. More than seven years later as this book goes to press, many around the nation and the world may not realize that residents of this region still have not returned to family homes, and many more still have not recouped the livelihood they once had before 2005. Rob Dowie spent much of his time in the Baton Rouge River Center shelter helping evacuees get reunited with their families after Katrina. As director and founder of Southeast Louisiana Aquatics (SELA), Dowie was on the board of the New Orleans chapter of the American Red Cross and a volunteer for the Orleans Parish learn-to-swim program prior to Hurricane Katrina. The Red Cross partnered with the New Orleans public school system and received a grant from the Save the Lake (Ponchatrain) Foundation to teach second graders as part of their P.E. curriculum how to swim. Every second grader in New Orleans was bused to the nearest pool to learn how to swim.

After Katrina, as a Red Cross board member, he was stunned to discover that the Save the Lake program in effect saved a life. At the center, a young boy, not much older than second grade, came running up to him and said, "Mr. Rob, Mr. Rob, do you remember me? You taught me how to swim, and I swam." Dowie recounts the rest of the story.

> I didn't automatically connect what he was talking about because in the shelter, as you can imagine, it is overwhelming. But come to find out he was in the learn-to-swim program. And I asked him in our brief conversation, "Who are

you here with? Did you ride a bus? Where are your parents?" And his response was, "Well, Mr. Rob, you didn't teach my parents how to swim."[10]

The Gulf Coast experienced two epic tragedies, very different, yet very similar. We often think of a crisis as a unique one-time event—this has not been the fate of the Gulf Coast. The Gulf Coast has been in a perpetual crisis mode ever since August 29, 2005. The perception is that the Gulf Coast must be jinxed, chock-full of victims who cost the American taxpayers billions of dollars within just one decade. Two equally complex crises have resulted in a steep S-curve of learning by all stakeholders—especially the journalists covering these history-making events. Since journalists write the first rough drafts of history, the story of the Gulf Coast did not begin with Hurricane Katrina, nor does it end with the oil disaster.

The dual disasters saw an unexpected spark to the fourth estate. Just two years before a global recession, it was already hard times for the news business. Public skepticism, online competition, and declining local revenues had many journalists believing the writing on the wall, that theirs was a dying business. Katrina, and then the oil disaster, bucked the trend, at least in the short run. More than ever before, the news, told by the region's journalists who know their world best, breathed new life into an economically threatened tradition, local news. The news of the region became innovative, groundbreaking, and economically viable in a time when big city newspapers were shutting down their printers and laying off reporters. In these two crises, the news mattered. It mattered because its users said it did as it saved lives, comforted the distraught, advocated for the deserted, and to this day championed the ever-present, ongoing struggle of the people of this region. It is this small but meaningful spark, a spark in the revered field of journalism that has arisen out of these crises, that this book hopes to illuminate. Just as the spirit of the region is to rebuild, despite the naysayers, news out of the Gulf Coast perseveres and pioneers in its field.

Overall, this book explores the quality of journalism within these two events and the effects it may have on the public and future disaster coverage. The media's role in a crisis is often to interpret the events to those viewers, listeners, or readers who do not experience the crisis firsthand. It is possible to have different media narratives. National news coverage and local news coverage for both Katrina and the oil spill took on very distinct tones. The local Gulf Coast journalists, who covered the spill five years later, were veterans and victims of the Katrina disaster. They had seen five years earlier how their Pulitzer Prize– and Peabody-winning coverage brought water to the dying and rescue boats to the drowning. Their burden of telling the story, when they too were victims, informed the kind of journalism that brought about a community response to the spill that paralleled the sense of oneness the Gulf Coast shared during the Katrina crisis. Meanwhile, the national media landscape continued with the usual narrative of trying to find who to blame: is it BP? Is it the Obama administration? The tenets of good journalism remain important in both, yet national and local media serve different masters and those loyalties can be exacerbated in crisis situations.

This book looks into the nature of and differences in the coverage of these two Gulf Coast disasters and the impact of the coverage on journalists and their audiences. The veteran journalists who have survived the Katrina disaster have reluctantly graduated to the coverage of a second disaster. The book captures this process of growth from the viewpoints of not only the journalists, but the public, the science community, and through an analysis of the journalists' own content. We explore the images and sound bites of Katrina and the oil spill. We ask the region's residents how they interpreted the media coverage of the events, and how they used the information journalists provided them. Finally, we examine whether the media coverage influenced good public and civic decisions. Media coverage affects the interpretation and the experience of an event. Our premise is that it all leads back to the fundamentals of solid journalism and the importance of following these tenets consistently in an enduring crises atmosphere—especially when the crises are just a few years apart.

One tenet in journalism is accuracy, and in this book when we are referring to the second Gulf disaster, you will find the terms gusher, oil disaster, and oil spill. The interchanging use of these terms warrants some explanation. In our interviews with the scientific community, they took exception to the term "spill" being used to describe what happened at the bottom of the ocean at the Macondo well. It was not a spill, they say, but a gusher. Bing's online dictionary defines gusher as "a free-flowing oil well: an oil well from which oil flows freely and in large amounts, without having to be pumped." The subsequent spill, however, stemmed from this sea floor oil gusher. The spill is what results on the beaches and in the marshes. The term spill is often referred to as any accidental release of oil, and traditionally has been thought of as a release from a tanker whose hull has been compromised.

As former journalists who were engaged in scholarly research for this book, we had a direct discussion about which terms to use, and while we wish to be accurate, we also do not want to be cumbersome. There are pre-conceived notions that come with each term. For example, the word gusher brings to mind images of a west Texas oil well or the beginning sequence of the *Beverly Hillbillies*. Using disaster instead of spill is also problematic because it is nonspecific and encompasses the entire situation, not just the seminal event. It describes the enormity of the situation, but not the cause. We also recognize that spill is not entirely accurate according to the scientists and by definition. However, the term spill is so enveloped in the lexicon of the event that even scientists said it in their own interviews with us. Therefore, we will use all three terms to describe it—spill, gusher, and disaster. Using all three terms helps us highlight the fact that this was, as you will see in the course of this book, a very different phenomenon.

We also want to be clear that this study of journalism begins and ends with scholarly research. We want our readers to be aware that the information presented in this book will toggle back and forth between the easy dialogue of the journalists and the layman's explanations of mass communication theoretical frameworks. Both are necessary to gain a richer, contextual view of the dual disasters.

As we travel back in time to the Katrina disaster, the media lessons from 2005 get vetted and revisited in 2010. It is our goal that readers can envision the transformations the region has experienced within five years based on the media's rough draft of events. We start this book with you, the mass consumers of news and information. In chapter 1, we analyze Katrina evacuees' news consumption patterns and their evolution as this first disaster unfolded. Media use is an important factor in decision-making during times of crisis; however, the game changes in a complete communications blackout. A digital revolution occurred, yet old traditional communication, like the landline telephone, resurrected in this crisis as well. Additionally, media use does not always mean the information is retained or practiced. Five years later, we discovered that Gulf Coast residents are still not where they should be in terms of hurricane knowledge, especially African Americans. A survey conducted while the oil was spewing into the Gulf found that the public knew even less about the processes of oil exploration and the effects the second disaster may have on the sea's ecosystems. Through the eyes of the viewers and readers we examined whether the media effectively transmitted the necessary information to the public, or the news they could use. We learned that the challenges to communication transmission were very different between the two disasters.

After studying the public's use of the media in Katrina and the oil spill, we turn our attention to media workers in chapter 2. Journalists pride themselves on being anonymous, emotionless, detached professionals. They are trained not to become a part of the news themselves. The one-on-one, in-depth interviews we were fortunate to conduct with Gulf Coast journalists that covered both Katrina and the oil spill are the crux of this chapter. We attempt to tell their stories, the stories that did not show up in the articles and television packages that the audiences in chapter 1 turned to. This chapter is unique in the study of crisis and disaster journalism because rarely do journalists and the subjects they cover experience the same catastrophe on the same levels. We argue that because Gulf Coast journalists were in essence victims of the Katrina disaster, it dramatically changed the way they reported the news. Then we revisit some of these journalists five years later as they cover the oil disaster. After becoming empowered from Katrina in their daily tasks as Pulitzer Prize–winning journalists, they had that power stripped away by a second crisis where the facts and events were controlled by a tight-lipped corporate entity. Here they tell a tale of frustration about this latest hit to the region's physical, economic, and emotional recovery.

That frustration was compounded by the fact that Katrina and the BP oil spill mesmerized the nation, drawing flocks of national and international news agencies to the Gulf Coast. While news is news for the viewers and readers, chapter 3 explains why local news matters. Both national and local, television and newspaper have different responsibilities. They serve different audiences, and the coverage is different. We dug back into hundreds of hours of television coverage of the oil spill and Hurricane Katrina and hundreds of newspaper articles of these two disasters. In comparing the local media discourse to the national media narrative, we reaffirmed that both news entities play different vital roles in a crisis. Both national and local outlets framed their coverage in a manner that highlights individuals without context and often results in blame being placed on victims. From the very first pictures of people wading through the water, race and responsibility became themes in the Katrina coverage. By coupling established scholarly themes and frames with media functions, we get a richer and often conflicting picture of the information being sent to the viewers. The media often overemphasize the negative and downplay the positive. While there was little positive to be found amidst Hurricane Katrina, the local media found a way to bring people together in what seemed like a hopeless sea of negative national coverage. Local television outlets and local newspapers often assumed specific roles that helped manage and guide a community through the tragedy. However, establishing the differences between national and local media is important because *most* of us experience crises from afar, or through a national media lens. Rarely do we get to understand what the crisis is like for those on the ground. The Katrina media experience of someone in Indiana is going to be different from the experience of a native Louisianan. In an age of corporate consolidation of media markets, we argue that all news is still local.

"Obama's Katrina" was used by the national media within the first week of the oil disaster, a knee-jerk media frame used to develop a narrative that pulls leaders in Washington into the unfolding regional crisis. In chapter 4, we explore whether the media's comparison was automatic or inevitable, or an oft-used narrative tool. More than eighteen hundred people died in Katrina and eleven in the explosion that caused the oil gusher. One New Orleans journalist compared the two this way: "we lost life . . . you are losing livelihood." A perceived delay in federal response to both disasters saw back-to-back U.S. presidents having their legacies tainted with apathy toward the Gulf Coast. Neither was the nation's first black president allowed to escape being painted as abandoning a predominantly black city and its surrounding areas when the oil spill first occurred. Through our analysis of the media's critique of responsibility for the Katrina and oil spill disasters we find surprising contradictions between federal and local leaders' actions and media characterization of them. The media frame of responsibility and blame takes on a different meaning between the two crises. Five years later, the critique of leadership of the Katrina recovery is ongoing, while the oil disaster cleanup process also challenges citizens for their part in the long-term health and vibrancy of the coast's ecosystem.

A story is only as good as its sources and in chapter 5 we explore the voices the media gave space to in both crises. We explore the use of officials, victims (whom journalists call the man on the street), and experts. In journalism those who hold positions of power in society often get their voices heard more often and in preference to ordinary citizens. Many times they are wealthy and white; the middle classes, the poor, and citizens of minority populations are sidelined. Katrina, and to some measure the oil spill, turned this pyramid upside down. The man on the street, the average American, the victim, was given prominence in local coverage of the Katrina disaster. In the oil spill, journalists, who were challenged by a very complex scientific narrative, turned to scholars, scientific experts, and academics to explain the disaster to the public. While journalists never fully abandoned their inclusion of powerful voices in society in providing information and context in the news reports, we explore several key story lines of these disasters, where journalists were forced to look to the less powerful for major facts in these two events.

Katrina and the oil spill are now part of an encyclopedic list of major American events. The public sketches these events in their psyche because of the images: the stills, videos, and other visuals that are first presented in the media coverage of any major historic event. In chapter 6, we sift through the thousands of visual images the public was bombarded with during Hurricane Katrina and the oil spill. What we found in surveying residents of the region is that a major historical event is not only defined by the media's iconic imagery, but by personal iconography. Victims of events recall imagery of the disaster that the distant onlooker may never hear of, or may never identify in the plethora of media-transmitted images of the event. With time, memories fade, we found, and the images repeated on anniversary news reports of these two crises endure. Yet, we end our analysis of the media's disaster content with visuals because to see is to believe, and to believe is to act. The powerful images of the flooding of a major American city and the Gulf Coast's oil-soaked beaches are a major reason Americans and the international community opened their wallets, phoned their elected officials, and joined in civil lawsuits against British Petroleum. The images of these two disasters are why the Gulf Coast is now viewed with sympathy worldwide. Yet for the region's residents, their own personal imagery is of their favorite local spots: a closed snowball stand, their grandmother's house, the Grand Isle vacation rental are the nostalgic memories they choose to hold on to in the aftermath of both crises, despite the catastrophic visuals of death and destruction that have come to symbolize the region.

Finally, in chapter 7 we advocate for local journalism in an era when corporate ownership is slashing and consolidating local news, in favor of the Web and its bottom line. For a region to experience two record-breaking disasters within five years, with consequences that will last for decades, the lives and livelihoods of local citizens depend on access to information and investigative journalism. Local journalists do not have to parachute in to a disaster to cover the story. They live it. They know the culture, the politics, and the geography. This last chapter is an analysis of what these two crises mean for the tenets of journalism as a whole. We assess where things stand now and how sustainable the current news effort is, given the state of the news business across the nation. We explore what aspects of journalism in these two crises are transferable for news workers in other places, in other tragedies. The final word coming out of Louisiana and the Gulf should not rest in reality TV. The very real issues that the people of the region must confront postdisaster require a robust and authoritative media to capture, spotlight, and champion the public's reality for those who are still watching, and for those who hold power but may have lost interest.

1

SEEKING INFORMATION IN DISASTER

We now live in a world of 4G news updates. The latest breaking news crisis can turn any one of us into an instant Anderson Cooper, the anchor man on the street of the next major crisis or tragedy. All we need is to phone a friend on our latest smartphone, text an "OMG!," capture eyewitness video and stills, and finally upload it to our own YouTube channels, Facebook walls, and Twitter feeds. Instantly, we are all our own personal newsmakers. We now expect information on anything and everything—when we want it and where we want it. Yet Hurricane Katrina, in user-sharing advanced 2005, rendered 4G a 1G.

Katrina was a perfect storm of winds carrying a technology blackout. Some victims described it as "apocalyptic." From local journalists to evacuees, cell phones and all their gadgets became useless as they scampered around a devastated city in search of working landlines, analog radios, and the small chance of a faint signal that would send a text message to anyone whose area code did not start with the dreaded 504. For scores of local journalists interviewed, and 250 victims and evacuees surveyed in the days and months after Katrina, technology in that summer of 2005 had failed them. Katrina remains a standout case study for what could happen in a technology blackout, but it is also a standout case for the coming of age of Internet journalism.

No longer a repository for rehashed print news, news organizations' websites became local, community portals—a way to inform and engage that had never before been used at this level. Users and communicators were forced to adapt in order to send and receive life-saving information. This adaptation mimicked a spiderweb rather than a triangle, in terms of the relationship between news providers and consumers. A stranded evacuee in St. Bernard Parish would text-message a relative on the East Coast asking to be rescued. That relative would post on the Nola.com blog that their family was stranded. The Nola.com blog staffer for the day would text-message a reporter in the field who might be embedded with the parish sheriff. The parish sheriff would text-message his crew at a post near the victim's home to go in search (anyone with the New Orleans area code of 504 could not be contacted directly). When the evacuee was brought to the nearest shelter, a journalist there interviewed him or her to share the rescue story. Neither of them was aware of the web in which they participated in the creation of news and the relay of information. Before Katrina, journalists sought out stories, published or broadcasted them, and users occasionally posted feedback after the fact, and that was as much of a flow as there was between the two entities. Hurricane Katrina turned this structure on its head, forecasting a view of how information and news may be transmitted in a technology-driven century when local communications infrastructures flatline.

Hurricane Katrina showed us the importance of having diverse media for information distribution, but it also highlighted the diversity of those affected by disaster and their information needs.

This is the story of how the victims, the displaced, the evacuees—those affected by the crisis—used the media. For those around the nation and the globe who watched the natural disaster and its aftermath unfold, the use of media and its available technology was quite different from those users at ground zero whose needs for the media and its information were far more crucial to their decision-making and, in many cases, their survival.

Diverse Evacuees

The victims of Hurricane Katrina used all forms of media, both national and local, traditional and online in three main ways. Also, where they were situated as victims corresponded with how they sought out and used the news. Three main groups provide a window into these three media-use trends. Trend one we named "early responders" because they travelled the furthest away from the storm, and ended up relying on more remote news sources, such as national news and displaced local news outlets sharing simulcasts with subsidiaries in other southern states. We labeled trend two "caught in the middle" because they were the last group to evacuate moments before the storm hit and only made it as far as the closest city such as Baton Rouge, in the Louisiana case. This group relied on a mixture of media sources as they still had access to local media and national media in the region. The third group we named "caught in the storm." For this group, media use resembled the spiderweb of information. Given a communication and technology blackout, this group was the most inventive in seeking, relaying, and transmitting information on the unfolding of the crisis in order to make life-saving decisions.

Survey Demographic Proportions

Graph 1

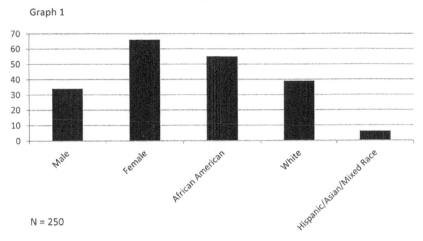

N = 250

Weeks after Katrina hit, we tracked down approximately 250 residents living along the Louisiana/Mississippi state line to the New Orleans metropolitan area to tell us the stories of why the news mattered for them in this crisis, and how they accessed the news. Their experiences reinforced the argument that information and the jobs journalists hold as conveyors is vital in a disaster.[1] A crisis like Katrina highlights the point that in an age of cynicism and supposed decline of the traditional press, media users in a disaster find that old-fashioned journalism is not outdated, yet. It may be adapted, but it remains vital.

Of the 250 Gulf Coast residents who told us their stories, 100 were "early responders," 99 were "caught in the middle" and 51 were "caught in the storm."[2] A window into their evacuation narrative helps explain their media use trends in the Katrina crisis. "Early responders" to the crisis were the region's professionals, business owners, public sector workers, and employees of major companies. They were the ones who could afford a week's hotel stay in Houston, Atlanta, or Birmingham, and who had practiced evacuation drills implemented in their households, dusted and rolled out every hurricane season, once their local weather forecaster or mayor announced a voluntary evacuation. Katrina being a mandatory evacuation, this group was the first to make plans and leave the area.

About two-thirds of this group converged on Baton Rouge and its surrounding towns in the first two weeks. The rest relied on geography much further than the nearest city. Many fled to Houston and Dallas, Texas, others to the Florida panhandle, some to towns in northern Louisiana, Mississippi, and Alabama. However, this was not a static group. Many moved several times across the Gulf Coast region in the aftermath of the storm as they strained their budgets staying at hotels they had only expected to hunker down in for a weekend and a few extra days.

The decision makers or heads of households of the "early responders" made the call for their families to leave the affected area before the storm, and then to return afterward. In the weeks and months after Katrina, once the city had reopened, roughly two-thirds of this group had returned, oftentimes with just one adult or part of the family, to live in outskirt towns of the New Orleans metropolitan area such as Kenner and in towns on the west bank of the Mississippi River that avoided flooding. Other "early responders," about a third of them, commuted to their jobs from rentals and relatives' homes in towns around Baton Rouge.

What informed the mobile lifestyle of this first group of evacuees was a shift in media use from a national account of the storm fed to them in hotel rooms to active search for local updates on the conditions in their area. Before the Katrina disaster, "early responders" overwhelmingly consumed local news reports on a weekly basis far more regularly than the other two groups at a rate of five to one. Local news helped them decide the best neighborhoods, where to send their kids to school, the state of the local economy, and which politician should have their vote.[3] Partly due to age, ranging from twenty-five to sixty-one in our survey, also due to income, local television was their main information source as residents of the region. When there was a partial local news blackout in their remote evacuation locations, this prompted information seeking on their part for news that helped them decide whether to bring their families back to uncertain conditions in the weeks following the crisis.

The second group, those "caught in the middle," are like the "early responders" in that over time they became active information seekers of local news content despite their quasi-remote locations camping on the outskirt towns of the city. Where they differ is in their demographics and prior media use before the crisis. We surveyed ninety-nine of those "caught in the middle," who had evacuated a little more than an hour away to the Louisiana state capital, Baton Rouge, and sought shelter with friends, relatives, or even slept in their vehicles at the side of the road or in public buildings around the city. Many residents "caught in the middle" were late deciders, who in the last windows available to evacuate the areas in the eye of the storm made a quick dash to the nearest exit points and only made it as far as the next largest city, given the bottleneck traffic heading in all directions of Interstate 10.

Half of this group we found enrolled at Louisiana State University for the fall 2005 semester as "visiting students." The state's flagship university made special accommodations for such students from universities in the affected area that were forced to close their doors for the rest of the academic year. LSU made two dorms on the campus available to specifically house them once they arrived, opened special sections of core courses for them to gain standard credits for transfer once their colleges had reopened, and waived tuition and other enrollment requirements as many of these students had already paid tuition at New Orleans–area institutions. Why this group is unique is because unlike the "early responders" and those "caught in the storm" roughly half of this group were not native to the Gulf Coast region; many were out-of-state students and employees, such as professors. Therefore, local news was not their go-to source for information.

Despite offers from universities across the country, including Harvard, inviting students "caught in the middle" to attend the semester there, these students chose to attend the university closest to the affected area, LSU. A major factor in this decision was the information and narrative students "caught in the middle" gleaned from local news accounts about the affairs on the ground.[4] This mostly young, ages eighteen to twenty-six years old, tech-savvy, Internet-using group had perhaps the most options to leave the crisis area and never return. The "early responders" and those "caught in the storm" had the most ties to the region—jobs, homes, and memories going back several generations of families—yet something prompted many "caught in the middle" Katrina evacuees to remain. Perhaps the information they received and shared during the crisis contributed to their decision to linger in the area longer than would be expected of them.

Finally, we found those "caught in the storm" to be of all age groups, but mostly of lower-income backgrounds. We found retirees, skilled laborers, the unemployed, single mothers, low-income families, and in some cases those overcoming addictions or mental and physical disabilities.[5] A small 10 percent of them had finished high school, and an even smaller 2 percent had college degrees and were working in fields such as nursing and education.[6] They rode out the storm, stayed behind to safeguard their homes, could not afford to evacuate, and in some cases told us that they had "rescued themselves."

Those whom law enforcement and other relief crews rescued found themselves deposited at organized shelters such as the Baton Rouge River

Center and faith-based shelters in Baton Rouge, such as one organized by Bethany World Prayer Center, a large evangelical church in the capital.

Those who "rescued themselves" tell of journeys in search of shelter where they waded and swam through water, losing loved ones to unknown suctions under their feet. Some broke into schools, headed toward police stations or parish government buildings and finally were told to go to the New Orleans Superdome or Convention Center. Once at these two notorious shelters there was endless waiting for supplies or information on their fate. A week into the aftermath they were moved to the Houston Astrodome awaiting a final destination. Many of them said they wanted to return to the state and took the first opportunity to be housed in one of the temporary Federal Emergency Management Authority (FEMA) trailer parks set up for evacuees on the outskirts of Baton Rouge. We were given official access to this group of evacuees at the FEMA trailer park in Baker, Louisiana. Again, this group had low income and education. Often, we had to read aloud the survey to them and write down their answers.

Their stories of escape and rescue shed light on what happened to those media users who experienced a complete blackout of information as the storm passed over and as they helplessly waited for word on their fates. They help us to understand the spiderweb of information relay that occurred in this crisis, and the power and need for the media in matters of life and death.

Media-Use Trends

"Early responders" used local news as a traditional news source, those "caught in the middle" used the Internet and national news, and those "caught in the storm" rarely used any media source consistently, before the Katrina disaster. Yet once nearly a million residents across the Gulf Coast got word that a major hurricane was coming their way, they told us that they all tuned in to local television news for information. The situation changed quickly in the days to come. Putting this volume of residents on the region's interstates and highways for roughly three days of intense evacuation provided a logical media-use transition. Residents told us they had few options but to listen to the radio reports as they sat in their cars in the parking lot that Interstate 10 had become. However, this was not the typical top-of-the-hour radio news report cutting off their favorite pop tune. Some noted they tuned in to the radio signal many television stations still broadcast through, but seldom listened to. Others noted that many music format stations re-aired or read local television and print news updates on the status of the approaching hurricane in longer news segments. For those placed at a dead stop on contra-flowed highways, or, as we will see later, left behind without power and becoming prisoners of accessibility, radio was their only lifeline.

Once evacuees reach their destinations, and the disaster is now in what crisis researchers call the "impact phase," we begin to see a divergence of media use among the three main groups. Some of those "caught in the middle" tech-savvy users lost their 3G signal once the storm blacked out cell phone lines, and for the first time, Internet use drops in accessibility and influence behind television, radio, and even newspapers.

It is in the impact phase where we begin to see a new user habit. Evacuees, in general, acknowledge that national news accounts were most accessible, meaning they could see it or hear it in public or residential spaces with ease. However, they pointed out that they actively sought out alternative media accounts, particularly local news. They were active information seekers, texting relatives out of state to check the websites of local news outlets of their cities for specific updates and accounts. Some "caught in the middle" evacuees sat in their cars to pick up AM radio transmissions from the affected cities once power went out in outskirt areas from the impact zone of the storm. For those who did not have cell phones with a 504 area code, they recalled being able to use their phones, powered by car batteries, to call in to local news hotlines to find out about areas where loved ones were left behind. Others texted friends out of state to call in on their behalf, given the jam to area cell phone numbers.

The impact phase of the crisis started the spiderweb of communication and information-seeking that flourished in the aftermath of the crisis, once the storm had passed over, leaving its devastation behind. This media usage is significant, supporting studies of prior disasters where victims actively sought out local news accounts because their confidence rested in local journalists' knowledge of their cities and conditions on the ground.[7] Where Katrina is different is that the information flow is far more complicated by the inability to communicate, both on the part of journalists, as chapter 2 demonstrates, and on the part of victims. When the media cannot speak directly to its primary users, in this case Katrina victims, we find that the relationship remains unshaken. It is these users who now find creative ways, through friend and family networks across the country, outside of the disaster zone, whom they alert to local news sources, to channel information to them or back to them. It is this that gives Katrina unique information use in an age of technology and interactivity online, and one that shows up in other disasters with communications blackouts such as the 2010 earthquake disaster in Haiti.[8]

In the aftermath of the storm, media use broke down across the three groups. "Early responders," who were the furthest away from transmissions of local news updates, relied on national television news reports. However, many turned to the television news stations in the cities they had evacuated to and found that the affiliates were carrying news packages from their affiliate stations in the Gulf Coast area. They recalled seeing local television reporters they recognized and even the anchors on set, cohosting with that city's anchor team. The reach of one New Orleans television station, WDSU, channel six, explained this account. The station's transmitter building flooded the Sunday before the storm hit but its affiliate stations took up its news reports. Its ABC affiliate sister-station WAPT-TV in Jackson, Mississippi, took in some of its staff, pairing anchors and meteorologists in the Jackson newscasts. Another sister station, WESH in Orlando, Florida, this time an NBC affiliate, aired WDSU's journalists' reports. WDSU's reach did not end there either. WDSU continued to air its coverage on other stations until the end of 2005 when its transmitter received a new, elevated building.[9]

Evacuees "caught in the middle" continued to use local radio because power had not been restored to the outskirt areas, restricting television use. The cellular blackout persisted, restricting smartphone access to the Internet. However, the visiting students made use of the Internet more than any other group. It must be noted here that while some areas of Baton Rouge lost power during Hurricane Katrina, the LSU campus did not. Many "caught in the middle" did not arrive on the campus until the announcement for open enrollment for displaced students went out. Therefore, this lack of power supports their claim. It also did not mean that a single text message, the main functioning communication tool for those "caught in the middle," could not also be used to get an outsider's take on national accounts of the event. However, in 2005, when text messages were not bundled in unlimited packages, many evacuees reserved texts for emergency correspondence, particularly to parents, in the case of students.

For those "caught in the storm" there was no access to any news source, unless they had a battery-powered radio or they "rescued themselves" or were rescued by law enforcement and taken to shelters. While only two "caught in the storm" respondents actually ran into journalists directly at their first rescue destination, others reported that without the media,

Table 1: Media Use During Storm %

	Evacuation	During	After
Local TV	73.30	-	33.9
National TV	7.80	-	29.4
Local Newspaper	5	-	2.2
National Newspaper	0.6	-	3.3
Doesn't Apply	0.6	8.3	1.7
Local Radio	8.9	-	20
National Radio	1.1	-	1.7
Local Internet	1.1	-	6.1
National Internet	0	-	1.1
Local Media	-	50.6	-
National Media	-	41.1	-
Other	1.7	-	0.6

N = 250

decision-making information came from "word of mouth," rumors, their "lovely wife," "the police," know-how from "past experiences," and in one case the "Holy Spirit." Once those "caught in the storm" had been moved from the Superdome to the Convention Center to shelters, the television sets were tuned to national cable news reports such as CNN and Fox News. They were similarly exposed to national outlets like their "caught in the storm" peers who ended up taken in by relatives in private homes or under-going extended stays at hotels.

"Caught in the storm" evacuees, now in shelters, had no choice but to watch what was provided in their "home away from home." Those we talked to stressed the desire for local information so they could find out what was going on in the city, how bad things were, and when they would be allowed back. Yet, even with the barrage of news from Geraldo Rivera and Ander-son Cooper, "caught in the storm" evacuees recalled not tuning in to these reports when it came to updates from local public officials. They recalled that national media carried more press conferences from Washington, D.C., before those officials arrived in the city. While helpful, the national TV news, they stated, failed to offer them the news they could use to return to the city, find loved ones, and identify their devastated homes in the aerial coverage.

Each phase of the disaster dictated the kinds of information local users sought out. There were reasons why evacuees had wanted to know what news and information was circulating in the local presses and on air-waves. As they evacuated, all groups sought the media for weather updates

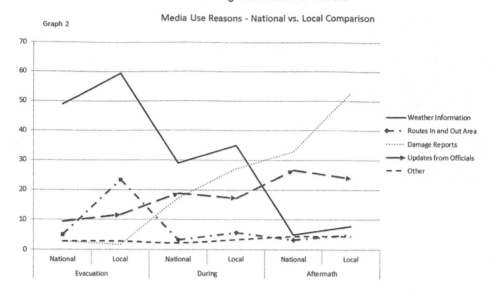

Graph 2 — Media Use Reasons - National vs. Local Comparison

tracking the storm. In the impact phase, residents used the media to learn the direction the storm had turned, the amount of inches in rainfall, the wind strength, etc., and how badly their homes and possessions might be hit. This mirrors results from prior natural disaster studies.[10] In past disasters, victims naturally turned to local media rather than national media to get their weather information in the two earliest phases. However, in Katrina, national media were more readily accessible in the impact phase, triggering active efforts by evacuees to seek out local accounts of the disaster. The divergence in media use occurred in the aftermath phase. Here, more than a quarter of respondents turned to national media to receive updates from officials, while more than half listed damage reports as the main reason they sought out local media reports on Katrina.

Those differing media narratives were more than informative, they began to shape attitudes, a dimension that studying the experiences of local journalists, as in chapter 2, explains the attitudes of the evacuees. Media exposure carried correlations for attitudes in favor of news coverage by different media sources. Evacuees who relied on or sought out local news and information expressed stronger attitudes of accuracy, satisfaction, and usefulness of the news content than those displaced residents using national news. However, both national and local news shared something in common. More than two-thirds of the displaced residents surveyed felt very concerned by both the national and local news coverage of the crisis.

The difference occurred in what they were concerned about. Those watching local news were concerned about their homes, possessions, neighbors, and jobs, while national news made them concerned about more generic aftermath conditions such as crime, public officials' handling of the situation, and the widespread damage. We found this difference supported as we studied news and information supplied between national and local media, further discussed in chapter 3.

Radio Makes History

These three groups of displaced residents paint a picture of how evacuees used media before the storm, during the storm, and after the storm. They also explain what types of information they were seeking out at different phases of the disaster and which media sources had the most influence on their actions and decision-making. These displaced residents also identified their attitudes toward different media sources as they gained information across the disaster and in the aftermath.

While the victims were very diverse, they all had a similar drive, what could be called a desperate drive, to seek information in order to make good decisions. Hurricane Katrina is often called the great equalizer. One displaced student said that when 80 percent of an American city is flooded, "It [the media] showed three- to four-story mansions with water up to the gutters. Katrina brought the rich and the poor to one level." The storm rendered moot other socioeconomic factors that could create a digital divide. Both local news workers and their affected immediate news consumers alike in those days and weeks returned to the tried and true communication means that served news updates for decades before the information explosion made them appear almost obsolete. At a time when many stranded people were able to take their own pictures of their homes flooding and needed to make pleas for help, there was no 4G-technology functioning to spread the word themselves. In August 2005, during a natural disaster that brought a technology blackout across most of the Gulf Coast, victims said goodbye to Fox News and CNN.com, and hello to AM radio.

A twenty-one-year-old sophomore New Orleans student packed a few items from her dorm room before heading onto the cramped parking lot that was Interstate 10 to make the roughly hour-long journey from New Orleans to Baton Rouge, a trip that took almost five times longer to make. As the storm blew over the shelter she sought refuge in, the hosts there kept the television channels tuned to the national news stations, primarily to get updates from officials. Yet the capital city one hour away could not prevent a massive power outage at their shelter, and the students were forced to return to their cars and listen to the only updates coming through from New Orleans radio news outlets.

A twenty-six-year-old white male construction worker from St. Bernard Parish, Louisiana, found himself moving from the Chalmette Courthouse to the police station to the St. Bernard High School in search of information when the storm knocked out his television access to local news. He recalled trying to seek out local news updates as he moved by foot from shelter to shelter and radio to radio, and when he was finally relocated to the River Center in Baton Rouge, a temporary holding site for those who were stranded, he recalled being dissatisfied with the national news reports being shown, compared to what he had learned from local news reports, mostly radio, while riding out the aftermath. That was the experience of a fifty-three-year-old white certified nursing assistant who stayed behind at her New Orleans home to care for an elderly relative and who recalled being "busted out" of her home and "taken to a school." It was local television news she turned to for advice for those staying behind with the sick and elderly, and it was local news she turned to during the storm until the power went out. She then switched to a local radio news report to help her pass the time as she waited in her attic to see if rescuers were passing near her home. In the middle of an American city, under water and off-line, the information age was usurped by the golden age of radio.

Radio was at the center of one of the more unique aspects of communication and information sharing in the immediate aftermath of the storm. Not surprisingly, five years later, in Haiti, radio once again made a reappearing star role[11] as it did in Katrina, underscoring that even new technology does not completely displace the old, and often fails citizens in times of crisis. Several New Orleans radio journalists interviewed separately recalled out-of-state relatives calling in to their programs to state that they received a text message from a stranded resident with their address. The relatives stated that they were listening to the radio station in their homes, and instructed the out-of-state resident, via another outdated technology, the landline telephone, to call in to the radio station's landline and inquire of the journalist to get word to any local relief crew for a rescue. The scope of this communication strategy by media users was so widespread that one Hispanic radio station owner in Gretna, Louisiana, who remained on air broadcasting in Spanish, received calls from as far as Guatemala and

Honduras not only from his relatives, but those of his trapped listeners, alerting him of rescues needed and asking him to alert authorities to their trapped family members.

The global community turned to "old" media and radio found its place in this historic event. WWL radio news director Dave Cohen said that it is the low-tech quality of radio that is a great feature in an emergency because just about everyone has access to it, and the stations, even in some cases operating remotely, found ways to stay on the air through this traditional medium, communicate directly with victims, and provide information.

> After the phones were down after Katrina people couldn't call 911 in many cases and they called the radio station and they could get through to us and they may have had a cell phone. We told rescuers where people were trapped in their attic, where they were trapped on their rooftops, and they were listening to us and going to those locations and rescuing those people.
>
> We can be heard by 42 states in the US so we have a big reach and we found out after Katrina we had people all over the country when the sun goes down our signal you can pick it up anywhere. All across the country people were sitting in their cars at night listening to us to figure out what's going on back at home. So we take our responsibility to provide information in an emergency very seriously and both at the programming level and the engineering level make sure that we can always stay on the air.[12]

Cohen was right; what radio accomplished in the life-or-death, decision-making moments of a crisis was something the much user-driven Internet and ratings champion TV could not do when a historic disaster struck.

All Things Local

Another commonality among the evacuees was the need for local news before, during, and after the storm. A twenty-eight-year-old general laborer who stayed behind in New Orleans was glued to his TV keeping track of what local officials were saying. However, as the electricity went out in his home, he recalled a news "media wipeout" and the information he now needed was unavailable. He felt helpless having so many questions: what local officials were saying, what the weather was doing, and how to get out of his area. His media blackout continued as he was eventually rescued and taken to temporary shelter, where the only source he could get proper updates from local officials was local news, whereas national news was only offering updates from federal officials.

With evacuees now scattered across a dozen states, local news in any form was highly sought after by them. The search for neighborhood and community news continued. The majority listed as reasons for seeking out local media such comments as "find out where evacuees were moved to," "stories on family," "locate family members," "how people died," "contact others," "look for updates on people," and "missing family." The locals had specific needs that the national media could not satisfy.[13]

Even a sixty-one-year-old retiree and his extended family who evacuated in advance to stay at a Hilton in Dallas, Texas, kept their channels glued to local Texas news stations only because they were carrying reports from their sister stations in New Orleans. Thanks to those Texas affiliates, he and his family knew that they could return to New Roads, Louisiana, to stay with a relative there and avoid the high hotel costs for weeks during the aftermath. National news reports were telling them that no one could return to the area in the aftermath, but from the feeds that were picked up from New Orleans, the family was able to hear a report from a New Roads official, and decided to take the chance and return to Louisiana.

Many of the evacuees who were either stranded in New Orleans or evacuated across the Mississippi-Louisiana state lines recalled actively seeking out local news sources, either by radio or by stopping law enforcement or camera crews to get information for making life-or-death decisions. Those who were able to leave the affected area to go as far as Texas and Alabama in the massive evacuation that took place before Katrina's arrival were being offered national news sources at hotels, shelters, universities, and relatives' homes. In the aftermath days and weeks to come, they actively shifted away from those sources to find local news reports online or turned to local television stations in those cities that were carrying the feeds sent in from their sister stations still operating in New Orleans.

Displaced residents revealed that many TV stations reminded the evacuees that they could stay tuned to local storm coverage via live streaming on the Internet. However, respondents claimed that national TV news influenced their actions and thinking the most. This could be attributed to two reasons. First, those who were in shelters outside the storm-affected areas at this time claimed their hosts mostly made national news available to them. The second explanation could lie in the types of information sought at this time, which were mostly weather updates. As researchers have found in prior disasters, during the impact phase victims use local media to stay connected and to help with a sense of loneliness and void during power out-age.[14] For those in shelters, there was a small community created to provide that sense of solidarity and comfort. For those who had power, there was an urgency to see which areas were being hit. The need for local community was mostly demonstrated during the impact phase among those who were left behind.

What displaced residents tell us is that local TV news was used the most in this disaster time. It continues the conclusions of others who have looked at natural disaster media use in asserting that residents will remain loyal audiences during a disaster, even if local media are less accessible than national media.

When a local story becomes a global story, such as with Hurricane Katrina, the definition of local news is expanded. Anchors from New Orleans TV station WGNO shared the anchor desk with Baton Rouge's WBRZ. WWL-TV, a NOLA Belo station, shared reports with affiliates and stations in the group across the nation. Others saw local reporters they recognized show up on NBC, CBS, and ABC reports of the aftermath. Evacuees many states over could see a report from a familiar face—a fellow "local." Others followed live streaming of WWL-TV via the Yahoo! Website. The concept of local news was expanded as their traditional news sources and personalities were turning up in national and even global media formats. Thus to narrowly define the presence and permeation of the local Gulf Coast media sources in those early days of the aftermath is to minimize the kinds of local information displaced media users were able to pick up from other sources.

Digital Maturation

Internet sites became more than just online newspapers after Katrina. Substantial changes in the media product were forced by the disaster that were more than anecdotal. While there remains a digital divide in New Orleans as noted by many of the journalists interviewed, the Katrina-accelerated shift from old media to "new" media was important in meeting the number-one function of the press in disaster—the information transmission process.

All residents, businesses, authorities, and the media found themselves without electricity, cell phone service was sporadic, towers and facilities were flooded—the infrastructure of communication was essentially decimated. The learning curve was steep. "I didn't learn how to text until Katrina. I had no idea so I had to learn," said WWL-TV's chief meteorologist

Carl Arredondo. His boss, Chris Slaughter, agreed. "Katrina was really a watershed event in terms of the Web and Web-based technology. E-mails are a very big part of it and Katrina opened the world of texting to us."[15]

Print journalists were wary of new media as well. At the time of our interviews, they saw the Internet more as a way to hastily put news out that distracts them from skillfully crafting news stories. They were also aware that the Internet is crucial to future revenues. Every one of the journalists interviewed indicated that they have completely changed their attitudes toward the use of the Internet in their daily routines. However, what is unique about their views is that they embrace community journalism and welcome it to their newspaper's website. More importantly, during the storm these journalists blogged, many times in the first person, about the details and reports they were receiving in the earliest stages of the aftermath. That constant exchange continues today. Some reporters who are not columnists even write articles that appear in print about how they and their families navigated the Katrina aftermath experience a year later. *Times-Picayune* editor David Meeks recounted his experience with blogging:

> I agree that the writing style became very personal and pointed, as has happened because that's just the way it was. It was so chaotic and there were so many citizens out there trying to find people and get help and I think the blog very much captured the mood of the people during those times. I do think our readers knew we were in a frenzied chaotic state, and the blog was almost a free-for-all for news, all sorts of things just got on the blog, because we found out about them. I don't know that we did stuff we couldn't check out, we tried to check out stuff as best as we could, but we had stuff get out there that turned out to be not quite right, or not true, that's the nature of the beast.[16]

While the outlets had online presences in 2005, Katrina forced them into territory where they had never been. Former news director Chris Slaughter said the website wwltv.com really came of age during Katrina because they were doing things with it they hadn't done before. The digital maturation process was enormously accelerated during Katrina when WWL-TV forged an unlikely alliance.

> History has shown that we can do this and we will always find a way to get material out of here . . . We basically streamed our signal on that site quickly and overwhelmed our own servers. At that point, in a five minute conversation,

we struck a deal with Yahoo where Yahoo put us on their front page and they streamed our signal and it was a huge success. That was something that most people can't do after two years of negotiations, [done] within a five minute format, that's because Yahoo saw the importance of it.[17]

That new landscape included websites that were community-based and encouraged participation from users as described by Slaughter.

In addition to people being able to visit our sites and find out about their neighborhoods we were monitoring the input to those and looking for stories. In other words, if a guy says you know I just saw the city park museum of art wing crumbling or whatever we could go out there and check that out. So it was the beginning of a true two way exchange of information that hadn't happened before . . . outside five years ago.[18]

And our respondents noticed this change. They had more access to the Internet, more so than physical newspapers. Yet, they found newspapers to be more influential on their actions and thinking than the Internet. The irony in this finding is that local Internet news would consist mostly of the posted reports of local TV stations and newspapers. Yet somehow, when readers and viewers saw those media in their traditional form, they were more influenced by the reports. Their use of local Internet sites perhaps suggests that residents were attempting to continue to use the newspaper's resources online, although this is more anecdotal than conclusive. It is possible that the Internet, at the time of Katrina, did not hold the same credibility with audiences as traditional media, even if it was the same content. Another reason for this could be, based on field notes, that there were blogs and postings on these official media sites by local residents themselves. Some residents stated that this allowed them to get a better insight about what was taking place. While it helps foster information and a spirit of community, perhaps, in their minds, citizen journalism on the Internet was not as authoritative as news reports by professionals in print or on the TV. The attitude toward this user-generated content may be different today.

The Internet leveled the playing field among outlets, but did not always reach its intended targets. Thus we learn that in a 4G world, a natural disaster that wipes out or handicaps technology finds those affected actively seeking out the tried-and-true local news sources they are familiar with on whatever platform available. With hurricanes past, local news media and their audience were not displaced to other cities, and those disasters did not receive the sustained national coverage that Katrina did. Neither did those disasters see the slew of national correspondents descending on the ravaged city, filing reports as if those news workers had as much intimate knowledge of the place as local news workers had. Five years later, we see a somewhat continued, but evolved, interaction between residents and the media as they navigate a life that it is in perpetual recovery.

These findings do not mean that displaced residents exclusively wanted to use local media; what it affirms is that in a crisis, those who are most affected are active information users, rather than passive. The fact that they used both local and national media suggested that they were willing to take and believe information from any news source, once it was giving them the information they needed for decision-making or other factors. What supports this, too, are their attitudes. They felt almost equally positive toward local media performance as they did to national media performance. Likewise, they felt almost equally concerned by both news sources' coverage. As one respondent indicated:

> The news about the aftermath was very concerning in that it made me worried and upset. However, I don't know if I was just overwhelmed with the negative images because that's how the media slanted it. I do believe it was bad and well worth being concerned, but I would suspect that many of the same images were displayed over and over creating stress for me as a viewer.[19]

However the users and communicators adapted, all the available technology will not work in a decimated communication infrastructure. Adjustments had to be made. Users and communicators could no longer be passive, but had to be aggressive in getting out and receiving information. The phases of use and technology during this disaster were brought full circle—we had to go back before we could move forward. While instantaneous pictures and reports were not possible at the beginning, new and expanded platforms opened up that allowed for local, community interactivity after the storm. And plans for future disasters were adjusted—with and without 4G.

Knowledge Gap

The 4G communication climate has given the illusion that access to information is a given, but access does not translate into use and use does not translate into information retention. The elderly couple in the New Orleans

Ninth Ward may be equipped with a wireless phone post-Katrina, but it does not mean they are any more aggressive about searching out information to prepare them for another disaster. The media does this job for the audience when hurricane season rolls around; as part of the news routine and its civic role, it does the work the public fails to do or does not have the time to do.

"The problem too now [is] that the public has all this information," said WWL-TV's chief meteorologist Carl Arredondo. "They're Joe Meteorologist now. They seem to know more than the hurricane center sometimes."[20] However, even with all the potential media available, use does not always translate into knowledge. When compared globally, the United States historically lags in math and science knowledge. And while our lagging might be more an indicator of the quality of our education system rather than the media's ability to educate, our vast multimedia networks are perhaps not making the desired impact in the quest to transmit information. The important aspect of using the media is making sure you get all the vital information you need to thrive in everyday life and survive in a tragedy. Then before, during, or following a crisis, once the information is transmitted via mass communication, it is up to the public to make solid decisions based on the information received. Odds would favor that Gulf Coast residents, because of repeated exposure, would have vast knowledge of hurricanes compared to other areas of the country. While such knowledge is often difficult to measure, a survey of Gulf Coast residents four years after Katrina showed a lack of basic hurricane knowledge.[21] More than five hundred residents were given a list of questions meant to determine what they knew about hurricanes. People were asked if they had a well-developed plan for hurricane season, if they had an evacuation plan, about the usefulness of different media outlets including television, radio, newspaper, and the Web, and how much they would miss different aspects of their communities if they had to evacuate. Knowledge about hurricanes was a composite of questions such as what are the different storm categories, what is the most dangerous category, and what kind of damage do Category 1, 3, or 5 storms cause such as power outages, downed trees, and flooding. Finally, they were asked how much confidence they had in government systems to protect them from the next storm.

The most troubling finding was the vast discrepancy in hurricane knowledge based on race. African Americans scored a "C," or 77 percent, on knowledge of hurricanes. Whites scored ten percentage points higher, or 87 percent. The more you know, the more likely you are to seek out information about storm consequences, preparations, and evacuation plans. This discrepancy in knowledge increases the risk to this population during a crisis. And to further stifle the flow, the information that is out there, due to the source, is not necessarily being trusted by black communities. More African American respondents said they do not trust the government systems in place to protect them the next time. This continued and robust mistrust is a difficult obstacle to overcome. The ramifications of the missteps of the federal government before, during, and after Katrina apparently are still being felt.

The findings also reaffirm existing research that African Americans trust and use their friends and families and community ties more as information sources. Every possible media outlet can be at your fingertips via a smartphone, yet some communities choose the face-to-face personal connections that they value and trust. What this means for media workers is that casting a wide mainstream media net may not be enough; more untraditional means of message distribution need to be considered. The information transmission process may be more successful if social networks are targeted, specifically family and interpersonal groups, such as churches and community organizations.[22]

Approximately a year after the hurricane knowledge survey, LSU once again found itself surveying Gulf Coast residents about knowledge of another disaster. In the weeks after the oil explosion and gusher, a survey of almost one thousand Gulf Coast residents most affected by the oil disaster indicated what they felt was the cause. With more than 70 percent saying they were very attentive to the oil disaster coverage, more than 23 percent of those in the Gulf Coast states surveyed believed the oil spill was a *natural* disaster and could *not* have been prevented by the industry or the government. They rejected the idea that the explosion, blowout, and subsequent spill could have been prevented. To most, the disaster was natural, not man-made. When asked what the effect of the spill would be on environmental conditions including coastal wetlands and wildlife protection, almost 34 percent of the Gulf Coast residents said "not much" or "little to no."[23] However, the survey showed that Gulf Coast residents were aware enough of the environmental implications to say that they were less likely to buy Gulf seafood because of it. Despite the sustained disaster, Louisiana residents surveyed were more supportive of offshore drilling than residents in other Gulf Coast states.

When it comes to users and communicators, the oil disaster was different from Katrina. First, there wasn't a communications blackout, but instead, an information barrier to journalists caused by a lack of science knowledge (see chapter 5). Secondly, there wasn't significant interaction between news workers and users for life-saving information. Katrina had an immediate threat on life. The oil disaster had a long-term threat to livelihoods. And thirdly, over time, interest in the story, other than the need to know whether to eat Gulf Coast fish, waned. Media use also did not vary according to the different stages of the oil spill. There was of course the initial spike in use when a crisis story breaks, but use continued in usual patterns as the crisis endured (variation in use was found in national versus local, which will be discussed in chapter 3). For weeks, if not months, Katrina victims had to put their lives on hold. They had to have an ongoing relationship with the news to know if and when to return to their cities and their lives.

2

JOURNALISTS LIVE
THEIR DISASTER STORIES

Peggy Gaddy of Belle Chasse, Louisiana, wrote to one of the *Times-Pica-yune*'s managing editors, Peter Kovacs, six months following Hurricane Katrina insisting that the paper's Living section columnist, Chris Rose, deserved a raise. The reason: "His column in Friday's paper made me laugh out loud when there was not much to laugh about."[1] Before Katrina, Rose had been somewhat of a local legend. His writings were quirky like the city, featuring local celebrity chef culture, the state's burgeoning film industry, and the goings-on of Mardi Gras, festivals, and the old rock 'n' roll scene. Now, Rose joked a year later, he was a national celebrity, a best-selling author, a finalist for the 2006 Pulitzer Prize in column writing, and undeservingly mentioned in the same sentence with his inspirations, columnists Leonard Pitts of the *Miami Herald* and Nicholas Kristoff of the *New York Times*. The main issue was that Rose did not understand why he had been interviewed on National Public Radio and asked to write essays for the *PBS NewsHour* with Jim Lehrer. Such exposure in public television was typically "TV news for smart people," a category Rose felt he did not belong to.[2]

Despite his national speaking forays, Rose was even more stunned by invitations to speak in the city of New Orleans itself, including eating lunch with the "super secret enclave" that is the all-women's group of the Orleans Club on St. Charles Avenue. He attended the event simply because no men are allowed, and Rose wanted to be the first male to claim to be inside the building, where the women eat lunch weekly and "wear white gloves." Another time, he was invited to speak at the relaunch of the Touro synagogue's monthly Friday night lecture series. He quipped that an Irish Catholic like himself probably had nothing relevant to say to the community, but went anyway because the organizers wanted him there to kick-start their series after the storm. And, finally, Rose was invited to address four hundred Catholic schoolgirls and forty nuns at the local Sacred Heart High School in the Uptown area of the city for a reading of his best-selling book at the time, *One Dead in Attic*. Recognizing how out of place he was, he kept apologizing to the nuns and students that the two short stories that were selected included the word "lesbian" several times.[3]

"I get invited to speak at all kinds of places I was never invited to once you start winning all these *'prestigious'* awards," Rose said quizzically to managers and editors at the 2006 Associated Press Managing Editors conference held in downtown New Orleans. Commenting on this newfound local and national fame, he said, "I guess I was considered both an influential and inspirational member of the community now—which is very frightening. A community that looks to me for inspiration is a community that is in dire need of [he laughs to himself], huh, addressing its problems."[4]

And the awards did pour in for the New Orleans press after Hurricane Katrina. A market often overlooked or seen as a brief stepping-stone to larger markets now received recognition for its nothing-short-of-heroic efforts before, during, and after the storm. WWL-TV, channel 4, like the *Times-Picayune*, took home its industry's most prestigious prize in April 2006—the George Foster Peabody Award. The *Times-Picayune* and the Biloxi *Sun Herald* shared the 2006 Pulitzer Prize for Public Service to their communities. The *Times-Picayune* also won the Pulitzer the same year in the Breaking News Reporting category.

WWL-TV stood out during the prize season of 2006, because it was the only station able to keep its satellite going, during, and after the storm. This took place thanks to its transmitter facilities housed in an unflooded location in the town of Gretna, on the west bank of the New Orleans metropolitan area. The station's competitors housed their transmitters in St. Bernard Parish, said Logan Banks, WWL-TV's weekend assignment editor and special projects producer. "And we all know what happened to St. Bernard Parish," recalled Banks, referring to the complete wipeout of the parish by storm surge and subsequent flooding.[5] The team that stayed at the station only evacuated on the Tuesday following the storm to join the rest of the staff set up to broadcast from the television station at Louisiana State University's Manship School of Mass Communication, and then later to the Louisiana Public Broadcasting station in Baton Rouge. Since theirs was the only New Orleans broadcast signal still running, thanks to the signal in Gretna, the station's engineers linked up to that signal in the city, while broadcasting from Baton Rouge. Given this remarkable feat, the company's corporate resources came flooding to their aid.

Lucy Bustamante, a young reporter at the time with WWL-TV in New Orleans, had nothing but praise for how the station's parent company stood behind the staff immediately after the storm. Before Katrina, Bustamante understood the rules of the television industry in terms of moving to larger markets to grow as a journalist and to have access to "bigger" stories that have impact, in order to advance her career. Katrina changed the way she viewed the New Orleans and Gulf Coast television media market:

> Belo Corporation treated us like gold. We stayed at the apartment complex . . . at the end of Siegen [Lane, in Baton Rouge]. And you know we were living like gypsies for a while. But our staff has never been closer. To see people leave and move away after the storm has broken our hearts on levels that it wouldn't have hurt beforehand.[6]

Weekend editor Logan Banks agreed. "We had a lot of support from our corporate base, Belo out of Dallas. We had what was called 'Belo-nation,'" Banks said. "We had satellite trucks, and photographers and reporters, and just all kinds of managerial help, converging on Baton Rouge."[7]

The *Times-Picayune*'s publisher, Ashton Phelps, Jr., as well as its owner, Advanced Publications, stood behind its journalists throughout the disaster and the recovery from the storm. From the beginning of the storm, Jim Amos, the executive editor, said the paper's owners saw the importance of keeping the paper functioning optimally with its most valuable resource, its staff, for the sake of the city in the years to come. He recalled:

> The most important support any worker can get is to be paid without any interruption. That was an extraordinary feat. First of all, it was a very generous act on the part of our owners to immediately guarantee that we would all be paid for the near future, until a decision can be made about the long-term future. And that we would even be paid on that first week when our auditing department, our payroll, was in complete disarray, just like everything else at the newspaper. So that was really a vital assurance.
>
> And then, longer term, our owners, they had no way to know what would become of our market. And I think faced with the circumstances they were faced with, a lot of other owners might have panicked, might have decided it was time to lay workers off, and our owners did none of that. Our owners supported us 100 percent and there was not a single layoff at our newspaper.[8]

While the corporate owners never imagined they would have to support their employees in such a way—nor did the journalists imagine covering a domestic story in such displaced crisis conditions—all knew what was at stake. This was a once-in-a-lifetime event that demanded super saturation of resources, time, and creativity to meet personal and professional challenges. With an event so impactful, so unexpected, a flare goes up in the newsroom signaling an emergency.[9] Gaye Tuchman[10] first introduced the concept of "what a story," which Michael Schudson[11] later termed the "holy shit" story. By designating a major event as a "what a story," journalists know how to produce a narrative that will garner professional success. Journalists go into routine modes, in that they know what routines will complete the story, and how the story should look, to fit the standard of success for their field.[12]

The economics of a news story on this scale is part of the "what a story" designation. Mass communication scholar John McManus[13] stated that newsrooms are at their best when the situation is at its worst. Likewise, viewership and readership are also at their best when situations are at their worst.[14] People flock to information outlets during times of crisis because it reduces their anxiety, feeding their need to know. The New Orleans market rose to the challenge successfully by covering the story with award-winning, compassionate journalism—compassionate because the journalists were victims of the crisis themselves. While the city was truly at its worst, the journalists and their corporate parents were at their best, and it was thus reflected in the coverage.

Using New and Old Media

The unprecedented nature of this disaster shifted traditional ways of thinking about information dissemination. Old and new media were used in new and unexpected ways. The importance of news during the Katrina disaster, and in the months following, was so vital that radio owners did the unprecedented for news formats. First, Clear Channel New Orleans and Entercom, long-time fierce rivals in the radio market of the region, teamed up staff, resources, and facilities. Under the umbrella name of United Broadcasters of New Orleans, their staff of disc jockeys, news reporters, talk show hosts, and producers worked in five-hour shifts to broadcast news for twenty-four hours a day in what seemed like a broom closet at the Clear Channel Baton Rouge facility.

It was through this team effort that one of the most unforgettable news events took place. As Entercom's Garland Robinette hosted his shift for the United Broadcasters of New Orleans, the mayor of New Orleans, Ray Nagin, gave his now-infamous interview, urging the federal government to "do something, and fix the biggest 'dah-gawn' crisis in the history of this country."[15] The interview, replayed on CNN and international media outlets, was seen as a breakthrough for getting people out of the Superdome and the Convention Center, and for sending more resources to rescue people off rooftops. Monica Pierre, then the news director for Clear Channel New Orleans, had just come off her morning rotation before Robinette came on and recalled the interview:

> When I found out that the mayor used the radio medium to have that impassioned, I'm not going to worry about how I come across, I'm going to be an emotional person, saying that this needs to happen right now, again, I never felt more proud to be part of a medium, especially where news was concerned, [radio] was pretty much a stepchild to television, for example.[16]

While radio regained prominence, the hurricane helped push forward the evolving new media environment. The *Times-Picayune* could not print or deliver the paper when the flooding damaged their presses.[17] Its online counterpart, NOLA.com, was traditionally known for Mardi Gras and event coverage, but its form and function changed after Hurricane Katrina. NOLA.com published information in a blog format for the community and the nation. James O'Byrne, director of content for NOLA.com, said they built neighborhood forums on the site for people to report what was going on in their area. Hurricane Katrina top-level officials even monitored this site to locate citizens around New Orleans.[18] Relatives in Idaho blogged on NOLA.com, writing where their loved ones were located in New Orleans and needed to be evacuated. Additionally, WWL news director Chris Slaughter says new technology created a crisis community bulletin board:

> The Web was able to drill down to the neighborhood level. It set up individual pages where people could go in and say, "Hey, has anybody seen the property at 3710 Bienville Street?" And they would say, "Yeah, I saw it had water" or "It didn't." In addition to people being able to visit our sites and find out about their neighborhood, we were monitoring the input and looking for stories.[19]

The site became a community portal at a moment in time when the potential of a news website to serve as an emergency community portal had not yet been realized. The *Times-Picayune* staff, online journalists, and citizen journalists came together to digitally update the nation, and in fact the world, about the havoc wreaked by the storm and the rescue missions.[20] According to O'Byrne, "I don't think anybody sat around out of design and said, 'Let's start a revolution.' I think it was just a response to the need to disseminate information and to have this venue in order to do so."[21] Today NOLA.com is a fully integrated site that serves the New Orleans community with news, weather, sports, and the option to follow this site on Facebook and Twitter. There is also a Hurricane Center that tracks the latest storms and an area where users can post their weather news.

The journalists had seen, through Katrina, how overnight their media market went from being a local one to being not just a national market at the time but an international one.

"We got like seventy million hits in a month," said Kevin Held, the Internet news producer for WWL-TV.com. WWL began streaming its coverage online for twenty-four hours the week after the storm and then for eighteen hours in September. The initial doubling of medium between television and the Web for its broadcast content crashed WWL's website on the first day, Held said.

> We got knocked out of the server here because a bunch of people flooded the site and were trying to get on all at once and that crashed the site. Then CBS . . . tried letting us use their bandwidth . . . and that crashed. It was Yahoo! who said they would host us streaming broadcast over the Internet and then we did not crash and that was how we were able to get so many millions of hits during September. They were like, hey you guys can come and use our stuff.[22]

For Yahoo! to directly stream WWL's coverage of Katrina from August 29 throughout the month of September, according to Held, is unique. For millions of viewers who were displaced and curious international onlookers to crash the WWL and then CBS's websites to watch the aftermath coverage of a local television station speaks to the importance of their ability to continually stay on the air. Those viewers could have chosen to watch CNN's coverage of Fox News, said Banks, the station's weekend editor, but they chose, even if it was online, to find the local station. Held added that the trend carried over into 2006, as many viewers were still displaced across the country. It made the Internet the transforming link, Held said, in turning a local television station into a national and international media source.

> My boss found we were getting hits from around the world, around the country, and people who had evacuated were coming to us because we were streaming our broadcast live. If you weren't in Baton Rouge, watching us on TV, 'cause

we were at a public access station . . . you had to watch us on the Internet. And I took a lot of pride in knowing that we on the Internet played a very large part in people getting information.[23]

Both radio and newspapers across the Gulf Coast saw how their Internet coverage took them to international market levels at least up to the anniversary of the storm. Jon Donley, the Web editor for Nola.com, and Kate Magandy, the online editor for the Biloxi *Sun Herald*'s website, said a year to four years after the storm the traffic levels online for their content tripled from what it was before the storm. For the *Times-Picayune*, Nola.com became an internationally known website for the first time, Donley said.

Traffic-wise, our servers are fortunately located in Jersey City, at our corporate headquarters. And because we get huge spikes of traffic, during Halloween, New Year's, and Mardi Gras, we have a big server bank. It's easy for them to boost us up to 50 servers, if necessary. And we have versatile bandwidth capability. So we went from an average traffic of about 808 page views a day, to a peak of 32 million page views a day. And over the long term, like the *Sun Herald*, we've basically settled in double the rate we were before the storm.[24]

New Kind of Journalism

The international and national attention on local news reports and the Gulf Coast journalists who produced them was a stark change as a result of Katrina, as Chris Rose humorously lamented in 2006. It created success for these newsworkers, in their given market, that they had never thought was possible before in local journalism. Mark Schleifstein, the environmental reporter at the *Times-Picayune*, had won the paper's only Pulitzer Prize for reporting before the storm for covering coastal erosion and the region's wetlands. He had spent many years at the paper with that coveted beat, shedding light on scientific and environmental concerns about New Orleans and the region. However, before the storm, his writings had a limited audience among universities, local officials, and science reporters. Following Katrina, his book, cowritten with his fellow reporter John McQuaid, titled *Path of Destruction: The Devastation of New Orleans and the Coming Age of Superstorms*, was a hit-seller not just in the state, but across the country.

Success had reached rookie reporters as well, not just the veterans. Trymaine Lee, the paper's police and crime reporter, had joined the

Times-Picayune only four months before the storm and was still on probation. He was unintentionally left behind at the New Orleans City Hall and
then at the Hyatt Hotel downtown when the paper evacuated its building the Tuesday morning the levees broke and the floodwaters rose. Lee
recalled that his editor told him before the storm that he would return to
pick him up, but never did, when cell phones and landlines went down. He
said he found out later that Tuesday evening, via a text message from a
friend in New Jersey, that Nola.com had posted a picture of *Times-Picayune* staff evacuating their flooded building in the backs of the newspaper's
delivery trucks. It was then that Lee left the flooding city hall and headed
to the damaged Hyatt Hotel, mostly without a plan.

As he walked into the crowded lobby, he came across a woman by the
name of Lucrece Phillips. Her story, the first to describe the horrors of the
rising floodwaters of those left behind, put "cub reporter" Lee on the cita-
tion list with roughly ten of the veteran reporters whose stories, together,
won the *Times-Picayune*'s second Pulitzer Prize in 2006 for Breaking News
Reporting.

"As a young reporter, being at the *Times-Picayune* when all of this was
going down, you end up getting a lot of success from this in one sense," Lee
said. "Then you have Pulitzers, and then the Spike Lee documentary, you
have all these things, and radio and TV interviews, and it's hard because
you're getting success on what I view on the back of so much struggles,
and that's the part I'm trying to grapple with." The difference for him and
his colleagues was that reporters elsewhere "might have the luxury of saying, 'hey, this is what we do,'" and patting themselves on the back. Lee felt
he did not have the right to accept praise, and even felt embarrassed that
such a tragedy had actually propelled his career. "People are still suffering," he said. "Fortunately, and unfortunately, I am emotionally connected
to the people."[25]

In fact, Lee's words have become the echoed mantra of Gulf Coast journalists. As far as the state of their profession was concerned, that was the
true success of having survived the Katrina experience. This connection to
New Orleans, the region, and to its peoples revolutionized local journalism in the post-Katrina media landscape. It is found not only on the front
pages, websites, radio broadcasts, and television reports produced since
the storm, but in the stories of survival and recovery of the journalists
themselves.

In-depth interviews conducted with thirty Gulf Coast journalists, editors, and media workers in 2005, immediately after the storm, and then in

2006, on the one-year anniversary, paint a telling picture of the local post-Katrina media world.[26]

The Katrina Media Experience

WWL-TV's Lucy Bustamante got a wake-up call as she covered Katrina. She thought that being the only television journalist of Hispanic background in the media market at the time brought some measure of uniqueness and valued point of view at her station. She recalled feeling embarrassed that, as a young woman and a reporter, she never spent more time, other than a quick crime report, in the city's more impoverished and hot-spot inner city areas. She recalled:

> We had always been reporting, in sections of town in New Orleans, basically, I'd go cover a murder at four o'clock in the morning in an area that I had never been to outside of work. And you know, shame on me, for talking about this place too, that's another thing I learned. I'd been going into bad areas talking about how people had died when I didn't even know how they'd been living. And that's an injustice to them.

Bustamante described Katrina as a great equalizer across the New Orleans metropolitan area, as if with one gushing wind, the storm wiped out all the superficial divides between rich and poor, white and black, and even Hispanic, Uptown, Gentilly, and the Ninth Ward, city officials and the homeless, and uniquely between journalists and their sources. They were all displaced, having lost their homes, and were hungry, smelly, and filled with a sense of hopelessness immediately after the storm. Many of the journalists interviewed were outraged by characterizations of evacuees at the Superdome, the Convention Center, and elsewhere, as they later found out from interacting with national journalists that had descended on the scene. Chris Rose recalled himself becoming a looter. He, along with other reporters at a makeshift bureau in the city, raided the Antoine's restaurant freezer in Uptown. They took 680 prime ribs and New York strips to cook for members of the California National Guard who were keeping watch on them, bringing water and military Meals Ready to Eat for them in the aftermath. He recounted how they went in search of a port-o-let at a construction site, and took it back to the makeshift bureau. Rose said a photographer even got them guns from a law enforcer—guns allegedly tagged as murder weapons, to protect themselves as they camped out in the abandoned city.

Rookie reporter at the time Trymaine Lee recounted not taking a shower for days until he finally ran into *Times-Picayune* photographer John McCusker, who took him to his parents' unflooded house on the west bank for him to take a shower and get something to eat. "I finally took a hot shower, and I was in the same clothes for days, it was a really bad funky situation going on," he said. Later on, when he got together with the rest of the *Times-Picayune* team of reporters at a makeshift bureau at a staffer's home, they would take dips in the pool of the neighbor's house to cool off from the summer heat and lack of air conditioning—a sort of necessary trespassing. In other words, it was not just the massive stranded "refugees" of displaced residents flashed on national television screens who were doing illegal acts at the time. The journalists found themselves in some of these precarious situations as well. They felt they were the last ones to pass judgment on their fellow New Orleanians.

Even before Lee found his coworkers, he spent the night of the storm at the New Orleans City Hall. As the floodwaters rose, unsure of what to do, he fled the flooding city hall along with the city employees, and walked over to the Hyatt Hotel where the city's leaders were stationed. He described a cramped and crowded hotel that was by no means luxurious, with dimmed lobby lights, flapping curtains, and no air conditioning. He saw and spoke with city officials such as Chief of Police Eddie Compass and his information officer, Marlon Defillo. He recalled all of these officials working tirelessly, rescuing trapped residents, never stopping to sleep, shower, or eat. They had all been wearing the same clothes since Monday, just as he was, and they all were "funky," as he described the smell of officials who had not been able to take a shower. They all slept on the floor of the Hyatt, or city hall, or wherever they were. Lee's reporting not only characterized the devastation differently but provided the shared situation of people from every corner of the metropolitan region.

Lee described the "kind of journalism" he was trying to do before as a new reporter on the scene as being dramatically changed post-Katrina.

After those experiences I'm no longer that "cub reporter" that just got here, I'm a little more seasoned. I always wanted to tell people's stories, especially from the community. I was a police reporter before, so the people I was encountering during Katrina, you know I was in the hood all day long, covering crime and police, so . . . I got a pulse of what the community was like. I had a kind of connection.

After Katrina, what I wanted to do before, those tools I was gathering up as part of my arsenal, made it easier. Because my heart was already with the community, trying to make sure I get the truth out, trying to make sure I peeled back the layers, and that we always expose the humanity of the circumstances of people.

Those early days, it was hard again, being the only black reporter here, because these are my people, first and foremost, and beyond all this journalism, beyond being a reporter, these are my people here, so to see that kind of suffering and to not be able to do anything about it, but use their voices to tell their stories. You know that was not more pressure, but it was more important at that point.

Lee and Bustamante were young reporters who were now beginning to identify with the city and region they covered, and yet were profoundly changed. They both found that covering Katrina brought another equalizer into their newsrooms between themselves and the veterans. Younger journalists had lost homes and possessions and endured the same circumstances as the veterans. They covered the Katrina disaster with the same intensity as the veterans and had emerged battle-scarred. To this day, in many of these newsrooms across the region, journalists hired after the storm are easily labeled as being "post-Katrina," and find themselves with an added level to live up to, in addition to being rookies.

However, Lee observed that the effect of the storm on veterans was even more obvious. Lee said that, as a black reporter in a predominantly black city, he felt connected to the people through his rounds in the inner city. However, unlike the veterans, he didn't quite get enough time to fall in love with the physical city itself.

"Early on, I didn't think that I had deserved the right to feel so bad, because I look around and people are dying," Lee said. "I also didn't have that love where I felt like I was going to cry: 'I can't believe New Orleans will never be the same,' I never had that feeling," he added, referring to the feelings of the veteran reporters at the paper.

However, as time went on, and the burden of covering the devastation every day for years to come set in, signs began to show. John McCusker, the same photographer who took the stranded Lee for his first hot shower three days after the storm, was arrested for attempting to commit suicide a year later after the storm. He reportedly asked police officers to shoot him, after he rammed several cars with his vehicle. He had sunk into a depression after receiving FEMA rejection letters, and had become frustrated with the insurance process.[27] He has since received treatment after his court hearing in 2006.

Even the laid-back Chris Rose had a public breakdown through his column. He said:

> I wrote a story in last week's paper where I outed myself on my mental illnesses and my treatments thereof. It's amazing. People were kind to me before, now everyone whispers to me, "How are you doing," patting me on the shoulder. I'm going, "I'm fine. I'm heavily medicated. Where were you in June? When I needed someone to break my fall."[28]

Some of the journalists recalled that as time passed, it was taboo to discuss their mental states. They all wanted to do the best job possible in the recovery and rebuilding of their communities. They sidelined the stress of gutting their homes, managed short-term debts from evacuating, dealt with spouses who had lost their jobs, and battled depression. Lee recalled:

> People dealt with it in various ways. Some people, during the initial days of the crisis, just had this adrenaline rush, you had your blinders on, just get the story, everywhere you turned you were focused, you couldn't look beyond this, so you were right here, you were focused on the story. And as time has gone on, we saw people crumble emotionally. Some people have had breakdowns, some people have had to do whatever, medicate themselves. Some people have turned to the bottle.[29]

The event that caused both personal loss and emotional strain resulted in a new kind of journalism, one many of them described but could not exactly name. This new journalism Lee described as different from the "kind of journalism," or perhaps traditional journalism, he was trained with at school. Lee said:

> I don't know if the classroom will ever teach you how to react and respond in these kinds of circumstances. Or can ever dictate how you're supposed to present the news. You know after something like this, you're talking about fifteen hundred, sixteen hundred people dead. You're talking about a city completely plunged into the depths of this crazy flooding. I think it's changed the approach in a sense but we have to know how to be chameleon-like and how to shift with the timing because in this place and time, this is what the community needs us to be.[30]

Lee is referring to the more aggressive and authoritative tone of coverage that had become typical of local journalism in the post-Katrina media landscape. When it came to television, Mike Hoss, the ten o'clock anchor with WWL-TV, applauded the fact that Katrina transformed local news from "soft" news about people to "hard" news about people.

"It has enabled us to do so many stories with such gravity and such importance in people's lives," Hoss said. "I have never felt more needed as a journalist, as a reporter, in helping people rebuild their lives, in being a watchdog over government and money, and all the factors that are happening poststorm."

Aside from a stark shift in tone and coverage on television and in print, this new "kind of journalism," has perhaps been the most dramatic in revitalizing news on radio. It had become a dying tradition in the world of music-only and talk-radio formats, said Monica Pierre, the veteran broadcaster in New Orleans who shifted from being the news director at Clear Channel New Orleans before the storm to cohosting the morning news show at Entercom's WWL-AM 870 radio station.

Pierre said she hoped that the type of aggressive news and reports that radio had been producing in the months immediately following the storm would put enough pressure on owners to balance news with the talk and music formats. She soon found out the effort would be short-lived.

> There was just this optimistic part of me saying, hey, we are going to sustain this. Because even as people started returning home, to New Orleans and to the greater metro area, they need this information. I was just shocked to learn that it didn't last very long.
>
> In fact, I remember speaking to my program director for the music station that we have to keep this information pipeline going. It's going to change; people will need different types of information. People need to know what's going on with the future of their city. I remember the person at the time telling me, but how will we stop the music. I'm thinking how will we stop the music? We stop the music![31]

Pierre said she proposed to Clear Channel a daily, one-hour news show that would focus on relevant information for the recovery. It was turned down, but Clear Channel did introduce a news-talk format, which she described as a positive outcome of the post-Katrina media landscape. Entercom, the company she shifted to after the storm, did away with some syndicated programming and kept the news segments.

"It was short-lived, the commitment to have local information-based programming," Pierre said. "We went back to just doing it on the Sunday shows, prerecording it, nothing live." The experiment with revitalizing news coverage on radio was an important one, given that displaced residents scattered around Louisiana, the Gulf Coast, and those trapped in attics could only turn to a radio station for information. She felt that should have signaled a return to more news on radio.

"We're missing a golden opportunity, especially now with this rebuilding . . . of keeping the local information pipeline going," Pierre said. "I don't know if corporations have the will to keep it going, on non music-talk formats."[32]

Gorden Russell, a city reporter with the *Times-Picayune*, described himself as becoming more "direct" in his writing since the storm. He, however, attempted to clarify how they, as local journalists affected by the storm, showed their aggression, as opposed to the national media.

> It's become sort of this cheap reflex to . . . get into these arguments with some
> of these politicians. Some of the Anderson Coopers, and Brians [Williams],
> some of those things, feel like editorializing or grandstanding a little bit. I'm
> not so crazy about that. I think you still have to be fair and balanced. The whole
> reason we're going through all this . . . is they're [the readers] depending on us.
> They don't want some wishy-washy bullshit when we're done, they wanna know
> what we found out. So I think that's a good development.[33]

David Meeks, the *Times-Picayune* city editor, had been the sports editor before the storm. He described how the connection sports readers had with the *Times-Picayune*, as the authority on the New Orleans Saints, had spread to the general readership view of the *Times-Picayune* as an authority on the city and region, post-Katrina.

> While we were a good paper before the storm, we've become a more aggres-
> sive paper after the storm. I think we feel very connected to our readers,
> I think they feel very connected to us. If you look at certain communities,
> I think there is a love-hate relationship with the local paper. They love that
> they have a paper, but they hate some of the things they do. I think the peo-
> ple of New Orleans, the whole metro area, view the *Times-Picayune* as looking
> out for the best interests of this community. And by that I mean, explaining
> to them the rules on flood elevation, explaining to them insurance, how to
> get things done.

I see the *Times-Picayune* right now as a practical guide on how to live here. It's hard to live here right now, if you have all these questions and no answers. And they see the newspaper, in an issue that has a lot of complexity, and a complicated answer, and they don't lend themselves to television, they lend themselves perfectly to print. We take the time to explain these issues carefully and I think people realize that, and they are very engaged because they want to get a good understanding of what the future's gonna be like here.[34]

For these journalists, the region was not just where they worked; Katrina made it their home. New Orleans can no longer be overlooked as a second-rate news market, said WWL's Lucy Bustamante: "This is not the best place in the world to raise your kids, but at the same time, the way I see it, my selfish purpose is that there's no better place for a journalist to be."[35]

Gulf Coast Journalists Predict Their Future

Monica Pierre was accurate in her assessment of the central need and the rebirth of local media years later after national attention had drifted away from the Katrina story. Where she was unsure was to what degree local journalism could sustain the new "kind of journalism."

David Meeks, the *Times-Picayune* city editor, said he started calling himself the Katrina editor because it remained the main news coming out of the city. "We've already talked about when will be the first *Times-Picayune* to be published without the word Katrina in it and we don't know when that's going to happen," Meeks said on the year anniversary. It is hard for a paper to stop covering a story, he said, when the story is the long-term reality of not only their lives but those of their readers.

A year later, when you're not back in your house, when you're still fighting with your insurance company, when you still can't get garbage pickup, or you're worried about police protection, or your streetlights turning on, that's when it starts to wear on people.

The burnout is not going to come from us so much focusing on Katrina, because it's not like we're focusing on something people don't see everyday. People here are still living Katrina. They will continue to live Katrina for quite some time. We know the newspaper is going to reflect what is going on in the community.[36]

It is not just that the paper is simply reflecting the community; it is also reflecting the lives of the Gulf Coast's journalists themselves. Gordon Russell, the city reporter, called Katrina their "double-edged sword." He recalled a coworker being interviewed for a job a year later and editors from different papers asking that reporter why he would ever leave a "story" like Katrina. The reporter recalled them saying, "It's the best story of your life." For Russell, and that reporter, Katrina is a story that never goes away, and sometimes a nightmare they see in the daytime. "It's Katrina, Katrina, Katrina, enough already," Russell said. "It's a personal story." He remembered housing some national journalists months after the crisis and felt like punching one of them in the mouth for their comments about the city and the people, as though it was "cool" to cover the disaster.

> They were so detached from it. . . . And then every now and again they'd go like, oh, sorry! I'm saying, sorry about your city. . . . And you realize that's the way reporters are, because they're used to parachuting in to wherever the latest thing happens. And if they took every one of them personally, I guess they'd go crazy. And if you don't live there, after a while it's just another disaster or whatever. And it wasn't that they weren't compassionate, you realize that it's a little different when it's the place that you live is being torn to pieces.[37]

John "Spud" McConnell, host of *The Spud Show* on Entercom's WWL-AM, put it more bluntly. "We will be discussing aspects of Katrina for ten years." McConnell rode out the storm at Entercom's building near the Superdome before he evacuated to Baton Rouge to work with the United Broadcasters of New Orleans. He said doing news, instead of talk, during the hurricane helped expand his listening audience and earned him the respect of his coworkers in the industry, particularly Garland Robinette, the veteran regional television and radio broadcaster. Since his show has continued on Entercom after the storm, McConnell's listeners still have a connection with him out of the shared Katrina experience, when he lost his home.

"I'm trying to get away from it as much I can, but you can't, because we're still devastated here, because we're still a mess."[38] Regarding most news topics discussed on his show, every decision the government or his listeners make has to be weighed against Katrina. That makes Katrina implicit, if not explicit, in everything he discusses.

> It's going to take years. Katrina will still have a physical effect on this city and this region, and Rita too, for at least another five [years]. And we'll still be

scooping up mud from it another ten years from now, not a lot of mud, but some. But ten years from now you'll be able to drive around somewhere and go, "That's Katrina, yeah!"[39]

Although many journalists and news managers see it as tragic that something devastating earned them loyalty and symbolism in their communities, they have realized that it would be irresponsible for them to just dismiss Katrina's impact on their profession. The symbolism of what Gulf Coast journalists did in providing nonstop news coverage across all media still resonated five years later, not only for media workers, but for their audiences as well.

Times-Picayune editor Jim Amos explained this best:

Usually what happens in newspapers is that reporters and photographers come into people's lives at a moment of great crisis and write about the crisis and the trauma, and then they go home. And the next day they come in and they maybe have a different assignment. And that's the paradigm.

In our case, we were in the crisis ourselves. And everything that was happening in our readers' lives was happening in our own lives individually. And we were going to see people who had lost everything and lost their houses and we're writing about that, and then we were coming home to our spouses, who had lost everything, and our own houses were gone.

I think this identification with our readers and the sharing of the same fate as our readers changed us profoundly. It changed our reporting. It changed the tone of what we wrote about, because we knew intimately what we were talking about. And spoke, I think with, we didn't have to force ourselves to be authoritative, it came naturally because . . . it was the collective life we led. And that has continued to this day. We are a very different newspaper now from a year ago. We are living through the recovery of New Orleans in the same way our readers are, and almost everything that we write about or that we cover in our newspaper is in some way connected to the hurricane and its aftermath. And I think it will be that way for some time.[40]

Post-Katrina Media Environment

Immediately after the storm, and even up to the one-year anniversary, Gulf Coast managers, editors, and journalists reenvisioned their devastated local market. While local media across the Gulf Coast received unusual backing from their corporate owners, and even thrived in the globally devastated media market as a result of the 2008–2009 recession, the realities of the economics became apparent in the calm after the storm. Newspapers and television stations across the country began massive lay-offs within the five years following Katrina, and many well-known big city dailies eventually folded.

The external changing nature of the news business, coupled with the internal downsizing of the outlets in the market, led to a leaner and meaner New Orleans market. The changes in the industry coincided with the two disasters. First Katrina hit, then revolutionary changes in the industry due to digital media and lower profit margins, and then the oil spill. The news resources available at the time of Katrina had slimmed by the time the oil spill came to the forefront of the media agenda.

Before Katrina, New Orleans was a "Top 50" Nielsen TV news market, which carries meaning in the television news business. In 2003, the National Association of Television Program Executives placed the Nielsen news market ranking for New Orleans at forty-two. Seven years and almost ten market sizes later, New Orleans is now the fifty-first news market. New Orleans fell from serving approximately 740,000 households pre-Katrina to just over 630,000 homes in 2010, according to Nielsen.

Within the television market, there are two very extreme cases. WWL is a traditional CBS station. It has been a longtime news leader in the market—owned by the Belo Corporation, one of the largest broadcast organizations in the United States. Belo owns twenty television stations across the United States from Dallas to Boise, Idaho. Belo is an example of how multimedia organizations have been downsizing in this age of the Internet. In 2007, Belo spun off its newspapers and placed some of this debt onto its television stations.[41] Some of Belo's top performing TV stations had pressures to perform at an even higher level and this included New Orleans's WWL. After losing market sizes, they now had to deal with the increased profit pressure from two different fronts.

In juxtaposition to WWL is Tribune's ABC station in New Orleans. By 2009, ABC 26 shrank from two anchors to one anchor per newscast and has begun to hire digital reporters—essentially one-man bands who can shoot, edit, tweet, and place stories and news promotions on the Web. This digital/multimedia shift does not just affect Tribune and its reporters; it is now a nationwide shift across the industry. In a recent Radio Television Digital News Association Survey of more than thirteen hundred television stations, more than 31 percent said they mostly use one-man bands.[42]

Before the storm, Gulf Coast journalists, particularly those in its largest city, New Orleans, felt that others saw their region as a second-rate news market. For sure, the region, and especially New Orleans, was well known across the country as a place for offbeat news, and, in its inner city, for crime. However, many saw the region as a stepping-stone in their careers to larger news markets, especially when it came to those in television broadcasting. Katrina may have initially shrunk the media market for the Gulf Coast region in terms of size, according to Jim Amos, the *Times-Picayune*'s executive editor, but in the long run, Katrina ironically saved local media. However, the *Times-Picayune* offered a buyout to senior staffers in 2009, and saw further reductions in 2012 due to a shift to more online.[43] Given that it's a big-city daily, the effects of the changing media environment could have been far more devastating for the paper had Katrina not strengthened its readership loyalty, even on the Web.

Another Disaster on the Horizon

In his address to the 2006 Associated Press Managing Editors conference held in downtown New Orleans, where he puzzled at his newfound fame, Chris Rose also made a prediction: "Who ever thought the day would come when the city of New Orleans would look to the New Orleans Saints and say that's how we need to be doing things around here. So the paradigm has been shifted upside down, somewhat dramatically I would say."[44]

Rose predicted correctly in 2006 about the symbolism of his newspaper in the community after Katrina. As the New Orleans Saints astonishingly went on to win the Superbowl XLIV in 2010, five years after the storm, the *Times-Picayune*, a paper that lost its presses to the floods and did not publish a print edition for three days after the storm, but did so online, was sold out of print editions for the first time in its history, the day after the Saints won the Superbowl. The newspaper even did the unprecedented and published additional copies of the Superbowl winning front-page edition. People drove from all across the state of Louisiana and even the Gulf Coast for that print edition. And national television captured Saints players holding up preissued front pages of the *Times-Picayune* on the winner's roster. The next day, local television coverage featured lines of readers outside *Times-Picayune* bureaus across the state, waiting to buy sometimes up to ten copies of the paper that included the coverage of the team's win.

The city was once again riding a high, finally vindicated, finally on a true road to recovery. Then, just months later, the city was hit with another tragedy of epic proportions. But this crisis was very different—less personal, less emotional, but nonetheless challenging professionally. It was a different crisis and a different time.

On the five-year anniversary of Hurricane Katrina, Rose wrote:

Because something feels off, way off, on this anniversary thing. Two letters: BP. The legion of doubt, the lingering questions lay you open, vulnerable in this period of such historical, spiritual, financial and emotional reckoning. Those bastards. But we're still standing. And when we get this part fixed, we really oughtta kick out the jams, old school.[45]

Getting "this part fixed" and covered journalistically would lend itself to new challenges for the Katrina journalists as they were dragged into becoming oil spill journalists. What we found when we went back to New Orleans to interview journalists in the summer of 2010 was frustration. Many journalists we interviewed in 2005 once again shared their insights with us. Additional journalists we reached out to for the first time were apprehensive about giving an opinion on the news, granting us access to their thoughts, and preferred to remain anonymous. In other cases, management restrictions were placed on identification. At the time of the interviews, the news was still unfolding and too fresh to discuss. And perhaps the journalists were back to being journalists now without opinions on the news? Whatever the reason, this tragedy took on a different feel—a different set of challenges to norms and routines—and of course, the expected fair and unfair comparisons to an earlier tragedy.

Journalistic Frustration

Three factors made covering the oil spill quite distinct from the Katrina experience for these Gulf Coast journalists. First, they faced the realities of a new nature of the business and market (less with more). Second, the scope of the disaster (offshore, coastline miles away) was local, but in a sense remote. And third, the private sector, instead of the local government, took control of the disaster, limiting news gathering to when they could get access to BP. Oftentimes, they were sidelined from access to the private BP, in favor of the national press.

In essence, the Gulf Coast journalists covered the oil disaster with less staff in a more volatile media environment. But this is where the New Orleans market found itself on April 20, 2010—facing another catastrophic event, but this time with fewer resources. So what happens in newsrooms when you have to cover the largest marine oil spill in the world with a weakened newsroom? One producer admitted that the national outlets had more resources to cover the story than they did in their own backyard.

This local producer summed up his dissatisfaction:

> The national people have the resources now to cover it better. You have the number one station, WWL, who should be a powerhouse, who is a powerhouse, and even they are running national packages from CBS at night and in the morning, on the oil spill, and they are in New Orleans—that says a lot.
>
> Nobody has the resources out there. They should have trucks out there twenty-four hours a day in places like Venice or right now on Barataria Bay, lower Jefferson Parish—that's where these people should be all the time. There should be someone out there all the time. The paper would have someone basically living out there. They would be the ones doing the story now. They [the national networks] have people stationed down there. They are pulling out a package every single day. They can do it, but we are not doing it. We are relying on them.[46]

Unlike Katrina, when the "Belo nation" rallied, the sense of urgency to cover the story appeared reduced. Again, the nature of the disaster lent itself to different coverage. Watching a rig on fire in the middle of the ocean, compared to watching twenty thousand people suffer outside the Superdome, is far less dramatic to remote audiences. Just as it took the national news some time to understand the full impact of the explosion and spill, perhaps parent companies and corporate owners' responses fit the nature of the images.

The networks' stories carried little to no background exploration of New Orleans or the affected region, the producer continued. The stories were short and marketed toward the entire nation, not the region that was experiencing the spill. The television producer continued, "They have a responsibility here to give people what's going on with the oil spill. It is a political thing. This is people making decisions on stuff lightly. This is only the biggest man-made disaster in the history of the United States."

As much as the producers objected to the scope and audience focus of the national networks, these national packages filled in for the lack of local reports on morning and nightly newscasts for Gulf Coast stations. The substitution was another sign of how the economy and the shrinking television news industry had reduced the ability of Gulf Coast journalism to entirely frame its own version of the crisis. To provide more local crews, Gulf Coast stations would have had to resort to pulling from their night crews, a drain they could not sustain for the entire summer of 2010.

Parachute Journalists and Sources

The return of the national journalists to the region stirred up old wounds and rivalries left over from the Katrina experience. While Katrina took days, it took weeks for the national networks to arrive in full force to cover the oil spill disaster. National networks and CNN hounded the local stations for news packages on the unfolding spill, but delayed sending their own teams, unsure of how big the crisis would eventually become. By the time the national news teams arrived, their presence upstaged the local veterans.

Local journalists felt slighted by the restricted access to coverage in what they considered their town. One reporter said, "I have seen Anderson Cooper in places that we weren't able to get into."[47] A local television assignment desk editor added, "Most [of the newsmakers] want to talk to nationals [media] more than they want to talk to us and then we get the feed from nationals. We haven't been able to talk to as many BP people or more of the higher-ups. The local people are very easy to reach."[48] This was in great contrast to Katrina, when the journalists saw the national media as allies, bringing international attention to the causes of the city, including coastal erosion, poverty, and governmental ineptness. With the oil spill, the local media felt second-rate when it came to access to information in their "own town." An analysis of the nature of both crises helps explain this.

With Katrina, the officials in charge of the crisis were part of the local infrastructure—mayor, governor, state police, parish presidents, etc. The local media had interviewed these newsmakers before, and the newsmakers had developed relationships with the local journalists. With the oil spill, the newsmakers were predominantly on the national scene. Louisiana and Gulf Coast officials were considered second-tier news and information sources in terms of managing the crisis. They did not belong to the standard group of officials being interviewed about the oil spill—from Doug Suttles, BP's COO for Exploration and Production, to retired United States Coast Guard Admiral Thad Allen. The oil spill's newsmakers naturally turned to the media sources they had dealt with in the past, and whose outlets carried the highest readership and viewership. Katrina's newsmakers were concerned that displaced residents received information and saw local media sources as their best shot. The spill's newsmakers were concerned with national perceptions of how the Coast Guard and BP handled the crisis. The outsiders created an enormous barricade to information and access on what should have been Gulf Coast journalists' own turf.

Frank Donze, who covered city government for the *Times-Picayune*, had been at the paper for thirty years by 2006. He said he found himself, in the immediate months after Katrina, cutting the mayor and the officials some slack. He understood what it felt like to be tired, blamed, accused, harassed, and labeled, sometimes unfairly, in the Katrina aftermath. Over time, he intensified his coverage of their recovery plans, but in those immediate weeks following the disaster "we all needed a break."[49] Five years earlier, Katrina journalists had access to sources. In 2010, oil spill journalists did not. Local oil spill journalists found few opportunities to cut sources "some slack" or even take them to task because of the limited access to credible sources.

There were some bright spots in the perception of the national media outlets from the Gulf Coast journalists' point of view. Perhaps it could have been that the Katrina experience had some effect on national reporters returning to the scene, and local journalists observed this. Local journalists saw this in particular with CNN's coverage, noting that the news organization was turning out stories daily on the spill, and the network's crews could be spotted throughout the community. One station meteorologist recalled:

> I have to say nationally I think of all the networks CNN has done a really good job. Anderson Cooper has been down here. They have had colleagues down here. From the cable networks I think CNN has made a really good friend in New Orleans—not only from Katrina . . . The other networks, ABC, NBC, CBS, they've been doing their thing as well, but life goes on in the big city and they pull out. They still report it, but not like CNN does. CNN is still here.
>
> They are here every night. They have colleagues reporting every night—local people hearing their voices . . . In the beginning, I think it was fantastic, but I think now it is kind of a story I can't say is getting lost, it is starting to get stale. But for us it's not people elsewhere, around the city. If it doesn't affect you, you are not really in tune with it.[50]

Studies show parachuting, or "out-of-town journalists," lack a measure of sensitivity to the community they cover.[51] Even after the national experience with Katrina, this trend seemed apparent for the spill, in some respects. National reporters may have had the resources but once again, some sources, particularly those in the scientific community, felt the reports of local journalists were more accurate. A Louisiana State University fisheries professor described what it was like to be interviewed by an NBC reporter:

> The national media coverage was irresponsible . . . they focused on let's scare, while the local media focused on let's inform. I have [a reporter from a network television news outlet] asking me if they are getting oily seafood and just how sick that will make people. I tell her that the waters are closed as a precaution against harvesting tainted seafood. She persists with "well, just how sick will that make people?" That is just how simple they get.
>
> And I ask can't we focus on something more positive? She said, "Thank you for your time," and hung up. They wanted to focus on the negative. By and large, the local media was receptive with what was the truth . . . The local people were real—"wait a minute, this was people's lives and livelihoods". . . I thought this was a big difference. The national ones were looking for sensationalism—the local ones seemed to have a better feel for the fishermen—the whole plight for the wholesalers and the retailers.[52]

A dichotomy exists between the Gulf Coast journalists' view of the national press during the oil spill crisis and the Katrina experience. While the Katrina journalists welcomed their national peers' help, during the spill the national presence hindered local coverage. The local journalists were now the "outsider group" and they both praised and maligned national coverage. Perhaps the bipolar attitude stems from their own inability to saturate the story.

Dr. Bob Thomas, chair in environmental communication and director at Loyola's Center for Environmental Communication, said, "Louisiana media have done an excellent job in relation to the resources they were able to apply. They felt limited and frustrated that they could not do more, but they did what they could."[53]

New Kind of Journalism, Hindered

Boat access was the only way to get to the story of both of these tragedies. The Katrina journalists never imagined they would need a boat to cover a story in their own city. For the oil spill, it was a given. The waters, in a sense, contained both stories. However, unlike Katrina, when the waters rose around them, the waters these journalists now needed access to, and thus the story, were at a distance. While New Orleans was officially closed to outside journalists in the initial days, Katrina reporters commandeered their own boats from somewhere or someone, gathered supplies and went; they did what they could do to get the story.

With the oil disaster, the waters that showed the most poignant damage were being guarded by a combination of private and public sector entities. Who was telling whom to block access is an answer that may never surface. However, what was clear and recognized at least by the national press was that the journalists' duties were being hindered by outside forces. The handlers for the oil spill journalists were federal government and big business. The blockage came from well-established and media-savvy groups that knew how to control the message. Across the country these were the headlines: the *Atlantic Wire*: "Are Journalists Being Kept from the Oil Spill?," NPR: "Reporters Face Security Hurdles," "BP, Coast Guard Officers Block Journalists From Filming Oil Covered Beach," the *New York Times*: "BP and Officials Block Some Coverage of Gulf Oil Spill."[54]

Across national media, journalists wrote about BP denying their fellow brethren access to cover the oil-saturated beaches. In one example, operators of a local aircraft contacted the local Coast Guard Federal Aviation Administration asking to fly over a restricted area. The BP contractor who answered the call denied access.[55] The wife-husband team who owned the aircraft said they were questioned extensively for wanting this access. Additionally, the three-week delay for BP to release the underwater oil leak images was also not acceptable to some scientists.[56]

The hindrance was so great that there was a call for citizen journalists to step in and help. Online a "Raw Story of Coast Guard Bans" appeared on YouTube. The "Louisiana Bucket Brigade," an environmental health and justice organization, made a call for citizen journalists, asking for pictures, e-mails, and texts related to Gulf fishermen and wildlife, in an effort to help map the breadth of the spill.[57]

Back in a local New Orleans newsroom, an anchor for more than thirty years said he was "voted down" and not allowed to do an access story. "I wanted to go challenge a road block and I was told no one cares about inside news business stories—I was told that's all about *us*, who cares?"[58]

Some journalists said that BP's control of the disaster, and in effect, the story, made them reliant on the company for information. It could have been, as a result, that the nation, including journalists, turned against the company. One journalist recalled:

The guys running the show, BP, have been able to tell the Coast Guard to restrict media access to certain areas, whether it be a body of water that's here or a certain marshy section or a sand bar out there. I think everyone has run into that, anyone that has covered the spill.

That to me seems to be enough to get them to say, all right, we are being made to look like we are covering things up and we better stop as it's not going to bode well for us in the public relations department at the end of things.[59]

One producer stated it plainly: "We are relying on a company, BP [for information]. This is symptomatic of bad journalism." During Katrina, the journalists became the experts, the sources of authority on what was happening because they were living the experience while they reported it. The oil spill rendered them observers. The authority they gained from Katrina was inadvertently transferred back to the newsmakers during the oil spill, particularly BP. Clearly, local journalists wanted to call things as they saw it, especially with regards to access.

It is likely that the effects of the Katrina experience still influenced the boldness with which they saw the task of telling their readers the truth. This "new kind of journalism," in theory, was hindered in practice with the oil spill, simply because the information remained out of their reach. Given the weakened media industry after the recession, many editors, it seemed, lacked the courage to publish or air stories that reflected editorialized grumblings about the local media's lack of access. They fell back on safety, and stuck to whatever information they received—even if it was sanitized by BP.

Despite the manhandling, Gulf Coast journalists aggressively worked to overcome these setbacks. They found ways to produce stories that reflected the background of the Gulf Coast region and place the oil spill in a local context. They still continued to frame the information from BP to reflect the effect of the spill on the community they understood so well. They may not have been able to report the developments of the attempts to cap the gushing well, but they were able to capture the mood of the community as it dealt with yet another blow.

Disaster Comparisons

Katrina and the oil spill were both unprecedented disasters that happened to hit the same region, within the same decade. Yet for the journalists who covered both, the experiences were as distinct as chalk and cheese. The comparison of these two disasters bubbled up suppressed feelings still lingering from

Katrina. Hurricane Katrina was more than just another disastrous story the region survived. It remains a story with the faces of their friends, family, neighbors, coworkers, and the misfortunes they knew so well and vividly remembered. It has become part of their own personal story of their lives, as the day they went to college, or got their first job—the day Katrina hit.

The contrast of loss of life and human suffering between the two disasters also shares no comparison for local journalists. Economic and psychological effects of both disasters still hold, but the nuances of both are in many ways their own.

One reporter said that at the peak of the oil spill crisis, a friend turned to her over lunch and asked, "I wonder if we should ask about the fish?" The reporter, a big seafood lover, realized then that this might be the biggest way the oil spill would affect her in the short term—her ability to enjoy a shrimp po-boy. With Katrina, her conversations were much more dire. She spoke constantly about the dead. "Katrina took about two thousand lives," the reporter said. "This is a big small town. My grandmother died post-Katrina. I had a friend commit suicide, who was a PIO, like days into the storm. One of my best friend's uncles drowned in his attic because he couldn't get out. We lost life."[60]

Another television producer said he too had reservations about eating Gulf Coast shrimp in the subsequent years. What might make the oil spill more of a challenge than Katrina might not be in the loss of life but in the widening of the stakeholders in the cleanup and recovery. "Katrina affected ninety thousand square miles . . . and all the people within that," the producer said. "The oil spill is supposed to affect the coastal areas of four states." It would take nature a longer time to repair itself from the contamination of oil in the Gulf than it would take Lake Pontchartrain to purge the waste that flowed in when the city of New Orleans flooded five years earlier.[61]

On the other hand, both Katrina and the oil spill had the hallmarks of man-made failures written all over them. One Web producer pointed out that Katrina spared New Orleans, but poor man-made levees ultimately brought the city to its knees. Likewise, man-made exploration and oil-well design led to the 2010 offshore disaster. Yet, there still needed to be a Katrina for a levee failure to occur. The oil spill was entirely a result of man's actions. "This oil spill would be considered a man-made disaster that could've been stopped," the Web producer said. "As much as I'm an animal and nature lover, I don't think you can match up thousands of dead to even thousands of animals dead."[62]

A local television station meteorologist, though, had a different perspective on the impact of the spill on the specific types of jobs it affected. Gulf Coast citizens who lost their jobs or homes after Katrina could move to other states and take up the same jobs elsewhere, if they were available. Fishermen who had scoured the Gulf for generations could not get another Gulf Coast and its waters back.

> In terms of comparing to a hurricane that devastated or a Gulf oil spill disaster that was man-made, I would have to say this is worse. The livelihoods of people you can't get back. With storms, you can rebuild and get your life back. This is a whole different dimension of wiping out a whole way of life.[63]

The glaring similarity between the two disasters: "People in this region have been smacked in the face again," said one local reporter. "Their livelihoods have been affected, their plans for the future. There is a lot of uncertainty." The comparison to Katrina, the reporter states, is because "this region has taken it on the chin a few times recently, and here's another one."[64]

The oil spill brought back the national gaze upon the Gulf South. Yet with Katrina, the story line was "Save Our City." For the spill, the story line was "Save Our Coast." One television producer observed:

> It's nice to see that people are paying attention not just to the coast of Louisiana, but to the ecology—that there is a real chance that this is really going to destroy some natural habitat that Louisiana has been screaming about for years, and that our coast's eroding, our wetlands are dying and *for the first time* we feel like we really have the nation's ear.[65]

The producer recalled that Katrina played a role in addressing the habit of journalists parachuting in and treating a local disaster as just another crisis without exploring the human toll. A story he came across at the time, by the *New York Times*, reflected on the unique attention the Gulf oil spill coverage was receiving, when similar spills occurred in Nigeria far more frequently. The Katrina experience, which brought a human face to a disaster, was reflected in the coverage of the spill five years later.

A year after Katrina, *Times-Picayune* Living section photographer Kathy Anderson had a similar revelation. She knew what it was like to be an international or national journalist parachuting into a local crisis. She had been at the paper for twenty-five years by 2006 and covered her share of disasters and turmoil, such as the volcano eruption that killed four thousand people in Armero, Colombia, in 1985 and the California race riots. Anderson, who took the pictures of the staff evacuating the *Times-Picayune* building through floodwaters, broke down in tears during an in-depth interview session in 2006, as she recalled driving around in a National Guard Humvee, and with a television crew, via helicopter, to take pictures of the devastation. In comparing the Colombia natural disaster aftermath, which had double the casualties, and the Katrina experience, Anderson said:

> I fast forward twenty-something years later, the same helicopters buzzing overhead, the whole city laying in ruins. Just the biggest difference for me was that in Armero I got on a plane five days later and I came home, and I guess I wasn't really thinking about that.
>
> And this is here, every single day, when I drive to work, when I go to people's houses. When I think in one day, how many people lost their homes, or their jobs. I have a friend across the street who was living in Houston, now living on food stamps, and unemployment, her business was wiped out in one day.
>
> It's humbling, and as a journalist, there is something really important about knowing what it really means to be displaced. And I can't say that I ever really knew that. Because none of us knew if we had houses, or cars, or if we had a job to go back to and I feel like I am a stronger journalist in that I'm more knowledgeable, because of this experience that I've had on a very personal level. So I think there is a strength brought out from having lived through this experience.[66]

The spill's access violations pushed journalists back to "distance reporting" in their own region—much like Anderson describes. What Katrina journalists reported in horrendous circumstances was stifled in the spill experience. Their authority and sense of outrage was hindered if not hampered by a story on their turf controlled by outsiders. Some of their coverage that focused on the community did receive praise, but it fell short of the true potential of their journalism that brought about far more quantifiable action post-Katrina. The oil disaster journalists were forced to report from a distance in a situation where they had the skills and experience to cover a local tragedy again at a level that saw action.

Gulf Coast journalists, within five years, faced two "worst-in-history" stories of their careers. The first, Katrina, left scars lingering, its memories at least demanding of Gulf Coast journalists that the oil spill be covered their way. It is in taking a closer look at the stories they wrote and produced that we get to see if "the new journalism" created by Katrina and limited by the oil spill holds water.

3

NATIONAL VERSUS LOCAL DISASTER NEWS

Wearing recycled newspaper hats saying "Save the Picayune," roughly a hundred citizens turned out one June morning in 2012 to let their local journalists know they cared. One homemade sign by rally protestor Jerry Siefken read "Publish seven days or sell to owner committed to the common good." The word went out like an echo across media outlets lining the Gulf Coast. Seventy civic and business groups signed a petition to get Advanced Publications to keep their hometown paper as a daily. From WWL-TV in New Orleans to KPLC-TV in Lake Charles, television anchors, radio announcers, and even local bloggers rallied citizens of all stripes behind Louisiana's leading news source. Word had just hit that the *Times-Picayune*, after 175 years, would no longer be a daily newspaper, birthing a love story between locals and their paper. The grassroots effort that was later organized under the Times-Picayune Citizens group hit the blogosphere, propelling "the *Times-Picayune*" as the number one searched item on Yahoo!'s Trending List on May 24, 2012, at 1:30 p.m.[1]

The scene at Uptown coffee shops was somber. The place where people come daily to swap sections of the newsprint was in an uproar. Businessmen turned up at a *Times-Picayune* board member's house to lobby the owners to sell to a local coalition. From the heads of Entergy New Orleans to the Ochsner Health System, from the president of Tulane University to local banks; they all tried in vain to hold off the pending plan of the paper's owner to print the paper only three times a week and to experiment with posting the news online instead.[2] It was not like the news was going away, but for Louisianans, and some in Alabama, where a similar experiment was taking place with three of its major newspapers, they felt like they would no longer be seeing a best friend every day.

In New Orleans, Tulane University President Scott Cowen wrote in the citizen group's press release that the local media remained a vital engine in attracting attention to major events in the city. Regarding the 2013 NFL Super Bowl, the NCAA Women's Final Four, the NBA All-Star Game, Katrina's ten-year anniversary, and New Orleans's three hundredth birthday, Cowen wrote that "these events, along with the downtown open-ing of two new $1 billion-plus hospitals, deserve a more robust approach to news delivery."[3]

Anne Milling, founder of Women of the Storm, reminded the owners of the importance of the state's leading news source when disaster hit. "A daily *Times-Picayune* has been the backbone of the community in our post-Katrina environment and provides the foundation for all civic dialogue and discourse," Milling wrote. "It is our hope that the owners will respect the voices and desires of the community which has been so loyal to the printed newspaper for generations."

Veteran New Orleans restaurateur Leah Chase of Dooky Chase wrote about how the paper best explained to outsiders the uniqueness of the city, and gave insiders the scoop on the local who's who. "People like Sheila Stroup, Judy Walker, Doug MacCash, and Brett Anderson provide me with information about the things I love, and I can relate to what they write about," Chase wrote. "For people my age, this will be a terrible loss." When it came down to dollars and cents, Michael Hecht, the CEO of Greater New Orleans, Inc., wrote, "New Orleans was recently named the '#1 Fastest Improving Economy in the Nation' by the *Wall Street Journal*. The drastic reduction of our paper is not only inconsistent with this economic renais-sance, it also sends a negative—and erroneous—message to the rest of the world."

Even the city's mayor, Mitch Landrieu, calling the paper "a part of our identity," made a heartfelt plea to preserve the paper he once tossed as a delivery boy.[4] "The First Amendment keeps America strong," Landrieu said. "We don't always agree, but the newspaper provides a critical service for our city by helping to keep the public informed."[5]

Ordinary citizens at the rally to Save the Picayune called the paper the "pulse of New Orleans," cited the jobs that would be lost, the elderly who do not have Internet access, and the need for a robust staff producing investi-gative reporting on the city's and state's affairs. One protestor shouted to the crowd, "This is about a bad business model. It's bad for the city of New Orleans, and it's about New Orleanians saying no."[6]

Yet some residents, recognizing that their love affair with their local paper was more a tearful send-off than a promising grassroots effort, rationalized their effort like Anne Milling of the civic group Women of the Storm. "You have to try," she told WWL-TV. "Who knows? Maybe they'll realize this community is different from the other markets they're talking about." It was former *Times-Picayune* columnist Lolis Eric Elie, now a writer on the hit HBO-TV series *Treme*, who articulated best the sentiment behind the uproar. Elie wrote:

> As the novelist John Biguenet told us shortly after the storm, the great enemy of New Orleans culture is American culture. The *Times-Picayune* used to understand this. Its coverage, even its very name, suggested a somewhat idiosyncratic perspective in keeping with our idiosyncratic community. It'll be hard to maintain such relevant coverage if decisions like these are made in New York.
>
> Long before the Internet, the daily newspaper was the virtual water cooler. Citizens from various walks of life and regions of the circulation area were brought together daily by a shared, though imperfect, vision of what was news, what was important, what was interesting. This thirst for community cannot be satisfied on a thrice-weekly basis.[7]

The argument was clear; the public, news outlet owners, and news managers want news that serves the public. Yet the response that Louisiana residents and media demonstrated in support of the state's leading news source underscores the role the local press plays in its communities. The nation's news leader, the *New York Times*, in obituary tones, reported the blow to the paper a week earlier as another casualty in the fall of big city dailies.[8] Yet the *New York Times*, for all its resources and accolades, does not carry the same sentimentality for New Orleanians as it does for New Yorkers.

What we learned from history, major events, and the study of journalism is that local news carries an additional role beyond providing information, news you can use, and an accountability role for those in power. Local news carries a linkage and a social utility role in communities.[9] In times of crisis, its ability to bring people together behind a cause is its linkage power, and its ability to get things done in a community is its social utility power. It is why when word hit the region that the *Times-Picayune*, along with several Alabama city dailies, were the next victims of the news industry's downsizing trend, local television and radio all advertised the upcoming rally in New Orleans, a growing Change.org online petition, and the budding movement to save the local icon. In effect, in this particular crisis, local media acted in a linkage role, getting citizens onboard to rally and petition, and a utility role, in working to see if anything could be done. Even the state's politicians were onboard, passing a Louisiana Senate resolution rallying behind the local fourth estate, often an adversary.[10]

The city's organized, diverse, and emotional plea to save its daily newspaper even surprised the new publisher, Ricky Mathews, the subject of a protest website titled "Ricky Go Home."[11] In response, Mathews told WWL-TV that "it is incredible so many people love the newspaper." However, the protest underscored the significance and essence of local news, a relationship solidified by both the Katrina and BP oil disaster. At the same time of the changes to the *Times-Picayune*, major papers in the state of Alabama, the *Birmingham News*, with a circulation size comparable to the *Times-Picayune*, the *Huntsville Times*, and the *Press-Register* of Mobile received a more muted outcry from citizens. One reason for this difference in response, we argue, can be attributed to the framing of the news in recent years, as observers pointed out. The framing of the Katrina and oil disasters by local news closest to these two events forged a solidarity with these news organizations and their audiences that expressed itself in loyalty in 2012 at the Save the Picayune rally.

Packaging the News

The media either knowingly or unknowingly use frames that affect how a story is told. Knowingly, journalists are taught efficient news writing and production skills. The constraints of time in TV and space in print limit the details and angles journalists can offer in a single news report. Secondly, the news is framed unknowingly, because journalists, despite being trained in objectivity and accuracy skills, carry their own biases and subjectivity of life, people, and events that, in small yet powerful doses, seep into the news report.[12]

The fact that the media holds this power to shape, filter, and organize the news is why locals reporting on a crisis can produce a product different from that of outsiders covering the same event. Like a picture frame, news stories or articles can only include some details that fit within the dimensions; a few are overemphasized, others left out. News frames package meaning into organized ideas, allowing the media to shape the way it tells the story and even the way a story is perceived and interpreted.[13] A subtle change in the wording of the description of a situation frames the context with which we understand the event.[14] For example, the calling of Katrina evacuees refugees changes the victim's story. News frames can therefore define problems, identify causes, make judgments, predict possible effects, and suggest remedies.[15] These frames influence public perception, yet they are typically unnoticed by the viewers.[16] The public's lack of awareness, along with their reliance on media for information and decision-making during times of crisis, makes audiences more likely to be influenced by framing.[17]

News stories can be framed by a journalist's work routine and a journalist's writing or reporting technique. Journalists' harried work schedules may cause them to cover stories as individual events, which scholars call "episodic" framing. Then, when given the time and resources, a journalist can cover stories in depth, framing them in what scholars call "thematic" treatment. Episodic news is unrelated "episodes," not connected or placed into a greater context, and usually focusing on events or personalities. Thematic news, in turn, gives an overall picture.[18] For example, during Katrina, an episodic news story could focus on a family that did not evacuate and was trapped in their home by the rising waters. However, when that single family is featured as part of a story on the largely ignored socioeconomic discrepancies in New Orleans or the lack of public transportation, the story is placed in the context of larger, more complex issues. The latter treatment of this same family becomes a "thematic" story. It provides the audience more background, offering contextual information that goes beyond the single family's episodic event of being rescued from their home.

By nature, television carries news that is more episodic. Locals, like the arguments of those rallying behind the *Times-Picayune*, received thematic treatment of the news from their local newspaper. Television coverage of Katrina, with its focus on victims and rescues, made it an episodic news affair, lacking in thematic treatment.[19] The tilted focus by television news on people rather than context leads audiences to focus on the individuals in a news story.[20] Presented with this situation, audience members are inclined to attribute responsibility to the people portrayed in the story as the root causes of problems and the drivers of solutions. In other words,[21] the blame is placed on the victim. Without a sense of the driving forces that bring people in a news story to the point where they are in an event, the audience is apt to dissociate itself from the "victims" portrayed in the news coverage, and takes for granted that those portrayed in the story brought their conditions upon themselves. Audiences also expect such individuals to either work harder to solve their own problems or endure the consequences of their actions. Episodic stories provide the audience little insight into the larger social and political circumstances contributing to the individual problem. The essential argument is that attribution of responsibility can become a frame for how people see a crisis and its victims.[22]

In contrast, news that underscores broader trends and social conditions (thematic framing) is thought to cultivate a sense of shared responsibility and encourage collective public action.[23] Audience members who view thematic reporting are more apt to recognize that government or other

institutions, such as the media, have a role in solving the problem. Therefore, thematic framing of the BP oil spill saw residents across the coast take
time off from their summer to clean up the beaches, care for the animals,
and purchase Louisiana seafood once again. Once the issues were fleshed
out, residents realized they did not have to wait on BP to act, but felt that
the revival of the coast rested in their collective action.

A journalist's reporting and writing technique also adds to framing.
Journalists call it the angle or the take, audiences may call it the slant or
the bias, but the hook that wraps a story provides the focus and direction
the news takes. Once a journalist selects this frame, it will determine the
facts, details, anecdotes, and quotes the audience will see, excluding all
other details. Scholars have studied dozens of such models, but the most
widely used by the media have been narrowed down to five. They are the
conflict frame (one versus one), the economic consequence frame (gains
and losses), the morality frame, the attribution of responsibility frame, and
the human interest frame. The attribution of responsibility frame seeks to
find out who is to blame in an event, while the human interest frame puts
a "human face" on an issue.[24] We delve further into the use of the attribution of responsibility and human interest techniques in the two disasters in
chapters 4 and 5 respectively. However, these five techniques can be found
in both episodic and thematic treatments of stories. A combination of
these five techniques can also be used in a single news story. The news does
not just fall haphazardly into the newspaper's pages or on the Web or in a
broadcast package. It is the combination of the journalist's time constraints
and training in assorting, organizing, and writing the news that dictates
what we learn of an event in the end.

Local versus National News

All news outlets are not created equal. National and local news have different responsibilities and news coverage is different between these two
entities. National and local news workers both ask the same questions. The
fundamentals of solid journalistic reporting—*who, what, when, where, why,*
and *how*—are baseline for both. But it is the *how* and *what's next* questions
that appeal to a more proximate audience. The locals require one information set, while out-of-towners, with no connection to an event or crisis,
require another information set.

Obvious differences exist between national and local television news coverage: the two groups have separate obligations, separate audiences, take different risks,[25] and often highlight different news values to determine which angles or frames to take in writing the news and which details to emphasize.[26] As such, news values help the outlets' specific viewers identify more closely with what is reported.[27] One obligation that is consistent across both media is the transmission of important information during times of crises. Both are responsible for providing timely, fair, and informative news concerning tragedies, which allows the public to make well-informed and educated decisions.

The fundamental difference between the national and local press is the kind of information they transmit. The national press has to reach a wider audience. One size fits all[28] national news, like that provided by *USA Today*, is often broad and nonspecific. The notion that all news is local is often not reflected in the coverage. Local television stations closest to the oil disaster found national feeds of the broadcast useless. They were offered "packages for people that want a minute-fifteen," just enough to update the status of the underwater gusher, one local TV news producer said. The details were left out by the national affiliate, because the short update was all "somebody in Oregon wants."[29]

National news outlets are also perceived as carrying more power, by the sheer size of their audiences. This allows them to attract better sources who offer greater credibility and in some cases more clout to their coverage of major events. Millions watched Fox News's Geraldo Rivera, with his tearful meltdowns as he took babies in his arms, pleading with the government to get to New Orleans, yelling, "This is Dante's Inferno" to describe the scene at the Convention Center.

Rivera got the attention he was looking for, but the national posturing during the Katrina disaster did not amuse locals. "We have a credibility issue if we start exaggerating the risk and the threat," said James O'Byrne, NOLA.com's director of content.[30] The grandstanding may get remote audiences to tune in to national accounts of local stories, said Chris Slaughter, the former news director at WWL-TV, the local CBS station in New Orleans. "The bigger problem" Slaughter pointed to is that "they parachute in at the last minute and they've got to get something on the air and they paint with too broad a brush."[31] Even more frustrating to local news outlets is that as fast as national news teams "jet in" to cover a local story, they "jet out," said Peter Kovacs, a managing editor at the *Times-Picayune*.[32] Their departure unfortunately signals to national audiences and national power brokers, that, in some way, the event is over. For local media, this is far from the case.

When a crisis hits, the motivations for news coverage by national and local news diverge even further. In 2011, when Japan was hit with the worst earthquake in its history, the ratings on that day for ABC's *Good Morning America* dramatically increased to some six million viewers. That was *GMA*'s biggest Friday audience in eight years.[33] Six years earlier, ratings surged for cable coverage and network news specials in the aftermath of Katrina[34] as Americans searched for information. Led by Fox News and CNN, cable news experienced high ratings for their extended coverage of Hurricane Katrina.[35] Because ratings increase exponentially during and in the aftermath of such events, national news organizations temporarily saturate audiences with rapid-fire information.[36]

Local crises are rather unstable times for local news outlets. With disasters such as hurricanes where mandatory evacuations occur, local news outlets may experience an audience exodus rather than a ratings bonanza. They may beef up coverage in the preparation stages of the disaster, but rely on contingency plans for news coverage in expectation of worst-case scenarios. The goal is "to give out fresh, important information from a meteorological point of view, from a public safety point of view, to help the viewers make an informed, sound judgment as early as they can," said WWL-TV's Chris Slaughter.

Good decisions are predicated on good information. Although the government distributes a substantial amount of information about hurricanes through the media, the public does not fully understand the nuanced meanings associated with scientific or technical jargon and relies on the media to provide the interpretations. The stakes are considerably higher for local media before, during, and after a crisis. Local television broadcasts are considered central for public officials to relay pertinent information to the public during times of crisis.[37] Local media become extremely powerful and increase in authority because officials are dependent on them and vice-versa. The relationship between officials and the media during a crisis is symbiotic. In this capacity, local media plays a "management role" in the relay of information.[38] They become a portal for disseminating instructions from officials, monitoring the storm, and making safety recommendations to the public.

Once a disaster hits, the media functions under a "recovery role." Local and national outlets focus their attention on the areas most affected and assess the scale of the damage. Then, local media serve as anchors for the community in the beginning of the "recovery" or rebuilding efforts.[39] The media's checklist, Chris Slaughter explained, shifts to the information needed for citizens to begin the recovery process. News of disaster recovery, Slaughter pointed out, must address the areas that were most affected, the timeline for residents to return, the locations of relief and aid, and even the ability to return with pets.

In the management and recovery roles the media play in a disaster, both national and local media outlets equally transmit this public information. Where the distinction occurs is that in these two roles, local media provide emotional support and facilitate social cohesion.[40] A study of prior natural disasters showed that residents had emotional connections to local media reports, beyond the basic information transmission.[41]

This distinction is made in a specific phase of the crisis. During the event, as the storm hits, the earthquake shakes, the tsunami submerges, or the World Trade Center towers crumble, the media stand in for the collective gasp of the audiences. This "linkage" function is the media's ability to unite people in the instant the disaster occurs. Indeed some communication technologies (TV, Internet, radio) have the ability to create stronger community ties and facilitate interaction between people despite real physical distance.[42] Technology coupled with the proximity of the local press caused viewers to demand site-specific, geography-specific, and topic-specific content during Katrina, said NOLA.com director of content James O'Byrne. It allowed people with similar stresses, such as those experiencing the impact of the same natural event, to become active participants in the community-specific conversation.

Katrina was different from other natural disasters scholars have studied because it was the first test case in how online news aided or transformed the linkage role of the media. Again, that new landscape included websites that were community based and encouraged participation from, as was discussed by WWL-TV's Chris Slaughter in chapter 2.

The Internet leveled the playing field among outlets, but wouldn't always reach its intended targets, thus hampering the first and most important function of the press: successful information transmission. Therefore, the community turned to "old" media, and radio found its place in this historic event. Dave Cohen of WWL radio said it is the low-tech quality of radio that is a great feature in an emergency because just about everyone has access to it and the stations find ways to stay on the air and provide information. While the Internet expanded the linkage role of the media, the initial

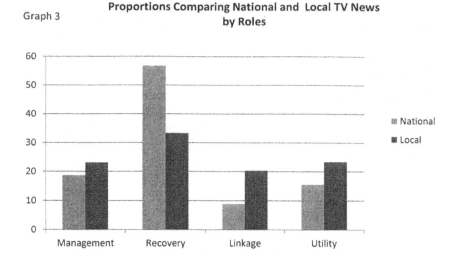

Graph 3

Proportions Comparing National and Local TV News by Roles

communications blackout during Katrina meant traditional media were not usurped by new technology.

The "social utility" role is the natural progression from this "linkage" role. After people are put together, the shared trauma from the experience can be harnessed and transitioned into collective action of some sort. During Katrina, the relay of information between audiences and local journalists demonstrated this linkage role, while the ability to comfort, grieve, and help residents in need was an example of the social utility role of the local media.

The emotional playing field between journalists and audience was on an equal level during Katrina, with both groups facing the same circumstances, as chapter 2 demonstrated. In past disasters, the local news workers were not always victims of the crisis their audiences were experiencing. Mike Hoss, WWL-TV anchor, said it was not empathy the local press was showing but emotional camaraderie.

> It has made us get back to helping people, you know, stories that have impact. We have gone back to our roots, so to speak, of journalism. It has enabled us to do so many stories with such gravity and such importance in people's lives. I have never felt more needed as a journalist, as a reporter, in helping people rebuild their lives, in being a watchdog over government and money and all the factors that are happening poststorm.[43]

"Linkage" and "social utility" are why local media serve as a fulcrum that holds a displaced, devastated, and beleaguered community together both during the crisis and in the aftermath. During all four roles and stages of shaping disaster coverage, local media reach out to the community, from official to regular people, increasing the human interest approach to the coverage.[44] The local media have the unique ability to create community and provide emotional support that adds another dimension to the media-audience relationship that has previously escaped the focus of natural disaster mass communication researchers. In an event such as Hurricane Katrina, the crisis raised the need and significance of national media to descend on the story.[45] Local television news, then, must carve out its place in the media landscape as the experts on and emotional supporters of their local communities.

Framing the Disaster

Hurricane Katrina confirmed the existing roles of national and local news in a disaster. In a study[46] we conducted of hours of national and local television news coverage of the Katrina disaster, we found that both national and local TV news performed management and recovery functions, but that local television news dominated in the community-specific roles. What was unique to the Katrina case was that, while both national and local news perfected different roles, their framing of stories was overwhelmingly episodic in nature. The irony for local television was that it captured the mood of its audiences, yet focused on events as they occurred with little contextual treatment.

Heavy episodic framing may have also contributed to the perpetuation of racial stereotypes of the mostly black, devastated population in New Orleans. Two-thirds of those affected by Hurricane Katrina were African Americans. The national coverage moved from one looting event to the other or from one rooftop rescue to the other, without context. Therefore, although race and socioeconomic status were not explicitly dealt with, event coverage may have helped single out negative stereotypes about minority groups instead of presenting "thematic" treatments of the affected region's poor.

Such broad strokes that failed to paint the larger issues may have prompted some viewers, in a survey of memorable images six weeks after Hurricane Katrina, to respond in a highly negative way toward the victims. "Those people should have left," wrote one student who participated in

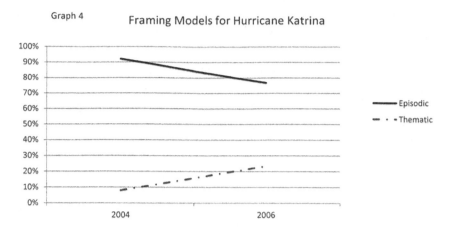

Graph 4   Framing Models for Hurricane Katrina

one of our surveys.[47] In this survey sample, some 20 percent were actually displaced by Hurricane Katrina, so their comments were candid and their wounds fresh. Another example of the failure to see the larger issues that surround poverty and transportation was clear in this statement: "All of the black people that were too stubborn to leave piling in the Superdome."

While research has shown that media frames are not recognized by the audience, one of the survey participants, a native Louisianan, noticed the lack of positive, thematic frames and wanted more from the media. "The images they were showing did not depict that of LA. It showed us during our worst time yes, but that does not mean we are like this all the time. I do believe the media could have spent more time showing the good."

The media, this participant critiqued, was television, and no distinction between local and national TV coverage was obvious when it came to episodic news. When comparing local television to local newspaper reports of the Katrina disaster, we came across the divide between episodic and thematic framing. Local Gulf Coast newspapers grew their thematic framing of the news significantly in the recovery phase of the disaster.[48] Herein lies the point where work routines of print and broadcast journalists differ, allowing the former the advantage of in-depth, nuanced reporting. For the broadcast journalist, the breaking news of the disaster was often live, with little time to frame and flesh out. Print journalists, while blogging online, could hold off to post, and then return to update a story with the context and angle it required.

The majority of the coverage of this disaster for both national and local news was spent in framing the recovery role. The damage to the region was so widespread and so severe that it took days, months, and then years to report the full toll. Both outlets offered information about what neighborhoods had been flooded and estimated damage to public and private property. Much of that role assumption was negative in tone as the outlets spoke about the damage in terms of loss and devastation.[49] Where positive news was found came in the local media's functioning in its linkage and social utility roles. The toll of the disaster on the journalists' own lives propelled these two roles to the forefront. As WWL-TV anchor Mike Hoss put it:

> We said stuff and did stuff because we were affected. It was our homes, and our lives. You would hear words like "we," "our," words you would never hear in a newscast. But in this situation, it was us. So I think in the weeks following, it was blurred because we were such a part of it. I don't think it's a bad thing, we were a part of the storm, just like everybody else. I think the viewers appreciate that and understood that we had homes that were lost too. So as a station, I think that in those weeks following and in the months following, that attitude kind of prevailed, the "we," "our" attitude that you probably would have never seen pre-hurricane.[50]

The national media serve a wider audience and make such community links in terms of connection and emotion impossible. What emotion did erupt from the reports of CNN's Anderson Cooper and Fox's Rivera was directed at national power players and less toward national viewers. However, national media were the purveyor of information for the people across the nation who wanted to help or donate. Therefore, linkage and social utility roles were filled in a broader context with the New Orleans community being the beneficiary.

By coupling some established scholarly frames with media functions, we get a richer and often conflicting picture of the information being sent to the viewers. The media often overemphasize the negative and downplay the positive.[51] While there was little positive to be found amidst Hurricane Katrina, the local media found a way to bring people together in what seemed like a hopeless sea of negative national coverage. In natural disasters, our studies showed local television outlets are assuming specific roles that help manage and guide a community through the tragedy. If national media are being heralded by some as a hero, perhaps local television can be considered the unsung hero of television coverage of this crisis.

Framing Models and Hurricane Katrina

In local newspapers where thematic framing was most prevalent, we were able to explore which framing techniques were most used in the Katrina recovery phase. Unlike the mixed results of the television analysis, the news from newspapers was good; there was a significant increase in thematic stories. In 2004, thematic news stories were considerably low in number and in length. This suggested that local journalists were expected to meet the reading needs and attentions of a local audience. However, a significant increase in length of stories and the overall number of thematic stories in 2006 indicated a clear change. In the interviews, these newspaper journalists stated that they now placed simple news events into the larger context of Katrina. For example, a crime was not an isolated event as it would have been reported in 2004. Instead, it was a crime that was part of the Katrina landscape, triggered in the aftermath and affecting a certain group of people. For these Katrina thematic stories, the reporters included analysis from experts and researchers nationwide and compared the issues to similar circumstances elsewhere. This helped solidify these Katrina connected stories as thematic in nature. They also did not merely write about news events from local government, but analyzed it through progress or lack of progress reports. The journalists stated that their reporting was aimed at helping readers understand what was at stake with any new development at this difficult time in their lives. Some of these thematic stories read like best practices guides, according to one editor, that helped residents rebuild their lives: "And by that I mean explaining to them rules on flood elevation, explaining to them insurance, how to get things done. I see the [newspaper] right now as a practical guide on how to live here."

> It's hard to live here right now if you have all these questions and no answers. And they see the newspaper in an issue that has lots of complexity and complicated answers that don't lend themselves well to television. They lend themselves perfectly to print. We take the time to explain these issues carefully, and I think people realize that and are very engaged because they want to get a good understanding of what the issues are going to be there.

These statements all explain a shift toward more thematic stories complementing episodic news accounts. At the time of our interviews, the attitude toward these Katrina thematic stories was ambivalent. Some reporters and

Graph 5   **Newspaper Change in Framing Technique**

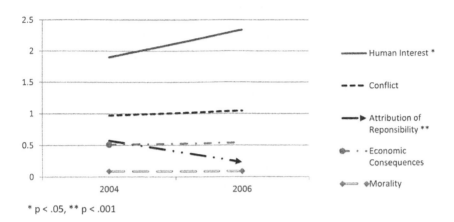

* p < .05, ** p < .001

editors described internal bets about the year in which the word Katrina would not be published in the paper or used as background in a story. Some reporters were resigned to the thought that it would be a long time before they could stop explaining Katrina anomalies.

On a trip to Boston a year after the storm, *Times-Picayune* reporter Gordon Russell could not help noticing how the rest of the country had moved on, particularly the journalism community. As Russell spoke to a journalist friend who contemplated moving away from New Orleans, his friend told him editors thought he was committing career suicide for moving away from such a huge story. During interviews, the editors told his friend, "You know it's the greatest story of your life." His friend's response: "I can't wait to leave this story. You know, it's just Katrina, Katrina, Katrina, Katrina, enough already!" The inability to separate your own life from your job had become too much, and no matter the career boost; Katrina had become a double-edged sword, Russell explained.

Thematic framing required the use of more techniques and reporting models to contextualize the recovery phase of the disaster. In using the conflict frame, economic consequences frame, human interest frame, morality frame, and the attribution of responsibility frame, the human interest frame was the most prevalent. The human interest frame included stories that emphasized the human or emotional dimension of a topic, issue, or problem. For Katrina, the personal vignettes in stories or visual information that evoked emotions propelled this frame to the top of the techniques journalists used to wrap the news of the post-Katrina dilemma.[52]

Before an event such as Hurricane Katrina, the media disseminate important information including storm tracking, preparation, and evacuation. During the storm, reporters in the field relay vicarious eyewitness accounts of the danger and damage. After the storm, the media play different roles such as "social linker," connecting viewers with government information and aid organizations. The common thread in disaster coverage is the focus on human beings and their needs throughout. It is why the human interest frame appears most often in post-Katrina news reports from local media. Is it part of the "new kind of journalism" discussed in chapter 2? Perhaps—a kind of journalism that experiences the story and puts it into context to serve not only the informational needs but the emotional needs of the local audience. Either way, the media experience between television and newspaper and local and national was very different.

For audiences, the difference between local and national news is like the tale of two sisters. Longtime local anchor Sally-Ann Roberts of WWL-TV and her sister, Robin Roberts, of *Good Morning America*, come from the same family. Gulf Coast residents know and can relate to them both well. Sally-Ann gets the attention of New Orleanians; her sister gets the attention of the president. New Orleanians see Sally-Ann Roberts as their neighbor, their friend, someone they greet every morning on their way to work, part of their daily routine. Her sister, Robin, the nation empathizes with as she publicly battles cancer. However, for most of the year, Robin remains a distant relative to local audiences, one to be visited on major holidays, Thanksgiving, or if the world was coming to an end. Both Sally-Ann and Robin covered the devastation of Katrina, with Robin parachuting in from *GMA's* New York headquarters to show the nation how her high school in Pass Christian, Mississippi, had been reduced to rubble. Yet locals will tell you it was Sally-Ann who helped them swallow the news that things would never be the same, like a bowl of warm gumbo after being weakened from a winter flu. A lot of chunky pieces in the stew, but a dose of reality was what the region needed, and Sally-Ann offered to pull the covers off and get going again. The affection creates trust, and was why in 2012 the protestors at the "Save the Picayune" rally turned out in support of not just any news outlet but what they considered the voice of their community. This is why national news and local news serve two different roles for audiences despite answering to the same corporate masters and bottom line.

Audiences wanted to get to the bottom line to hold someone or something accountable for the causes of and responses to both disasters. In the next chapter, we discuss in detail the attribution of responsibility frame and ask the question: who runs this disaster?

4

WHO RUNS THIS DISASTER?
THE MEDIA AND THE BLAME GAME

In *A Concert for Hurricane Relief* on NBC on September 2, 2005, rapper Kanye West uttered the now infamous quote, "George Bush doesn't care about black people . . ." Five years later, George W. Bush wrote in his 2010 book *Decision Points* that the backlash from Hurricane Katrina, more so than his administration's handling of the Iraq war, was the all-time low of his presidency. In 2010, on the anniversary of Katrina, Bush poured out:

> Five years later I can barely write those words without feeling disgust. . . . I faced a lot of criticism as president. I didn't like hearing people claim that I lied about Iraq's weapons of mass destruction or cut taxes to benefit the rich. But the suggestion that I was racist because of the response to Katrina represented an all-time low.[1]

As *Today* host Matt Lauer pushed Bush in the NBC special *Matt Lauer Reports* to explain what he meant in his book, Bush was quite clear about what tone of the Katrina media discourse he found inaccurate, if not downright unfair. "He [Kanye West] called me a racist," Bush tells Lauer. "And I didn't appreciate it then. I don't appreciate it now. It's one thing to say, 'I don't appreciate the way he's handled his business.' It's another thing to say, 'This man's a racist.' I resent it. It's not true."[2]

What Grammy Award–winning rapper Kanye West was actually feeding off in his finger-pointing, off-script monologue to President George W. Bush was in fact his interpretation of the nonstop twenty-four-hour coverage of mostly cable broadcast news of the crisis days into its unfolding. Standing next to Canadian comedian and actor Mike Myers of *Austin Powers* film fame, West, despite a clearly stunned Myers, went off script in the celebrity telethon. Since the 2004 tsunami crisis, major cable and network news outlets have turned to these charity events, interspersed with news updates, to provide a break in the nonstop coverage. Showcasing well-known humanitarian celebrities garners audience as well as provides a civic role in raising funds for relief organizations such as the American Red Cross. *A Concert for Hurricane Relief*, carried also by NBC partners MSNBC and CNBC, featured New Orleans musical bonafides Aaron Neville and Harry Connick Jr. and Hollywood headline makers Leonardo DiCaprio and even Lindsay Lohan. Clearly, West had plans that differed from those of the rest of the who's who lineup that Friday, September 2, 2005, four days after Katrina made landfall in southeast Louisiana. As Myers began to recap the events that had blacked out the Gulf Coast, West dived in:

> I hate the way they portray us in the media. If you see a black family, it says they're looting. See a white family, it says they're looking for food. And you know that it's been five days, because most of the people are black. And even for me to complain about it, I would be a hypocrite because I've tried to turn away from the TV, because it's too hard to watch. We already realize a lot of people that could help are at war right now, fighting another way, and they have given them permission to go down and shoot us.[3]

A confused Myers then tried to steer West back on course by guiding the narration back to the teleprompter. "And subtle, but in even many ways more profoundly devastating is the lasting damage to the survivors' will to rebuild and remain in the area. The destruction of the spirit of the people of southern Louisiana and Mississippi may end up being the most tragic loss of all." But Myers was unsuccessful and West refused to hold back his now infamous "George Bush doesn't care about black people."[4]

MSNBC producers then cut to dazed comedian and actor Chris Tucker, who was cued in a few seconds early as West's voice could be heard trailing in the background—he obviously wasn't finished.[5]

But President George W. Bush was and still is not laughing. He told Lauer five years later as the clip was played to him:

> Yeah. I still feel that way as you read those words. I felt 'em when I heard 'em, felt 'em when I wrote 'em, and I felt 'em when I'm listening to 'em.
> **LAUER:** You say you told Laura at the time it was the worst moment of your presidency?
> **BUSH:** Yes. My record was strong, I felt, when it came to race relations and giving people a chance. And it was a disgusting moment.
> **LAUER:** I wonder if some people are going to read that, now that you've written it, and they might give you some heat for that. And the reason is this—

BUSH [interrupting]: Don't care.

LAUER: Well, here's the reason. You're not saying that the worst moment in your presidency was watching the misery in Louisiana. You're saying it was when someone *insulted* you because of that.

BUSH: No, and I also make it clear that the misery in Louisiana affected me deeply as well. There's a lot of tough moments in the book. And it was a disgusting moment, pure and simple.[6]

West has since apologized during a subsequent interview with Matt Lauer in November 2010, citing getting caught up in the emotion of the moment.[7] And he was not the only one apologizing to the president. The network issued a disclaimer right after West's comments in 2005:

Kanye West departed from the scripted comments that were prepared for him, and his opinions in no way represent the views of the network. It would be most unfortunate if the efforts of the artists who participated and the generosity of millions of Americans who are helping those in need are overshadowed by one person's opinion.[8]

However, not everyone in those heated and frenzied first five days of the Katrina disaster was onboard the national mea culpa bandwagon for the finger-pointing and name-calling—certainly not a defiant New Orleans *Times-Picayune*, and certainly not the city's mayor, Ray Nagin.

Spurred on by a distress call made by Mayor Nagin to New Orleans radio broadcaster Garland Robinette, the *Times-Picayune* took action as a local news organization and called out the federal government. The paper's executive editor, Jim Amos, recalled in an interview with one of the authors a few months after the crisis that:

I think that the newspaper's news report always has to be fair and accurate and that you can't advocate in the news columns, no matter how passionately you feel about something. The place for advocacy is on the opinion pages of the newspaper. And we, on one occasion this past fall, took that advocacy in the form of an editorial and placed it on page one, which is normally the place of the news report. We felt so strongly about what needed to be said, at that point, namely that the federal government owed it to New Orleans and to this region to come to our aid in a way that they hadn't yet. And that that needed to be said as forcefully as we possibly could say it, namely on page one. And so some people in journalism might think that that is a blurring of the line. I think it's very clear to readers where we draw the line. And I don't apologize for that.[9]

In its open letter to President George W. Bush, published on September 4, 2005, the newspaper, with biting sarcasm, rips into the administration. The letter affectionately begins "Dear Mr. President," but that is as much love as Bush was to receive. The not-so-love letter reads:

We heard you loud and clear Friday when you visited our devastated city and the Gulf Coast and said, "What is not working, we're going to make it right."

Please forgive us if we wait to see proof of your promise before believing you. But we have good reason for our skepticism.

Bienville built New Orleans where he built it for one main reason: It's accessible. The city between the Mississippi River and Lake Pontchartrain was easy to reach in 1718.

How much easier it is to access in 2005 now that there are interstates and bridges, airports and helipads, cruise ships, barges, buses and diesel-powered trucks.

Despite the city's multiple points of entry, our nation's bureaucrats spent days after last week's hurricane wringing their hands, lamenting the fact that they could neither rescue the city's stranded victims nor bring them food, water and medical supplies.

Meanwhile there were journalists, including some who work for the *Times-Picayune*, going in and out of the city via the Crescent City Connection. On Thursday morning, that crew saw a caravan of 13 Wal-Mart tractor trailers headed into town to bring food, water and supplies to a dying city.

Television reporters were doing live reports from downtown New Orleans streets. Harry Connick Jr. brought in some aid Thursday, and his efforts were the focus of a "Today" show story Friday morning.

Yet, the people trained to protect our nation, the people whose job it is to quickly bring in aid were absent. Those who should have been deploying troops were singing a sad song about how our city was impossible to reach.

We're angry, Mr. President, and we'll be angry long after our beloved city and surrounding parishes have been pumped dry. Our people deserved rescuing. Many who could have been were not. That's to the government's shame.

Mayor Ray Nagin did the right thing Sunday when he allowed those with no other alternative to seek shelter from the storm inside the Louisiana Superdome. We still don't know what the death toll is, but one thing is certain: Had the Superdome not been opened, the city's death toll would have been higher. The toll may even have been exponentially higher. It was clear to us by late morning Monday that many people inside the Superdome would not be returning home. It should have been clear to our government, Mr. President. So why weren't they evacuated out of the city immediately? We learned seven years ago, when Hurricane Georges threatened, that the Dome isn't suitable as a long-term shelter. So what did state and national officials think would happen to tens of thousands of people trapped inside with no air conditioning, overflowing toilets and dwindling amounts of food, water and other essentials?

State Rep. Karen Carter was right Friday when she said the city didn't have but two urgent needs: "Buses! And gas!" Every official at the Federal Emergency Management Agency should be fired, Director Michael Brown especially.

In a nationally televised interview Thursday night, he said his agency hadn't known until that day that thousands of storm victims were stranded at the Ernest N. Morial Convention Center. He gave another nationally televised interview the next morning and said, "We've provided food to the people at the Convention Center so that they've gotten at least one, if not two meals, every single day."

Lies don't get more bald-faced than that, Mr. President. Yet, when you met with Mr. Brown Friday morning, you told him, "You're doing a heck of a job." That's unbelievable.

There were thousands of people at the Convention Center because the riverfront is high ground. The fact that so many people had reached there on foot is proof that rescue vehicles could have gotten there, too.

We, who are from New Orleans, are no less American than those who live on the Great Plains or along the Atlantic Seaboard. We're no less important than those from the Pacific Northwest or Appalachia. Our people deserved to be rescued.

No expense should have been spared. No excuses should have been voiced. Especially not one as preposterous as the claim that New Orleans couldn't be reached.

Mr. President, we sincerely hope you fulfill your promise to make our beloved communities work right once again.

When you do, we will be the first to applaud.[10]

The newspaper's anger did accomplish one outcome: the president's "Brownie," his affectionate name for FEMA head Michael Brown, got the memo and tendered his resignation a few days later.[11] All the while an exhausted and no longer politically correct New Orleans Mayor Ray Nagin had some choice words, many expletive laden, for the federal government. Veteran television and broadcast journalist Garland Robinette managed to get the mayor on air on local radio being simulcast throughout the Gulf, for a quick update on the status of supplies to the stranded. Nagin abandoned all composure as Robinette probed him and let loose in an interview reaired by CNN and which triggered a much-needed coordinated effort between federal, state, and local forces. Nagin's most memorable line from the interview remains, "They [the federal government] need to get off their asses, and fix the biggest *doggone* crisis in the history of this country."[12]

Robinette pressed Nagin to elaborate on his phone call with the president and Nagin was livid about the response.

NAGIN: I told him we had an incredible crisis here and that his flying over in Air Force One does not do it justice. And that I have been all around this city, and I am very frustrated because we are not able to marshal resources and we're outmanned in just about every respect.

You know the reason why the looters got out of control? Because we had most of our resources saving people, thousands of people that were stuck in attics, man, old ladies. . . . You pull off the doggone ventilator vent and you look down there and they're standing in there in water up to their freaking necks.

And they don't have a clue what's going on down here. They flew down here one time two days after the doggone event was over with TV cameras, AP reporters, all kind of goddamn—excuse my French everybody in America, but I am pissed.

ROBINETTE: Did you say to the president of the United States, "I need the military in here"?

NAGIN: I said, "I need everything."

Now, I will tell you this—and I give the president some credit on this—he sent one John Wayne dude down here that can get some stuff done, and his name is [Lt.] Gen. [Russel] Honore.

And he came off the doggone chopper, and he started cussing and people started moving. And he's getting some stuff done.

They ought to give that guy—if they don't want to give it to me—give him full authority to get the job done, and we can save some people.

ROBINETTE: What do you need right now to get control of this situation?

NAGIN: I need reinforcements. I need troops, man. I need 500 buses, man. We ain't talking about—you know, one of the briefings we had, they were talking about getting public school bus drivers to come down here and bus people out here.

I'm like, "You got to be kidding me. This is a national disaster. Get every doggone Greyhound bus line in the country and get their asses moving to New Orleans."

That's—they're thinking small, man. And this is a major, major, major deal. And I can't emphasize it enough, man. This is crazy.[13]

Monica Pierre, who headed up the news unit with Clear Channel New Orleans at the time, shared in an interview with one of the authors that the outcome of the Nagin interview was vindication for the aggressive reporting tone the combined staff of Clear Channel and Entercom had taken in the early days of the crisis. As radio had become a sort of 911 hotline and direct feeder between those in distress and those in power, Pierre recognized that the interview would have the national impact the crisis required. Once the mayor's interview had produced some national results, it empowered the radio journalists to follow suit, calling out other organizations and parties to get the relief and rescue moving much faster. Pierre recalled:

The mayor was on, and that interview was heard around the world, whether it was rebroadcast on our station, whether it was actually heard on television and around the world, it was a turning point . . . it really made things go in a different direction. . . . With our broadcast, we were able to hold the Red Cross's feet to the fire, on the air. And on this particular Sunday morning, to get the director, at the time, with the Red Cross to come and explain why people were on hold for eight hours, just trying to get a human being to talk about processing the checks. And they put this young person, I'm sure, just started working at Red Cross. And I said, well, you tell your boss, that the way it's set up, great ideas or not, great intentions or not, it's not working. Again, you began to see some action behind some of those great sound bites. It was a turning point. You saw the National Guard come in. You saw relief come in, when the mayor said get down here. . . . Citizens of this country, we don't deserve to be hungry, and thirsty, two days later, five days later. We don't deserve to be on rooftops, to be in the Superdome and the Convention Center, under deplorable conditions. You get down here. And again we saw the immediacy of radio.[14]

Those early days solidified a combined effort that put aside old grudges—local media and local politicians—at least temporarily in staring down a common, greater opponent, the federal government. The relationship created a honeymoon that lasted at least two years following the disaster.

In a 2006 leadership roundtable, Jim Amos of the *Times-Picayune* and Stan Tiner, his counterpart at the Biloxi *Sun Herald*, made a joint appearance on a media panel with their respective mayors, Ray Nagin and A. J. Holloway.[15] On the Biloxi side, both mayor and editor mutually described a strong work relationship between government and media that emerged out of the crisis in an effort to support the rebuilding process. In the case of these two newspapers, such courtesy among former foes had solidified and extended out a year and a half after the storm. On the New Orleans side, the editor spoke of forceful leadership under the mayor, yet surprisingly the mayor found the paper to be just as critical of local government as it was before the storm. Nagin did clarify, admitting in the panel discussion that his "words seem to get" him "into trouble." He recalled that it was more his sharp tongue and comments such as "chocolate city"[16] that generated the negative articles. Nagin also felt that the local media had become more activist in its recovery solutions, pressuring local government to consider development options through its reporting, as opposed to simply reporting the recovery plans of Nagin's administration, a more passive traditional role.

Mayor Nagin was onto something; times had changed and Katrina had altered the way local media played the blame game. Yet what remains a scar on President Bush's legacy, five years later saw President Barack Obama finding that a similar media label was beginning to stick as the Deepwater Horizon disaster took place. In the roughly seven hundred articles from the Biloxi *Sun Herald* and *Times-Picayune* archives we were given access to,[17] it is clear that before Katrina and after Katrina power relations had chilled between local leaders and those who report on them. The indication is that the storm called for working together, and sometimes in competition, rather than as adversaries.

During February of 2006, President Bush made his State of the Union address to the nation. The talk around the towns in Mississippi was that they remained unmentioned in the president's address. Residents called in to the *Sun Herald*'s "Sound Off" hotline asking of the paper, "What will it take for the whole United States to realize that it was not only New Orleans that was affected, but the number-one area was the Mississippi Gulf Coast?"[18] Local politicians were united along party lines. Representative Gene Taylor, a Mississippi Democrat from Bay St. Louis, told the paper's Washington correspondent Adina Postelnicu: "I deeply regret he said almost nothing about it. . . . Maybe they have been forgotten by the president." While Republican

Senator Trent Lott was also critical of the federal response, his spokesman, Lee Youngblood, told Postelnicu at the time that "Mississippi's delegation, including Sen. Lott, will continue making sure no one in Washington of any political stripe forgets Mississippi's recovery and rebuilding needs." The state's other senator, Thad Cochran, gave the president a bit more leniency, telling the reporter that President Bush had "given a great amount of personal attention" to Mississippians in the Katrina aftermath. In fact, the president did. Postelnicu pointed out in the same report that the president had been to the state nine times after Katrina, and even two weeks before his State of the Union address. Yet as far as the federal government agenda was concerned, citizen e-mails and letters to the *Sun Herald* indicated they were no longer on the president's radar.

Around the same time in New Orleans, an article by *Times-Picayune* Washington Bureau reporter Bill Walsh further inflamed local and regional opinion that the White House was responsible for the Katrina disaster. In a report that eerily echoed pre-September 11 warning signs of an impending attack on the World Trade Center, Walsh reported that the Department of Homeland Security e-mailed a forty-page "Fast Analysis Report" to the White House Situation Room. The time of transmission: 1:47 a.m. on August 29, 2005. Katrina made its second landfall on continental U.S.A. at 5:10 a.m. on the Louisiana/Mississippi border.[19] The report was a fortune telling dead-on. Its alerts: levee breaches, a submerged New Orleans, a "communications blackout" that could frustrate "rescue efforts," one hundred thousand people stranded, a city under water for weeks, if not months. The *Times-Picayune* had obtained a copy of the PowerPoint presentation of such a scenario presented within FEMA on August 27, 2005. The slide show even pointed to current events at the time alerting viewers that the "exercise projection is exceeded by Hurricane Katrina real-life impacts." Walsh attempted to frame the findings for the readers with the analytical paragraph in his story: "The report raises an important question: If the highest levels of the government knew the likely impact of Hurricane Katrina, why was the initial response so slow and uncoordinated?"[20]

Walsh then reminded readers that "Four days later, President Bush said on ABC's *Good Morning America*, 'I don't think anyone anticipated the breach of the levees.'" Roughly six months had passed since Katrina, and across the Gulf Coast, President Bush and his administration, particularly FEMA, still was a sour taste, not just with residents but with state and federal politicians.

On the first anniversary of Katrina, the media of New Orleans and Biloxi took slightly different nuanced tones toward the president's attempts at reconciliation with the region. A behind-the-scenes look at newsroom opinions within the *Herald* and the *Picayune* sets this contrast up clearly. In the news report, *Times-Picayune* reporter James Varney says that the president and his wife "sat down to a hearty meal of traditional New Orleans fare—and some frank and heartfelt discussions on the slow and painful recovery from Hurricane Katrina." He was joined by Louisiana Governor Kathleen Blanco, Mayor Nagin, and parish presidents for two hours at local Central Business District restaurant Mother's Next Door for some étouffée.[21] The president remained mum to reporters, but the mayor declared defiantly, "I will not be neutered." Nagin was critical of the slow trickle from the $110 billion set aside for Katrina recovery across the Gulf Coast and came under fire for describing the World Trade Center site as a "hole in the ground." On the first anniversary of Katrina, Nagin remained unapologetic.

"I applaud him for the dollars that have come," Nagin said. "But I'm always reminding him that he needs to keep it up. . . . This is not a quick fix. It's unprecedented, and it's going to take some time." The mayor's explanation for the slow flow of cash to the city: "I've said it before, if it had been a bunch of rich people struggling in New Orleans, it would have been different."[22]

It is no wonder that on the first anniversary of Hurricane Katrina the president opted for the Mississippi Gulf Coast first before touching down in hostile New Orleans territory. Ricky Mathews, the *Sun Herald*'s president and publisher, described the president as rolling up his sleeve at a "power lunch" also at a local staple, the Schooner restaurant in downtown Biloxi.[23] The guest list included Mississippi Governor Haley Barbour and the state's congressional delegation, including Senator Lott and Senator Cochran, both Republicans. Mathews recounted the meeting and sized up the leaders.

Barbour facilitated the meeting. And as usual, he did an excellent job. The thing that those of us who have worked in the recovery trenches with the governor have noticed most about him, outside of his incredible focus on getting the recovery job done, is his super-human grasp of the details. He is a man who does his homework. He has a mind like a steel trap. That quality serves him well in this complicated, precedent-setting world we are in today.

And on the president, Mathews makes this distinction:

Listening to the intense discussions about our recovery efforts, I was once again struck by the dedicated, competent leaders in this state who remain focused on finding the answers to the difficult challenges we still face.

The meeting was not designed by the governor to be a feel-good session with the president. It was a straight-talk meeting designed to help the president understand one of our most difficult challenges—housing—and what we are trying to do to address this challenge.[24]

While Nagin felt that the White House dismissed New Orleans as not being as rich or of as much national worth as, say, New York City, Barbour wanted to "help the president understand" Mississippi's needs in the aftermath—a slight nuance in coverage tone on both sides of the state border, but one that can be explained by a study of pre-Katrina *Sun Herald* and *Times-Picayune* coverage.[25] The *Sun Herald*'s coverage was community based before Katrina, with the bulk of its nontraditional thematic stories including military and personality profiles. The *Times-Picayune* was city based, heavy on sports and entertainment in addition to its politics and crime based reports. Politics in the *Sun Herald* was episodic in nature, in that it reported the day-to-day events and plans of Mayor A. J. Holloway. This changed in 2006, as the coverage the mayor received became longer and more thematic, or detailed in its treatment of the mayor's plans through additional reporting or context. Likewise, the *Times-Picayune* also increased the lengths of its political reporting, yet not more statistically significant than before the storm.[26] It is clear that measuring blame or critique of leadership is a value that is quite subjective. When compared to other major frames journalists use, such as human interest storytelling, conflict, morality, and economic contexts, attribution of responsibility or blame remains the most obscure. For both 2004 and 2006, it received the weakest score (on an index designed to measure it) compared to all other framing tools journalists typically use. Readers are not always clear of the tone and intent of the news report when it comes to the blame game. Outside of the Katrina coverage, it was a subtle reporting tool buried behind facts, data, and context.[27]

The most remarkable change in tone toward those in power can be found in the *Times-Picayune*'s coverage more so than with the *Sun Herald*. Mayor Nagin's radio interview with Garland Robinette was still spurring local media on, and local officials were celebrated in the early months following Katrina. As Hurricane Rita threatened the state merely weeks after Katrina's devastation, the *Times-Picayune* wrote in its mix of news, journalistic diaries, and citizen reports that muddied its traditional news makeup in late 2004:

> Bravo to Mayor Ray Nagin of New Orleans, Jefferson Parish President Aaron Broussard, Kenner Mayor Phil Capitano and the many others involved in the successful hurricane evacuation.
>
> The calming, yet informative joint press conference on Tuesday morning was needed because of the uncertainty of a Category 4 hurricane possibly headed in our direction. Fortunately it didn't hit the metro New Orleans area, but we now know that millions can evacuate in a timely and calm manner.[28]

By year's end, the New Orleans mayor is portrayed as a brash crusader and fighter for the city of New Orleans, extending his love-hate honeymoon with the city's leading news source as he successfully sought reelection. His opponents are framed as being detractors with no real support base strong enough to unseat the incumbent, and Nagin comes across strong, unapologetic, and inevitable as the city's champion for rebuilding.[29] Once Nagin had won his reelection, the *Times-Picayune*'s coverage portrays him as a uniter, willing to put aside petty reelection politics, especially with Lt. Governor Mitch Landrieu who would succeed him in 2010, and whose sister, Senator Mary Landrieu, was a needed ally in Congress in Nagin's effort to obtain more federal funding for the recovery effort. Nagin told supporters in his victory speech, "It's time for us to stop the bickering" and become "one New Orleans." To his opponents he offered an olive branch, stating, "Me and Mitch can work together. Me and the governor can work together. I'm bringing everybody in because this is a big job."[30] As Nagin proceeded to try and turn the city around in his final term as mayor, the *Times-Picayune* used words such as "optimist," and "making progress," as well as "improvements" to measure the mayor in contrast to the unprecedented challenges he faced.[31] The local newspaper that before the disaster had been pointedly critical of its politicians had continued to do so but cushioned in the context and compassion of the magnitude of the challenges the local and state leaders were facing. Gordon Russell, who covered the mayor's reelection, explained in an interview the root of the initial change in coverage toward local leadership.

> . . . there were times when I would be interviewing the mayor, the council president, or some other official, and they would just break down and cry. They would say, "I don't know when we're going to get this up and running, or that

working." They would even share their own personal problems with me, every-thing they'd lost, how they were going to rebuild their lives. I never experienced that before. Sometimes, I just had to take a step back and give them a moment. I'd say we were a bit sympathetic with them in the beginning. I mean nothing like this had ever happened, as far as I know, in America. We were sympathetic with them, or you can say, we cut them some slack. There was kind of a honey-moon period. But those days are over. Now it's about holding them accountable for what they do or don't do.[32]

Five years later, the Deepwater Horizon oil disaster was to once again restart the finger-pointing. President Obama's first trip to the oil spill was so short that national news commentators called it the "daiquiri summit." Once the president's team realized the first trip did not play well with the media, he returned, this time to roll up his sleeves and pick up tar balls off the beach, albeit before flying off to a family vacation. As a *New York Times* reporter commented on *Hardball with Chris Matthews*, "I mean, at some point, he has to be smart enough to realize that he has to do better by the people of south Louisiana, or you're going to get to the point where you're going to have a Kanye moment, where somebody's going to say, President Obama doesn't care about bayou people."[33]

The press early on labeled the Deepwater Horizon disaster "Obama's Katrina." Justified or not, this reference came during the first week when the enormity of the leak was not yet realized by the public or the media. The level of disconnect President Obama's administration initially showed the region to the events on the ground echoed President Bush's response to Katrina when the scope of the oil crisis failed to receive national priority in a similar fashion. When interviewed in the summer during the oil gusher, Gulf Coast scientists had strong feelings about connecting the current pres-ident with this disaster. "Absolute bullshit," said Frank Rohwer, program leader at LSU's Wildlife and Fisheries in the School of Renewable Natural Resources. "I don't think it is anywhere near the level of incompetency of the response to Katrina." The Exxon Valdez spill created the protocols for handling such a man-made industrial disaster, and so the federal govern-ment only had in place what it learned from that disaster.[34] Louisiana State University fisheries professor Lucy Lampila believed because the media was being sensitive to how Bush's timing appeared to the region, they framed the news as "oh here it goes in New Orleans again."[35]

As is the case with many disasters or crises, there is plenty of blame to go around. The oil disaster expanded this narrative, adding corporate responsibility to government responsibility. Instead of it being only an "Obama's Katrina" narrative, Dr. Julie Anderson squarely put the responsibility on the oil company British Petroleum.

> . . . this was clearly BP's disaster, and also because the federal government response was pretty good, though certainly not perfect, this time, whereas the federal response to Katrina was absolutely appalling. I thought it was really unfair to call this "Obama's Katrina" and to imply that the government response was anywhere near as bad this time.[36]

Early on, however, it became clear that there were external factors that could affect the quickness and size of the response. Many of those factors were in the control of BP, not the federal government. On May 1, eleven days after the Deepwater Horizon oil rig exploded, and nine days after oil began spewing into the Gulf, the Coast Guard had still only released a single image of oil leaking a mile beneath the surface—an out-of-focus photograph of a broken pipe releasing oil. But inside the unified command center, where BP and federal agencies were orchestrating the disaster response, video monitors had already displayed hours of footage they did not make public.[37]

On June 3, just a few days after the oiled pelican images emerged, *ABC World News* investigative reporter Brian Ross explained how BP wouldn't allow the White House or the Coast Guard to release video of the disaster. For a major global corporation to "*not allow*" access to information shifted power and control over the crisis away from the government, placing it in the hands of this private business. The collusion or perception of collusion between the government and the energy giant to withhold vital information was shocking to many journalists and observers following the story.

Then, once the video was finally made public, the media accepted the government's and BP's estimates of the volume of oil gushing underwater. The information proved grossly inaccurate. On May 12, NPR's Richard Harris was the first to report that figures released by the U.S. government and BP underestimated the size of the Deepwater Horizon disaster. It had taken almost a month for the media to realize their trust had been misplaced. But it was not only the news outlets that did not understand the depth of this disaster thanks to BP's visual gatekeeping—scientists also weren't allowed to understand the disaster's enormity. This new information changed the direction of the response. The visuals did not lie. The untruthfulness, failure, and unpreparedness of BP and the government became swift undercurrents of the disaster.

The size of BP's obstruction of information continued to come out more than a year and a half later in disclosed company correspondence. A federal lawsuit revealed internal company e-mails that showed experts informed BP on April 22, 2010 (the day the rig sank), that the ruptured well would trigger a disaster the maximum of eighty-two thousand barrels a day. According to internal messages, BP executives chose to keep this information secret and not inform those preparing to respond to the disaster. On April 24, BP gave the first "official" estimate of the disaster—a flow rate of one thousand barrels a day. Some would call this spin, others a ridiculous, intentional lie. The true amount was closer to the April 22 prediction. Later in the disaster, an expert task force put the flow amount at that time at sixty-two thousand barrels a day. A *Times-Picayune* editorial remarked that "the new documents are the first public indication that BP had a very good idea early on that the disaster could be enormous."[38]

However, BP was not the only power player performing a disappearing act. A video content analysis conducted of the oil disaster showed that the lack of Obama's presence in the Gulf region may have contributed to the persistent blame frames appearing in the oil disaster narratives.[39] President Obama did not visit the Gulf Coast region in the first week of the disaster and therefore he was absent in the television visuals we analyzed. Obama did not visit until May 4, two weeks after the initial rig explosion. In contrast, President Bush's first visit to New Orleans came five days after Katrina. This fact seems shocking when you think about the criticism Bush received for his now infamous thirty-five-minute "flyover" of three states on August 31. It was only two days after Katrina hit but came to embody Bush's perceived detachment from the suffering of the region. In reality, his response was quicker than Obama's. With the media already calling the oil gusher "Obama's Katrina," the researchers expected the Obama administration to be cognizant of the need to react quickly. However, Obama's presence in the visuals, while greater in week six, remained minimal.

Networks had one relevant image of him that they relied on—Obama bending down on the beach to look at oil on his second visit. Other than that, the networks relied on generic video of Obama. This video led to the discussion on MSNBC's *Hardball with Chris Matthews* by a *New York Times* reporter, who is originally from Louisiana, questioning Obama's perceived commitment to the "bayou people."[40] While the Obama images were few, it is important to discuss this finding in itself: that Obama did not appear as a salient image in the first and sixth week of the Gulf oil disaster coverage and this could have contributed to the initial displeasure with governmental response.[41]

Some local reporters, veterans of Katrina coverage, were in fact willing to give Obama a break. "Only so much the government can do. People complain about Obama, but only so much Obama can do."[42]

Just as with Katrina, local authorities were looked to for leadership and action, and local politicians again became champions of the region but also targets. While Democratic Governor Kathleen Babineau Blanco was questioned for her response and abilities during Katrina, Louisiana's new Republican Governor Bobby Jindal was poised to show action and did so. On cue, Jindal even criticized the Obama administration for its slow response. In turn, Jindal was criticized for not activating fast enough six thousand National Guard troops that the federal government had authorized. It should be no surprise that with the scientific complexity of this disaster, additional criticism of Jindal came from unlikely sources. Whereas criticism was lacking from the aggressive journalists of the Katrina experience, the region's scientists observing the media discourse became more vocal. Bob Thomas, a scientist at Loyola University, recalled that:

> The governor slightly rolled up his sleeves and took his coat off and followed the cameras into the wetlands. He had photo ops holding a vacuum hose, standing on a milk crate speaking to a group of people, and otherwise appearing tough and in command. He vilified the scientific community and attempting to spend $400 million to build berms that the best wetland scientists in the world said wouldn't work for the value of the dollars spent. He didn't even consult them, although they all work or have worked/earned degrees in Louisiana universities. I very much appreciated his engagement but regret his tactics and (as usual) hard-headedness. When challenged about his decisions being uninformed, he chose to just repeat his mantra: "The berms are doing what they were designed to do." Why? Because he knows the masses will say, "Leave him alone. His plan is working"—regardless of what the intelligencia is saying.

Thomas went on to criticize local officials for being pressured into rash and uninformed action. In the effort to demonstrate they were getting something accomplished, local leaders sidestepped experts who could offer informed recommendations for cleanup, water testing, and marine life care. The emotional rhetoric of local leaders, Thomas added, fanned the flames of Gulf Coast residents' emotions and did little to educate the population on what was needed in the aftermath. "They failed the lessons of a good Mardi Gras krewe captain," Thomas said. "They didn't look back to see if a quality parade was following them; they simply led the masses down the yellow brick road."

In the effort to transmit information, the media can frame issues to influence others, win over public opinion, and as we have seen above in crisis situations, to assign blame.[43] Past research of disaster coverage has found more government blame than praise in both local and national news outlets.[44] Since the press early on dubbed the Deepwater Horizon disaster "Obama's Katrina," when evaluating blame during the first and sixth week of the Deepwater Horizon disaster, we also coded for an attribution of responsibility frame.[45] Our observations were confirmed, and the study also reaffirmed past research. Operating in a conflict mode, the national press aired more interviews from sources that attributed blame and responsibility than the local media. In the hostile political atmosphere, many of the sources blamed the lack of federal oversight for the explosion and took issue with the Obama administration's perceived slow recognition of the disaster and subsequent response. Additionally, there were just as many criticizing BP for its lack of oversight and painfully slow, ineffective response. It is prudent to remember that this is a man-made disaster caused by mistakes of many, not just a few. So the very nature of this disaster warrants a search for responsibility.

Almost two years later, in 2012, that media narrative moved from social science studies and the court of public opinion into the court of law. Assigning a monetary blame figure is proving to be difficult and time consuming. There have been a number of reports issued from investigations spreading the blame fairly evenly between BP, Transocean, and Halliburton. However, a key federal report by a team of the U.S. Coast Guard and the agency that regulates offshore drilling (BOEMRE) puts the ultimate responsibility on BP, citing a series of faulty decisions leading up to the explosion.[46]

Still to be decided are just how much oil leaked and how much should be paid to the federal government and those who make a living off of the coast through wildlife and tourism. BP received court approval to finalize a $7.8 billion settlement with more than one hundred thousand businesses and individuals just days before the second anniversary of the rig explosion. The settlement, which could be adjusted higher, covers private economic and medical claims for such victims as fishers and hotel operators.[47] The liability trial began in February 2013 to help determine the cause and assign blame. ". . . [A] massive civil trial that pits BP and its corporate partners on the doomed Deepwater Horizon rig against the federal government and a half-dozen Gulf states, as well as possible federal criminal charges related to the disaster."[48]

Also, in the week of the second anniversary, the first of perhaps more arrests was made. Former BP U.S. engineer Kurt Mix was charged with trying to destroy evidence related to the size of the oil gusher. His arrest could lead to determining exactly how much oil leaked into the Gulf by revealing the company's own internal estimate—an estimate the company, as we have noted, has refused to share.[49] At issue are the fines that could be levied under the Clean Water Act that will be decided by the amount of oil that flowed into the Gulf—if negligence is found. At up to $4,300 per barrel, penalties could go as high as $17.6 billion.[50]

The government's case may be helped by the disturbing pictures of shrimp without eyes and cancerous-like lesions and fish with deformed gills that were taken by fishers and scientists almost two years later. It's unclear if the oil or the dispersants are to blame.

Even with numerous reports putting the blame on a triad of global companies, the press continued questioning of the federal government's role.

> While the federal investigative team lays blame on decisions made by the companies, it does not address the government's own role in approving some of the questionable decisions. The federal agency that oversees offshore drilling signed off on many of the calls made by the companies, sometimes in minutes, and accepted an outdated and erroneous oil disaster plan for the well that discussed protecting species that did not even exist in the Gulf of Mexico.[51]

Those with the most responsibility are the ones who are looked to for action. In crisis situations, the public looks to leaders for answers and to the press to take those in power to task if the response is not adequate. Oil and gas remain the American consumer's untenable addiction and its expanded exploitation the subject of political polarization. However, even among Gulf Coast residents who survive off petroleum profits but still suffered from this disaster, responsibility and accountability remain a vital part of the media discourse in the fallout from the oil spill. As we have seen, sometimes it is just the perception of quick action that pleases people, even if the chosen path is questionable. The role of the media, although not always accomplished in both of these crises, is to ensure the spotlight remains on those institutions who must answer to the public when disaster strikes.

In the news coverage of Hurricane Katrina and the oil disaster, different sources were used to interpret the events. In Katrina, official sources were not questioned in the beginning. In the oil disaster, uninformed sources confused the coverage. Chapter 5 explores who reporters used to find the answers in tragedy—answers that led to both justice and understanding.

5

SOURCES AND ACCURACY IN DISASTER

Sources say what the journalist can't. During Katrina, sources said what the journalist wanted to. Boxed in by an ever-increasing skeptical public and a twenty-first century abundance of cable talk show pundits, pick-your-cause alternative media, and digital user-generated news, journalists have held their heads above the fray simply because they hold to the credence that they are fair. But scholars have always known there was an imbalance in the *"he said, she said,"* of newswriting fairness of who finally ends up being quoted in print or through sound bite. The VIPs—the presidents, governors, mayors, and their spokespeople and public information officers—get showcased first in news reports; and should the editor or producer extend the reporter some generosity, an advocacy group director—and really generous—the "man on the street" can see him- or herself on the nightly newscast or in the next day's headlines. Human interest stories, those that chronicle the struggles and trials of everyday folk, often feature these less powerful, if not equally important, news sources as prominently, or even more prominently, than the "official" sources who typically dominate the order and content of a traditional news story.[1] Yet, the quotes of unofficial sources must then be weighted and legitimized by the corroboration of official sources in order for the journalist to dispel reader doubt and live up to another elusive credo: accuracy.

Katrina journalists across the Gulf Coast were faced with a communications blackout, and while some were embedded with local and state officials, in the first five days of the storm it was the "man on the street" who had the "facts on the ground." The *Times-Picayune* and SunHerald.com, rolling news blogs from August 29 to September 5, 2005, gave equal weight to unofficial eyewitness accounts while posting word for word the statements, releases, phone calls, and quick television interviews by officials. On the *Times-Picayune*'s rolling weblog *NolaLive* on NOLA.com, its affiliate website, the subheadlines for news updates showed who the news sources were on the ground as events unfolded. One subheadline read "From Folks Who Evacuated from Houston," and another read "Katrina Tales."[2] In one news update on August 29, 2005, it is the residents of the lower Ninth Ward who provide the legitimacy to Mayor Nagin's announcement on local radio that the Florida Avenue pumping station had gone down, resulting in a toppling of that levee system. As Nagin could barely confirm the scope of the flooding, the residents do. In "Water tops 9th Ward Levee system," the residents tell *Times-Picayune* staffers that "houses were taking in water on Reynes Street at the Claiborne Avenue bridge." The residents then add further detail:

> Not all of the 9th Ward, however, appeared to have water problems.
>
> A group of about a half dozen families, some with severe hardships, were riding out the storm near the corner of Feliciana and Marais streets. Among those who stayed was a mother with a son paralyzed in a recent shooting and a 56-year-old man with a broken leg.
>
> "The wind's pushing pretty hard here," the man, Paul Garrett, said in a 7:15 a.m. phone interview. "But it doesn't seem to be destroying any rooftops. We're doing OK."
>
> Garrett said he stayed to help other families, as did his neighbor, Arnold Scott, 49.
>
> "There's a little guy that's paralyzed down the street, and he and his mother didn't get a chance to get out," Garrett said. "We didn't want to leave, and then come back and find them dead or something. I made some rafts so I can get down there as fast as I can if I need to. I'm just hoping the water doesn't come in one big surge."[3]

As that first day of the storm progressed, it was these unofficial sources who provided legitimacy and a strong measure of accuracy about the impact and scope of the storm damage. Christy Franchi, who rode the storm out on Dumaine Street in the French Quarter, is quoted by reporters in a news item titled "Katrina Tales." "It looks like the winds are calming down," she said around 10:30 a.m. "The Quarter isn't flooded. The building manager on the third floor, his balcony railing is in the street, and there are plants everywhere. But, so far, it doesn't look too bad. [The Quarter] is holding up pretty well."

Phyllis Wagner-Bolger and her family members who weathered the storm at Ursuline Academy on State Street let the journalists know that Uptown was spared, and Shawn Gwin in River Ridge, another citizen "weather man," reported to journalists that it was just "lots of debris—tree debris" on his side as well.

The lack of communication access to officials emboldened many local journalists to break with tradition and become a quasi-source themselves.

After all, they were seeing the destruction with their own eyes, and the news had to be reported, so why not use their own testimony? This is how it appeared in the weblog:

Howard Ave. area, New Orleans, Monday, 3 p.m.

Reporters didn't have to travel far from *The Times-Picayune* offices on Howard Ave. to witness the storm's destructive force.

Within four blocks of the office, the storm scenes were still raw and astonishing. A handful of cars in the parking lot had their windows and sky roofs blown out. One sports car had its hatchback glass blown out, the backseat headrest protruding from the back window like a shark's fin.

Several concrete light poles along I-10 were snapped in half. Billboard signs were shredded and flailing in the wind. Dozens of sheets of aluminum siding were twisted around tree trunks and fences. Street signs were bent at 45-degree angles. Several trees were uprooted. Several large tree branches littered both lanes of Howard Ave. Windows at a General Electric maintenance building were blown out on both the first and second floors.

Dozens of buses and vans at the New Orleans Tours depot appeared to be in good shape, their windows intact thanks to owners who left the front doors and side doors open to reduce the pressure on the glass.

The wind was still gusting to tropical storm strength, churning the floodwater to white caps along open roads.

The floodwater was as deep as four feet in some places, rendering roads in and out of the area impassible to all but the highest-riding trucks and SUVs.

The floodwater was knee-deep under the Jeff Davis overpass near Xavier University.

A middle-aged Mid-City couple who had evacuated to Baton Rouge was stranded in their Honda Envoy under the overpass. The couple had evacuated to Baton Rouge for the night but could not reach their house because more than 5 feet of water surrounded it. Fortunately, the house was raised above the water level and appeared dry, the man said. The couple had chosen to wait out the storm in the relative safety of the overpass.[4]

And the journalists also attempted to verify the rumor mill being spread by callers on radio and television. One weblog update titled "Looting, New Orleans 2:15 pm" began:

Returning from a fact-finding expedition at the newspaper's Howard Avenue headquarters, a group of reporters and photographers stumbled onto a parade of looters streaming from Coleman's Retail Store, located at 4001 Earhart Blvd., about two blocks away from *The Times-Picayune* offices.

The looters, who were men and women who appeared to be in their early teens to mid-40s, braved a steady rain and infrequent tropical storm wind gusts to tote boxes of clothing and shoes from the store. Some had garbage bags stuffed with goods. Others lugged wardrobe-sized boxes or carried them on their heads.

The line going to and from the store along Earhart Boulevard numbered into the dozens and appeared to be growing.

Some looters were seen smiling and greeting each other with pleasantries as they passed. Another group was seen riding in the back of a pickup truck, honking the horn and cheering.

No police were present in the area, which is flooded heavily with standing water two to four feet deep on all sides of Earhart Blvd.[5]

When word hit that the flooding had reached Hurricane Betsy proportions, as in residents were now seeking rescue via their rooftops, the paper used its own reporters to corroborate the first hours of this iconic scene. In the weblog update titled "Despair in the 9th Ward, New Orleans, 9th Ward, 2:30 pm" readers learn that:

Times-Picayune photographer Ted Jackson waded into the Lower 9th Ward Monday afternoon and reported a scene of utter destruction. The wind still howled, floodwaters covered vehicles in the street and people were clinging to porches and waiting in attics for rescuers who had yet to arrive.

In one home on Claiborne Avenue near the Industrial Canal bridge, Jackson saw a man peering from a window in his attic. The man said rising water in his house had forced him, his wife and two children into the attic.

Jackson estimated the water's depth at 12 feet.

"He was very calm," Jackson said of the man in the attic window.

Jackson said he couldn't get across the street. The water was too deep and the current was too fast.

Nearby, three children and three adults were clinging to a porch, trying to stay above the water, which they insisted was continuing to rise.

"They were really scared. They said they had been clinging to that porch since 8 a.m."[6]

Gulf Coast journalists did not realize then that they were breaking all the rules that confined traditional reporting; in fact, they found that the rules had to be broken in order to get the accuracy, truth, balance, and fairness that the readers needed in what they saw were life-or-death situations in those early moments before the waters rose. *Times-Picayune* city editor David Meeks pointed out that "you didn't have the ability to check your information. There was no police information officer to call to check things out. No office to go back to to fill out your story, to flesh out the details, to get some contacts, to double-check things, all that was gone. All you can do is write down exactly what you saw in front of you, and turn it in to people that you hope will be able to use it in some way."

When it came to sources, Meeks, who functioned as an assignment editor for a team of the paper's reporters who stayed behind in the city when their building began flooding, said that the journalists had to make decisions as they went along. They debated where to eat, where to have a news bureau, where to meet up, how to write up what they saw. They even wrangled over the decision to return to the new building to get equipment and supplies. "I went with one of the reporters, and we got a kayak, and floated stuff out of the paper," Meeks recalled. "So those [were] very, very fundamental stuff in those early hours." Neither was there much time for fact-finding those eyewitness reports, as his reporting team would dictate "stories off the back of envelopes," and craft the story while calling it in over the phone. There was no time or electricity to write or type as deadlines were instant. As the reporter saw the news it went on *NolaLive*, with a few edits from the paper's team holding the fort down in Baton Rouge. The *Sun Herald*'s makeshift blog master Don Hammack, affectionately called the "bloganator," embedded himself with first responders, and as he fed his reports back to the *Herald*'s online editor, Kate Magandy, he too had become a source in his own blog. "He talked about walking down the street and seeing what people were doing and as people started coming out and seeing what the devastation was, he sort of just gave a bird's-eye view of what it was like to walk though downtown Gulfport and see what had happened."

Typically, television reporters, unlike radio and print, have images to support their stories, as seeing is often believing. Yet without the ability to contact official sources, they simply ventured out of their flooded stations to get the word around town to fill the twenty-four-hour news update cycle format. WWL-TV anchor Mike Hoss remembered that "[w]e couldn't call the mayor's office, we couldn't call New Orleans Police Department . . . we couldn't call the Northshore. We had a guy, a reporter over there, and we couldn't call him and he couldn't call us. Communication, for a business that's in the communication world, it was life and death. . . . We couldn't communicate with anybody, we didn't know that the 17th Street Canal levee had collapsed to the extent that it did." Hoss said "old-fashioned reporting" is what they resorted to.

> We overcame it by reporters and photographers going out as far as they could, gathering the information, bringing it back to the station, sitting on the news set, and telling us here's what's going on. So it was pure, unfiltered, I went here, here's how bad it is. All right, next reporter, I went here, here's how bad it is. That's how we drew the picture of the storm, just by word of mouth. We had no communication. It was just word of mouth and word of mouth from our reporters who were in the field.[7]

Radio journalists went beyond the call of merely gathering information, but relayed the news back to official sources who were unaware of events on the ground. KGLA 1540 AM in Gretna was a constant flow between sources, journalists, and officials as the mostly Honduran Spanish-speaking population on the West Bank of New Orleans, as well as in Mid-City, was cut off from official updates in English of the aftermath damage. The station owner and announcer, Ernesto Schweikert, found himself pressing Mayor Nagin for supplies to Spanish-speaking residents by directing his relief efforts to specific locations these families were seeking refuge in. Families called in from overseas to Schweikert's continuous coverage to direct him to where stranded loved ones were, as all this played out over the air. In some cases, he tried getting hold of the Coast Guard or the National Guard for help. In another case, like the television and print journalists, he got a boat and went out with a friend to see for himself, not just to report, but to save a life. In one of the more poignant recollections of those early days, Schweikert said:

> [T]here was an old lady that didn't want to leave, she had two dogs. And she lived in Mid-City. So her nephew came from Guatemala, and he called me and he said, Ernesto, you have a media pass? They are not letting me in. I know my aunt stayed there because we spoke with her before the hurricane passed by. And I really want to find out, you know, but her house is under water. But I know that if you get me to this point, we can maybe get a little boat. I said don't worry about it, we called some of the people with the National Guard. I went to meet him at La Place. I brought him into New Orleans, all the way into the line between Jefferson Parish and Orleans Parish, they had a boat, we went on the boat, all the way to Mid-City to the house.

It was a one-story house. She had opened up the thing to go up into the roof, el attico, the attic or something. We went into the attic, you know, it was the saddest thing, you know, we saw. The lady was laying down on the top of the attic, she had broken a window, she had a white cloth, you know to wave for help, 'cause the lady was old, she was dead, and the two dogs were eating her. It was very, very strong, you know.[8]

As the weeks rolled on, access to official sources improved. Many of the journalists across all media in the region felt they had seen enough of the facts on the ground with their own eyes to legitimize their reports. "You start reporting . . . as a news person, seeing all this devastation there, plus you see bodies of people floating on the water," Schweikert said. There was no way any official source, be it local, state, or federal, could deny to them how bad the situation was. *Times-Picayune* reporter Gordon Russell said as time went on, readers expected local journalists to sort out the facts for them and to be able to cut to the chase, picking apart the truth from the rumor mill. "I think part of our job is to go root out all the stuff and say ok this guy screwed up, and I'm gonna say he screwed up. 'Cause I've interviewed everybody, and he screwed up." It became even more clear who Gulf Coast journalists considered having the final word on the events as they unfolded in those early Katrina days, the "man on the street," and at least up to 2006, the region's journalists became allies with their unofficial sources in reporting the news or the facts as they saw it.

Who's Who in Gulf Coast Katrina News

Researchers have many names for the man on the street. They are often called nonroutine, unofficial, and, more recently, unaffiliated sources. The final term describes them best because at the moment of being quoted for a news story, they do not wish to identify themselves with any entity other than themselves as individuals.[9] It works as such. If a reporter interviews the CEO of Entergy New Orleans about storm power outages, then the CEO is an affiliated source, speaking on behalf of the company. However, if a journalist comes across the same CEO and interviews him about the state of the damage in his neighborhood as a resident for a story unrelated to Entergy, in this capacity, the CEO is now an unaffiliated source, or a man on the street.

Additionally, affiliated sources fall within a hierarchy for journalists. At the very top are government-affiliated sources, such as elected officials

Table 2: Nonroutine Sourcing Means

	2004	2006
Source Affiliation		
Unaffiliated U.S. Citizen*	2.05	2.45
Foreign Citizen	1	3.33
Other	1	1
Source Agency/Institution		
Nongovernmental/Nonprofit	1.6	1.65
Educational	2.11	2.26
Civic	1.39	1.62
Other**	2.05	1.42
None*	2	2.5
Source Status/Rank		
Position Not Specified	2.5	2.4
Worker/Employee/Member	1.61	1.78
Victim	2	1.75
Eyewitness	1.45	1.56
Common Man/Man on the Street*	1.91	2.4
Other	2.07	2.08

* $p < .05$
**$p < .01$

and their spokespersons, whose facts are considered the most accurate and whose inclusion makes a news item more credible, journalists believe, with the readers. The second level is often corporate and academic sources, who often put forward data to support the information they provide journalists. At the bottom of this list are nonprofits and community or civic groups. They are perceived as carrying the agenda of a minority or niche group and hence journalists are less trustful of their interpretation of the facts.[10]

As Gulf Coast journalists shifted the types of stories they wrote about after Katrina, so too did their reliance on affiliated sources. In New Orleans, in 2004, the year before the storm, 32 percent of stories featured "cops or courts," followed by entertainment or "other" story categories at 18 percent, then "local/city government" stories at 10 percent. In 2006, stories about "cops and courts" declined to 21.3 percent, with those in the "other" category dominating the news report at 27.5 percent, and "local/city government" stories increasing to 18.7 percent. Over in Biloxi, military stories comprised the bulk of the "other" category, given the Seabees post located near the city. In both cities, stories in the "other" category, which comprised the bulk of the daily news, were about Hurricane Katrina.[11]

With Hurricane Katrina, by nature a human interest event, given the toll on lives, possessions, and livelihoods of the region's residents, nonroutine, unofficial, unaffiliated sources increased significantly from 2004 to 2006.[12] Sources from what were traditionally considered less credible affiliations, such as academic, nonprofit, and civic entities also significantly increased the year after the storm.[13] However, the largest increase from 2004 to 2006 came from sources who were designated as "victim," "eyewitness," and "resident" with no affiliation.[14]

It was not just stories about Hurricane Katrina that brought more of these unaffiliated sources into the region's news reports; stories that focused on local and city government also saw a significant increase in quotes from the man on the street.[15]

Katrina forced Gulf Coast journalists to source the news in more diverse ways. Initially, a communication breakdown with official sources pressed the region's journalists to go seek out the facts themselves and to give credibility to the eyewitnesses they had encountered. As communication was restored, aware of the national and in some cases international attention to the local news report, many journalists felt pressured to ensure that official or affiliated sources were reintroduced. This decision had less to do with their own personal opinion of the facts, but to ensure that outside audiences felt that their news organizations were credible. As *Times-Picayune* city editor David Meeks put it:

> They want to believe that if I've read the *Times-Picayune*, that I'm reading an earnest honest attempt to get me the best possible information and they're transparent, they're telling me where they got their information. No, we're not bloggers, we don't throw stuff out there randomly, we don't just read other media and comment on it, our job is to tell you the information and to tell you where we got it.[16]

Katrina, Meeks added, despite its extraordinary conditions, was not a "license to forget everything we've learned in journalism." In fact, Meeks admitted, "I think we've learned some things about journalism," and that is not just sticking to the facts, but that their readers appreciated when they commented or qualified those facts. It is this new sourcing that provided the much-needed diversity in the post-Katrina dialogue of the needs of not just residents, but of officials.

The change in sourcing led to a shift in the reporting of a major story plaguing New Orleans and federal reaction to it. For New Orleans, the nation's "murder capital" before the storm, this change was to come to "cops and courts" reporting in the local media narrative of the FBI stepping in over the NOPD.

NOPD Gone Amok, Citizens versus Officials

Nowhere else in all of the case studies of post-Katrina news coverage can the role of unaffiliated, nonroutine sourcing prove more effective than in the public and then court of law trials of the New Orleans Police Department's conduct during the immediate aftermath of the storm. In the ultimate power test of the "*he said, she said*," it was through nonroutine sourcing that these issues came to light, and it was through nonroutine sourcing that New Orleans media championed the cause of everyday citizens in the bringing to justice of the city's law enforcement's biggest homicide cover-up since a similar spate occurred in the 1990s.

The first incident is ironically alleged to have occurred between Race and Religion streets. New Orleans's majority black citizens have been pitted against a mostly white NOPD law enforcement unit to which the latter has been treated as the credible official source, and the former a dubious unknown entity who have contributed to the city's crime rate. Since Katrina, particularly from 2006 and onward, the city's journalists, who rode out the storm among the city's black citizens, have begun advocating the facts according to their fellow residents, and have questioned the accounts of the NOPD. By 2010, the *Times-Picayune*, along with Public Broadcasting Service's *Frontline*, and ProPublica, a public journalism online outpost, have been partners in documenting the many cases of misconduct during the Katrina aftermath in an ongoing series titled "Law and Disorder: After Katrina, New Orleans Police Shot Frequently and Asked Few Questions."[17]

The first incident occurred on September 1, 2005, and was noted by journalists when two currently unknown men lay dead despite police stating they were released alive. The same day Keenon McCann was shot, but not killed, by two police officers who alleged he had a handgun. Police also took McCann into custody but later released him. Then on September 2, the homicide with the widest cover-up took place when Henry Glover was shot in Algiers. He was brought to an NOPD outpost by a passerby to seek medical attention, but instead his relative and the driver were allegedly assaulted by police officers while Glover lay bleeding to death in the car. Later Glover's body was discovered burnt, along with the car, a few miles away. On September 3, 2005, Danny Brumfield was shot and killed near the New Orleans Convention Center by NOPD from a cruiser passenger side window. The same day Matthew McDonald was shot and killed by an NOPD officer but his family was told he was killed by a civilian. Finally, on September 4, the incident with the most victims and witnesses, the Danziger Bridge shooting, occurred when two men, Ronald Madison, who was mentally challenged, and James Brissette, a teenager, were killed, while a family was seriously wounded at the hands of NOPD officers.[18] To date, more than a dozen of the city's current and retired officers have been brought to trial and face as high as life sentences. Even the NOPD's well-respected spokesman and number-two top law enforcer, assistant superintendent Capt. Marlon Defillo, who had a warm relationship with the city's journalists, retired in the summer of 2011 amidst a Louisiana State Police investigation into his handling of the Henry Glover case.[19]

The evolution of local reporting, first on the Danziger Bridge shooting and then the Henry Glover case, demonstrates this shifting allegiance in the use of sources among New Orleans media. Having been hunkered down with the city's law enforcers, *Times-Picayune* reporters Ron Thibodeaux and Gordon Russell chronicle the attitude of the NOPD in *7th Day of Hell—A Week of Horror Ends with More Evacuations and Uncertainty*, published on September 5, 2005.[20] The veteran cop reporters chronicled the mood of the local law enforcers with little critique or foresight, portraying them mostly as tireless heroes and dangerously stressed-out mavericks. The reporters wrote:

> For the city's police officers in particular, Sunday was the first day to get something like a breather after working around the clock for the past eight days. "Today is the first day you will see a smile on some of the officers' faces," said NOPD Capt. Marlon Defillo, who was taking a break on the neutral ground of Loyola Avenue with Detective William Charbonnet. "This has been a tremendous challenge for members of the police department, but they've held their ground. They've given their hearts and souls."
>
> New Orleans police officers sent up a cheer at one point Sunday at a report that their colleagues had engaged in a shootout with an armed group on the Danziger Bridge in eastern New Orleans, with several of the suspected marauders—but none of the police officers—being hit. Deputy Police Chief W. J. Riley said police shot eight people, killing five or six of them.

Defillo said police morale had hit a low point around Wednesday or Thursday in terms of the stress on officers, who had to try to keep the city safe without a working communications system amid increasing anarchy. While it was harrowing, reports that hundreds of police officers abandoned ship are false, he said.

"There was a report that 60 percent of our officers bugged out and hadn't been seen since Monday night. It is totally untrue," Defillo said.

What happened, according to Defillo, was that the NOPD's communications system crashed in the wake of the storm, making it impossible for officers to contact one another.

"We had to work on the buddy system, two guys staying together," he said. Defillo acknowledged that "there were some people who bugged out" but he didn't have an estimate of their numbers. Defillo himself was feeling better after shaving for the first time in a week and taking an impromptu bath in the green, leafy water of a backyard swimming pool. He was wearing a clean pair of acid-washed jeans and a polo shirt that he "found."

The scene was more intense in flood-ravaged St. Bernard Parish, where rescue efforts still lag behind those of New Orleans. Sheriff Jack Stephens authorized his haggard deputies to shoot to kill looters or anyone else who poses a threat.

Small gangs of heavily armed career criminals are roaming the parish's isolated eastern half and looting buildings, Stephens said.

"These are the same a—who have been testing us for 20 years," Stephens told his SWAT team at a security briefing. "Today is the day they are going to listen to us or we're gonna take 'em out."

Seven days into endless reporting, it did not occur to Thibodeaux and Russell to query the nature of the Danziger shooting, or to express concern about Sheriff Stephens's vigilante-style approach to dealing with civilians even in a major crisis. This report was almost 95 percent sourced by official sources, in an "us against them" frame that placed local law enforcers in a legitimate power struggle with the undefined "same assholes" that Stephens is alluding to as the source of the looting. Russell looked back in 2006, before the FBI trials began, and expressed some regret about the early coverage. He said, "We and everybody sort of overreported the mayhem and then we did a story that debunked it. I still wonder though that there was more mayhem. The debunking that we did was very well sourced unlike the initial stuff we did, but I'm not totally convinced that some stuff didn't totally happen. . . . it still kind of keeps me up at night sometimes."[21]

Russell did make major corrections as one of the lead *Times-Picayune* reporters in the PBS/ProPublica investigative reporting project, but a closer look at the paper's coverage showed that other journalists were beginning to question the NOPD early on as they incorporated not just citizen sourcing, but their own personal eyewitness accounts of NOPD behavior. By month's end, staff writer James Varney, in a story on officers being suspended for deserting their duties during the storm, wrote that the acting police superintendent Eddie Compass "came under fire this week for hyping reports of crime and violence among desperate survivors stranded throughout New Orleans after the storm, reports that were believable at the time but were subsequently shown to be overblown."[22] A day earlier Varney had reported that eyewitnesses and journalists corroborated a story that NOPD officers were themselves looting, taking Cadillacs from the Sewel Cadillac Chevrolet in the CBD.[23] Once Compass resigned, the coverage of the NOPD began to become more critical of the credibility of the organization. Varney wrote:

> Compass had come under fire for a variety of other reasons after Katrina. At first, he seemed invisible, holed up in the Hyatt Hotel with Nagin and other city leaders. As anarchy threatened to overwhelm the city, cops on the street said they "had no chief."
>
> Widespread looting, some of it conducted by police officers, branded New Orleans worldwide as lawless, and almost 249 officers left their posts without permission.
>
> After that first week, however, Compass became a seemingly omnipresent fixture in media accounts, and was feted by broadcast news stars. After the crisis was in full swing, Compass was a virtual quote machine, offering a down-home mix of empathy and bravado.
>
> "I'm still standing. I'm the ultimate warrior," Compass was quoted two weeks after the storm. "I'm going to be the last person to leave the battlefield."
>
> While his tearful interviews made him a compelling local face of the horrors of the storm, his decision to leave the city and flip the coin at a New Orleans Saints game in Giants Stadium on Monday Night Football on Sept. 19 was criticized by some of his rank and file.[24]

From the first few days to the first month post-Katrina, the local news in New Orleans had begun to unravel the credibility of an official source. And as early as 2006, the *Times-Picayune* began to pick away at the Danziger Bridge shooting, despite its early failure to question the official sources in the September 5, 2005, Thibodeaux/Russell piece. As Brendan McCarthy and

Laura Maggie write on June 19, 2011, regarding the state of the Danziger Bridge shooting and current trial, six years ago "uncertainty flooded everyone's mind." When NOPD officers alleged that an officer was "down" on the bridge, the officers sped to the scene in a Budget rental truck and fired recklessly; "dozens of lives changed forever." With five officers on trial, another five pleading guilty, and one more charged separately in a cover-up, the reporters wrote that while it had taken five years to get to the truth "some facts are indisputable: Two people, forty-year-old Ronald Madison and seventeen-year-old James Brissette, died from police gunfire. Four other people were wounded." While in 2007, the Danziger seven officers marched triumphantly to the Orleans Parish jail to be booked on murder and attempted murder charges, surrounded by a hundred officers lining the street to hail them as heroes, the reporters substantiated the claims of the wounded Bartholomew family while exposing the weakening story of the NOPD officers.[25] It may have taken local journalists some time to balance the narrative, but by 2006, the local news gave the unofficial sources as equal a treatment as official sources in the Danziger case, who continue today to be accused of having favor with the city's coroner's office and other prosecutors.[26]

The weight given to an unaffiliated, unofficial source becomes even more prominent regarding the Henry Glover shooting on September 2, 2005. Despite the story first being broken by ProPublica in a report in 2008,[27] once the *Times-Picayune* came onboard the story, staff writer Laura Maggi gave a report that was heavy on the testimony of one man, an unofficial source. In a round-up article on the indictment, Maggi wrote:

Much is at stake: Unnamed New Orleans police officers stand accused by the car's owner of contributing to Glover's death, abusing others who tried to save him and stealing the car before it was destroyed.

The case was brought to the NOPD's Public Integrity Bureau and FBI by William Tanner, 41, a maintenance man who tried to save Glover's life after he was shot during chaotic conditions on the fourth day after Katrina hit. Tanner said his efforts on behalf of a complete stranger were stymied by the police officers he asked for help. Instead of offering aid to the wounded man, they left him to bleed to death in the back of Tanner's car, Tanner maintains.

A police officer wearing a tactical uniform eventually drove off in Tanner's Chevy Malibu—with Glover's body inside, according to Tanner. He said he found the car a couple of months later on the riverside of the Mississippi River levee, behind the NOPD's 4th District police station. The car was mired in the batture mud, burned and inoperable, he said.

> It's a shocking story, but the details Tanner related about the body's dis-
> covery seem generally to jibe with an autopsy by the Orleans Parish coroner's
> office. Glover's remains, mostly charred bone fragments, fit into five biohazard
> bags examined by pathologists at the D-MORT autopsy facility in St. Gabriel
> after the storm, according to the three-page document.[28]

Maggi's reporting here in 2009 empowered unofficial sources not just by the journalist's framing, but in the order they are placed in the story, and by the journalist's supporting of the unofficial source's claims with documents.[29] This may seem like standard journalism. Yet for a practice that had statistically changed post-Katrina to still show its head in 2011 when it comes to Katrina and "cops and courts" stories demonstrates that the average citizen and residents of the region are being championed. For the most significant news stories that make the headlines of the local news, five years later the least powerful of sources continue to be given proper space in the time slots and pages of their local media.

Accuracy and Sourcing Five Years Later

Five years later, the initial enormity of Hurricane Katrina remained unparalleled in the United States. The widespread effects of the flooding—suffering, death, and displacement—were not matched by the disaster of the Deepwater Horizon. The effects of the oil disaster were no less important, however, as these effects reached global proportions—beyond coastal and fishery preservation—to the conversation about energy that drives American global politics. This was a very different narrative that ended up with a distribution of sources different from Katrina's—and more often than not, elite and official. What the journalists found was a complex scientific narrative that mostly lived at the first and second levels of sourcing with government officials and corporate spokespersons and academics. But often at this second level were "analysts" with some credentials, yet no expertise in oil or the environment. This was a main difference between the oil disaster and Katrina: the suffering of the "man on the street" was not as prevalent and revealed itself only over weeks and months instead of days as with Katrina. What was left out of much of the television coverage were those people below the surface, those who live and die by the seafood and tourism industries. Nationally, they were replaced by pundits with lots to say, but no real scientific knowledge.

A content analysis of two selected weeks[30] of national and local television news coverage of the Horizon disaster showed that visits to government officials dominated the top of the source food chain. Nationally, 44 percent of sources in oil disaster stories were state or national government officials, 24 percent were academics, political analysts, and BP corporate officials, while only 13 percent were victims. This compared to the local news coverage where 48 percent were government officials, a lateral 23 percent were academics, etc., and only 7 percent of the sources in the stories were victims of disaster—a stark turnaround from local media that had learned the importance of featuring the "man on the street" in counterframing the realities of an unfolding crisis.

What is telling is how the victims' stories changed over time. During the first week of the Deepwater Horizon coverage, national stations showed the fiery pictures of the rig and used sound bites from Coast Guard officials to tell the tragic stories of the eleven victims that died in the initial explosion. As time progressed, the outlets realized the enormity of the situation and that victims were beyond the rig. As the victims' stories moved into the sixth week, the networks traveled to New Orleans and added "real people"—the stories of those being directly affected by the consequences of the spill. Once the national networks were on location they were able to add a sprinkling of faces to their coverage. Rig workers' wives started to appear on air with family photos of those who died on the rig.

Surprisingly, the local stations relied less on victims' stories. The stories of the businessmen and businesswomen who made their living through the coast were told mostly through fishers, shrimpers, and tourism business owners. If they were present, most told of frustrations with British Petroleum and the claims process.

Additionally, which is a surprise to no one, more white male officials were included in both the national and local coverage as compared to minority sources. This is a robust finding, especially in the context of crisis coverage.

Finally, both local and national news outlets relied most on political sources to frame the oil story. The local outlets relied on state politicians, which is intuitive given the audience they serve. National outlets, however, relied heavily on political analysts to frame this story. Oftentimes, the scientific stories of the spill would alternate back and forth from science to politics. Political analysts regularly appeared on national outlets to discuss the moratorium on drilling or whether President Barack Obama was strategically doing the right thing. It is interesting, with such a complex scientific story, that both national and local news outlets chose to use more political sources than scientific experts. Additionally, scientists and BP officials were interviewed in almost equal numbers by national news outlets. Scientists from Louisiana State University and Tulane University were interviewed both locally and nationally for science-framed oil spill stories. National as well as Gulf Coast marine biologists were interviewed to explain such ideas as the chemical makeup of the seawater. Scientific sources helped flesh out what had happened, but, given that they were competing with political sources and corporate sources, they were unsuccessful in advancing the scientific nature and consequences of the disaster.[31]

Media Trips Over Science

From the very beginning in covering the Deepwater Horizon oil disaster, the media got it wrong. It started with the very slug of the story. The media began the narrative by comparing the Deepwater Horizon rig explosion to the Exxon Valdez spill. The Valdez spill was near the shoreline, yet the Macondo Well was "far from land and a mile beneath the surface."[32] The Deepwater Horizon oil flowed in and under the water. As Dr. Robert Thomas, at Loyola University's New Orleans Center for Environment Communication, put it: "The disaster was labeled a *spill* by the media, but was actually a *gusher*."[33] This is because spills, as in the Exxon Valdez case, originated artificially from a tanker vessel leaking oil near the shoreline. In the case of the underwater Macondo Well, the gusher was a natural free-flowing phenomenon that BP was unable to contain. Scientists told us it was nearly impossible for journalists to explain the complexity of the disaster in just a few inches of newspaper or minutes of TV. It was easier to call it a spill, because gusher would have needed explanation at every reference. Once the "spill" was established, journalists did not know the science behind the gusher in order to explain it. A New Orleans television journalist interviewed during the summer of the Deepwater disaster noted that journalists had to do homework just to keep up. "We are trying to read more on the subject," he said. "We have had to do more research to break it down for the viewers. I don't think any of us are trying to be chemical engineers."[34]

A test case in using chemical engineering lingo came in furthering the scientific narrative of the BP's attempt to combat the disaster. Journalists tied their tongues in explaining Corexit, the dispersant used to break up the oil flowing out of the Macondo Well.[35] The contradictive nature of the coverage was evident during the first six weeks of the oil "gusher" coverage. *CBS*

Evening News[36] aired a story with sources who claimed dispersants were not harmful and within days aired another story with different scientists that said dispersants could shut down a person's lungs. A confused public asked, which is it?

The dispersant complexity proved to be the most difficult science issue of the story. Scientific observers like LSU's Dr. Chris D'Elia, professor and dean of the School of the Coast & Environment, felt journalists never asked the questions that would help explain the science in layman terms.

> I think the most important question early on to us is how do dispersants behave at depth—when you are down five thousand feet at very cold tempera-tures, the conditions are far different than they are at the surface. And disper-sants are normally used at the surface, that's where spills occur. That's what so bizarre about this spill—it's a deepwater spill. There has never been one before . . . This made the science difficult. There wasn't data on this. It had EPA confused as to what to do. They were under the gun to make decisions based on very little scientific information . . . So people made up things and in the environmental business you got very polarized opinions and whoever sways the reporter, sways the story so that's what you'd see.[37]

The dispersant confusion had a direct impact on one of the Gulf Coast's greatest industries—seafood. Gulf Coast residents hold emotional connec-tions to their "southern food" and the safety of seafood guided the news coverage and remained the focus a year later. There was a fundamental misunderstanding perpetuated by mostly national press accounts concern-ing how seafood was evaluated, according to Dr. Julie Anderson, an assis-tant professor and fisheries specialist at LSU's AgCenter and Louisiana Sea Grant. The average consumer would smell petroleum in their food, as it has a sharp smell.[38] Scientists sniffed and tested food during the oil disaster, but, she said, this was not the normal process. "Suddenly we had to justify to the media why seafood was safe and at the same time explain how sea-food was tested."

Seafood is rarely tested and the government does not have routine test-ing for toxicity.[39] In the past, when contamination was found, the seafood industry would shut down and everything would be retested before the waters would reopen. Seafood recalls and shutdowns are rare, although some fishing waters were closed for a time because of the oil disaster, Anderson recalled. The main health concern to be reported from this disas-ter, Anderson said, is a long-term cancer risk, a point the media glossed over in favor of the "eating toxic fish" narrative. "Most people assumed it was an immediate health risk. Really you could eat quite a bit of oil on something—it might give you an upset stomach, but it isn't going to kill you immediately."

Dr. Lucina Lampila, associate professor and seafood specialist in LSU's Department of Food Science, agreed. Some media outlets wanted her to take an extreme point of view as an academic source, offering a worst-case scenario regarding health. "They wanted gory details on how it was going to happen and they didn't want to listen that it wasn't going to happen," Lampila recalled of her experience with journalists. In one account, the black lining that flows down the back of shrimp, the digestive track, was mistaken as oil, Lampila joked.[40] "I have issue with the media making a foregone conclusion that seafood was going to make people sick and it was going to kill people. The local media got that, but the national media didn't."

Scientists, the Celebrity Sources of the Oil Disaster

With interviews in China, Finland, and on the *Late Show with David Letterman*, coastal expert Dr. Ed Overton, LSU professor emeritus of the School of the Coast & Environment, could barely keep up with the media demand.

> When they called and asked me to be on [*Late Show with David Letterman*], I said, well, this is not a joking matter and I am not a comedian and they said oh no, we want a serious discussion. Letterman has got to joke about something, but they wanted a serious discussion. So virtually everyone who talked to me was asking for a kind of scientific opinion. I think they were trying to get that; unfortunately I think they also got people who tended to be pretty articulate and a lot of these weren't really knowledgeable about oil spills or the ecology of the environment.[41]

That's because the media failed to distinguish "among true scientists, science educators, activists, government authorities, policy wonks, politicians and industry personnel" said Loyola's Dr. Robert Thomas.[42] Unlike Katrina, at issue with the media in the oil disaster, according to the scientists, was *who* they chose to interview.

For an appearance on a television panel on the unfolding oil crisis, Overton sat with an activist. The person's presence there was more because he made for "good TV" on the issue as opposed to knowing the facts. This nonexpert appeared to be a successful source because this activist was better on camera. LSU's Dr. D'Elia concurred with Overton on his encounters with nonacademic sources who received excessive exposure in the media narrative.

> I saw a lot of people sort of winging it. . . . I think our group, by and large, was very measured in what we said. We were very careful. We tried not to engage in hyperbole. We tried to speak in some balance—talk about the pros and cons of different arguments, things like that, so I was really proud of what our scientists did.[43]

Politicians and bloggers were also part of the shouting chorus on the oil disaster. Billy Nungesser, president of Plaquemines Parish outside New Orleans, did try in the year after the spill to capitalize on his media face time as a source by running for lieutenant governor. Nungesser was a regular on CNN Anderson Cooper's reports from the Gulf Coast in 2010, and the local talk was that his criticism of the federal government's response was part of an unsuccessful campaign strategy to seek higher office in 2011. He lost to incumbent Republican Jay Dardenne.

Likewise the blogosphere was lit afire with pseudoexperts on the crisis, all perpetuating their own take on the news that filtered back through the mainstream discourse. It was an "open mic" online, Dr. Thomas recalled, to nonjournalists who "are perceived by the public with the same legitimacy." In Thomas's assessment, "They are biased writers who have an agenda, and the agenda is not fair coverage."[44] The influx of experts muddied the science presented by oil and environmental scholars, making the findings of the event more a debate than a truth-seeking narrative.

Academics Grade the News

Local accounts of the oil disaster were perceived to be more accurate than national accounts in their treatment and use of sources according to the scientists we interviewed. If there was an untrue or misinterpreted headline, Dr. Julie Anderson found, local media would often retract the story. She said this was not always true with national news outlets. The national media chose sources that allowed for a focus on the negative, scientists recalled, and national journalists would call, ask for an interview and, if the scholar would not support a particular disaster headline, they would no longer be interested in an interview, Dr. Anderson recalled. Given a focus on the big, sensational headlines coming out of the oil disaster, scientists said the local reports centered on community issues. Additionally, scientists clearly were more comfortable speaking to print than to broadcast journalists. The news routines of print journalists best suited the scientists' narrative, and Dr. Anderson, for instance, was able to go back and forth via e-mail on the details. With television news "sound bites don't always translate to the full story," she said.

The lack of follow-up earned many national news outlets a failing grade by academic sources. Many had reported the findings of non–peer-reviewed studies as fact, and did not frame the numbers and statistics in their appropriate contexts.[45]

The narrative of the oversight of offshore drilling also missed the mark. Investigative journalism on the dangerous practices of oil companies was missing early on, according to Dr. Thomas. When evaluating the catastrophe of the Deepwater Horizon, there appeared to be failure of the Minerals Management Service (MMS) now called the Bureau of Ocean Energy Management, Regulation and Enforcement.[46] "A thirty-year-old record of relative safety in the Gulf operations lulled the agency to sleep," said Dr. Ed Overton, and the former MMS did safety checks on the Horizon merely to make sure workers were wearing their hardhats. The Deepwater Horizon rig even received an award for safety the day of the explosion.[47]

> Here was a case where they were finished drilling that well. They were closing it up and getting ready to move the drilling rig away and put a production rig on. This was the last thing—literally the last day. They were cementing it, sealing it and moving out so somebody else could come in. They had the group on the rig that were celebrating completion of the well.[48]

Unlike in the auto industry, where one button can stop the flow of an entire assembly line should a faulty car go by, as Dr. Overton points out, this was lacking in the Horizon oil disaster. "There were people that could have enacted that blowout preventer," Overton said. "You shut it down before the accident takes several million dollars to get back where you were."

These are the kinds of media narratives that should have emerged long before the explosion, according to Dr. Rowher. The questions must be asked before disasters happen.

Sometimes, answering science questions and answering news questions can clash, as *Times-Picayune* managing editor Peter Kovacs found in a conversation with a scientist.

He said one thing that's—the difference between science and media is that the way scientists work is that they write something or they have a theory and then they peer-review it and if you are a scientist you sort of expect all these geniuses in your field to tell you about crap you didn't think of or math you did wrong or whatever and then you repair it and he was telling me how in this . . . all that rhythm doesn't exist. They want you to show up in Waldenberg Park in an hour and stand next to Anderson Cooper and explain what this is doing to the rare blue fin tuna and the answer is we really aren't going to know in five years, but that doesn't really work on television. What works on television we are going to know in five minutes. I'd say having more reporters trained in science, but I don't know if you could ever be trained in science—you'd have to have a Ph.D. in this stuff in order to be in the same league as the people you are interviewing.[49]

Celebrity Sources Look Back

Although experts in their fields, the science sources accept that they were partly to blame for the often faulty news coverage.[50] Academic-speak does not always translate to media discourse; however, it was not an excuse for these expert sources to shy away from dialogue. Dr. Lucina Lampila knew she was out of her league when she found out that more than five hundred tickets had been sold to a Smithsonian event in which she was a speaker. She took a rare step and went to a number of outlets to get media training. The training made her realize science-speak was unacceptable. "Sometimes scientists get so lost in the technical they don't get the message through," Lampila said. A public relations specialist asked the question of her "and that means?," helping her to understand that the jargon can go over the public's head. One morning LSU's Dr. Ed Overton received a call for an interview at 5 a.m., a definite change in pace to how academics work and see their civic role in society as knowledge communicators.

The science world often takes time to get the data ready for interpretation. Lack of funding and the lag time between an event and conducting research are the main obstacles in how they do their work. "That process just flat out doesn't work for an emergency like this where all of a sudden you have the largest oil spill in history," said Dr. Frank Rowher, the program leader in Wildlife and Fisheries at the LSU School of Renewable Natural Resources.[51] By then the impact of the crisis has faded and the science is "far too little and far too late."

Science can learn from journalism and journalism can learn from science. In times of disaster, perhaps science needs its own disaster plan much like newsrooms have on how to cover breaking news. The scientists we interviewed were savvy about media—more than media appeared to be savvy about science.With journalists being required to increase their workloads in a new competitive media landscape, "the first thing to go is strong, in-depth reporting," said Dr. Thomas.[52] When faced with the possibility of another crisis, scientists like Dr. Rowher are pessimistic about the current news landscape having the resources to accurately cover it. "Look at the state of journalism . . . newspapers are folding left, right and center. I am impressed that the [Baton Rouge] *Advocate* still has an environmental reporter."[53] LSU's Dr. Chris D'Elia thinks the issue is more with the nature of journalism than with its current economic woes.

> I see a press corps that is poorly educated in the sciences. A lot of times people go into journalism because they don't like the sciences, they like to write. My own son was in journalism . . . He works for New York media and all that sort of stuff now and he says, Dad, I really regret that I didn't have more science in my background, and I think that's a problem—a huge problem.[54]

Journalists understand that the public has a short attention span, and as Dr. Rowher points out, the public is "not interested" in any explanations past thirty seconds. Neither is science their cup of tea, Dr. D'Elia felt. With its focus on facts and details, the public gravitates to stories about human beings and that is what journalists give them. "They want it neat and pretty—they don't want it in dribs and drabs. They want the fast food version of journalism." That is why the Katrina narrative remains compelling to media audiences today, and beyond the immediate shock of the oil disaster, its lack of human emotion leaves viewers wanting.

The Legacy of Disaster

Parallels between the scope of the oil disaster and Katrina are not often easy to make. Katrina launched a new era in the region, but a year later, people were second-guessing the scale of the oil disaster, according to the *Times-Picayune*'s Peter Kovacs.

> There is not a single person in New Orleans of the million and half or whatever it was . . . who didn't have their life impacted or changed by Katrina, and the

oil spill doesn't have that quality—even though people followed it and they were involved in it, it didn't deprive you of your ability to stay in your house or send your kids to school. You know it messed with some people's employment, but nothing like Katrina, where you had to figure out how to put your life back together and where to put it back together. That was true in the oil spill of a limited number of people, but it wasn't really true of like everybody who would be a reader of your newspaper and like all your neighbors and everyone you ever knew.[55]

What is similar about these two events is that no one had ever seen disasters like these before. The events are historic, unprecedented, and have legs—stories will be generated from these events for decades to come. And while journalists aren't covering the Deepwater Horizon disaster in the Gulf as religiously, there are many questions still left unanswered. Scientists say there are specific long-term issues that need attention, such as the volume and form of hydrocarbons left in the sea, how these hydrocarbons affect the Gulf's food webs, and the negative effects to the ecosystem, as well as human health due to the oil and dispersants used in this disaster.[56]

To date, sources in this oil disaster narrative agree that the scope and ranking of the spill may have been overstated, but also caution that this disaster could produce effects not yet realized. "All these questions are still up in the air," Dr. D'Elia said. "We have no basis for comparison than the historical record." As Dr. Overton pointed out:

The environment is a lot, *lot* less damaged today than it was last summer—and that is just one year . . . We don't totally know some damage . . . little critters and microscopic animals. If you screw those guys you don't see the impact on other animals for several life cycles out.

By the second anniversary of the oil disaster, even more disturbing scientific findings had been reported in the media. LSU researchers now believe oil, not dispersants, is negatively affecting marsh fish on a cellular level. The oil, they believe, is causing a reduction in estrogen levels as well as deformed gills in the fish.[57]

In terms of human impact, another 2012 report placed carcinogenic levels up to ten thousand times more than what is considered safe by the FDA in Gulf shrimp. According to the Natural Resources Defense Council, the FDA severely underrated the risk of contaminants from the oil disaster.[58]

The story of the Gulf now appears to be deep within the water; the story headline, according to scientists, is now about future life cycles. Scientists who study the Gulf of Mexico in its entirety—hundreds of thousands of miles—said this area is now being put under an intense research microscope. "Any abnormality gets attention," LSU's Julie Anderson said. "It is survival of the fittest. Most of those animals you'll never see. A lot of that we will never be able to directly measure."

The strength of a source can be directly measured. For Katrina's Danziger story, success is measured in alternative voices speaking the truth and resulting in justice. For the oil disaster, it may or may not be fair to measure the audience's scientific knowledge or lack thereof. A story is only as good as its sources. What we have learned from these two disasters is that sources must be fair, informed, and diverse of status, ethnicity, and thought, in order to give the story context and texture. Anyone can be a source on a story. But journalists, in the absence of subject education or time, must choose voices that contribute to the story because, given this digital landscape, these voices will be forever linked to the event. The "man on the street," thanks to human interest events like Katrina, will continue to be a voice to be reckoned with. Expert sources, likewise, now know their worth, thanks to the oil disaster, and understand that their research is as important in the halls of academia as it is to be transformed so that the "man on the street" gets the facts too.

6

VISUALS OF DISASTER

The power of pictures is undisputed. A single snapshot can sum up all meaning, above and beyond the cliché word "iconic" (the term of the experts) and the less eloquent "unforgettable" (the term of the masses). At the height of photojournalism, from the World War II era and onward, a single still frame could embody social and cultural meaning, becoming its own marker in time. Disaster visuals are in a category of their own: the aerial view of Columbine High School as armed police escorted students with raised hands down the sidewalk, the airplane striking the South Tower of the World Trade Center, the FBI agent escorting children with their eyes closed from Sandy Hook Elementary School. Journalists captured these visuals and news agencies replicated them, embedding them in the national and global psyche. Now, in the twenty-first century, iconic images have evolved with media technology, and the masses now own a part of them, defining them through YouTube hits, Twitter trends, and Facebook shares. The public now shares the selection and transmission process that once was the exclusive domain of mainstream news agencies. What exists today is a symbiotic relationship as news agency–generated visuals are shared across cyberspace, and on the other end, user-generated visuals go viral and become news in a traditional sense. In either case, be it still photos or moving frames, common denominators remain—mass recognition, identification, celebration, and in some cases mourning—and all come together to enshrine an iconic visual.

When disaster strikes, the media's use of imagery goes beyond the story, taking users to an evocative, emotional level. It is no wonder that not only can people recall exactly what they were doing as they watched United Airlines Flight 175 strike the South Tower of the World Trade Center, but exactly how they were feeling. The media landscape in 2001 for the coverage of 9/11 was still a traditional one and acted like a choir singing in unison. Viewers who tuned to the networks or cable stations saw the anchors singing the same tune in harmony. While the September 11 attacks harken us back to the same recollected visuals in our heads, four years later we found Hurricane Katrina left a disjointed collective memory. During Katrina, the media landscape was in discord. The picture of this natural disaster was heavily regionalized, personalized, new-media driven, and user-defined in terms of meaning and importance. Even in 2005, the media environment was still relatively traditional. Facebook was in its infancy and Twitter didn't exist. Smartphones didn't have video cameras. Yet the use of new media and the importance and necessity of information redefined the coverage and the visuals. No longer did the anchor "voices of God" impart on the public how to understand what it was seeing. For the oil spill, the pictures were for the most part out of reach. All of the technology at our fingertips in 2010 could not bring pictures of a story that was forty miles offshore and almost a mile under the sea to the social media surface. Hurricane Katrina and the oil disaster offered up their own visual firsts in the world of iconography.

The media has much experience routinizing nonroutine stories, even seemingly out-of-control disasters such as Katrina and the oil spill. News management knows the amount of resources needed to cover a story of great impact and interest, what sources to interview, and even what visuals to obtain. Media take stories and visuals and place them in familiar contexts that are easy to understand and their meaning falls into place.

Additionally, crisis situations usually have standard themes and visuals that allow the stories to become somewhat routine and predictable. Certain visual narratives are expected. For example, the obligatory extreme wind reporter live shot will take place for every hurricane. For oil spills, the public expects to see pictures of helpless animals head to toe in black ooze, only the whites of their eyes showing. Similar images across disasters neatly package the events, help the public process the information quickly, and help make sense of the tragedy. However, the news media landscape is evolving, both technology-wise and in how the roles of the journalist and consumer are increasingly becoming blurred. In 2005 and 2009, the routine use and treatment of disaster visuals expanded the concept and process and, in turn, affected the meaning-making for these mass consumed images.

Water-Soaked Images of Disaster

Weather reports are the number-one reason viewers are loyal to their local stations, and in New Orleans, storms can be a station's bread and butter. Chris Slaughter, New Orleans's WWL-TV former news director, started at the CBS affiliate as a desk assistant back in the late 1970s. Some thirty years later, and at the helm of the number-one station in the market, Slaughter led his news staff to numerous awards for their Hurricane Katrina coverage. Of all the hundreds of thousands of images he saw through his work that fateful week in 2005 and firsthand when he finally returned to his own destroyed home, Slaughter named the definitive memorable image of Katrina, for him, as the waterlogged and abandoned houses marked with a solemn X.[1]

X marked the spot not only on the abandoned houses, but in Slaughter's mind for Katrina. It was the system the authorities used to communicate with each other if a flooded house had been checked and what or who was found inside. Of note is that Slaughter could have encountered this image in real life, in WWL-TV's video footage, online on the station's website, or a combination of all three that his memory had fused into one image. At the makeshift media triage that was the converted LSU Manship School of Mass Communication's "Hurricane Katrina bunker" for stranded Gulf Coast journalists, we knew that as early as Saturday, August 27, 2005, there was something different about the visuals we were streaming.

In a state prone to storms and flooding, the dialog in the makeshift bunker suggested with each passing day that the visuals being showcased outside the Gulf Region were not the ones being memorialized locally among this subgroup of affected journalists. If the journalists were at odds with what was iconic about Katrina, it begged the question: what about the people across the Gulf and the nation who were watching the disaster unfold? Were we all remembering the same visuals? Within weeks of the disaster, we asked the viewers—both victims and nonvictims of Katrina—to name the most memorable images from the disaster. In giving our respondents free rein to define iconic imagery, meaning-making, and symbolism, we learned that memory, when empowered by new technology, can transform iconography.[2] While many of the images shared by participants were predictable, the personal comments on the visuals were insightful, interesting, and sometimes disturbing. Four years later, the study was replicated to find out what images endured.[3]

In 2005, survey participants did not list Xs on searched homes as a memorable Katrina image. Yet Chris Slaughter, the veteran newsman who had experienced the storm firsthand, predicted this visual would emerge in some people's minds as representative of the disaster four years later—and it did. This represents one of the few changes in image recollection between 2005 and 2009. For the participants surveyed in 2009, Katrina had been an evolving story, from evacuation to search and rescue to a never-ending aftermath and recovery. The Xs on homes were a symbolic selection on their part, signaling that perhaps many of them still have not returned to

Figure 1. This X on a flooded home was part of the X-code—symbols used by search-and-rescue teams to mark searched property after Hurricane Katrina. The symbols communicated what they did or did not find inside the homes. Credit: FEMA image provided by IllinoisPhoto.com

where "X marks the spot," where their treasure, their homes, lives, and family memories have been buried in bureaucracy with insurance companies. Katrina left an enduring ink stain on the landscape of the city and along the Gulf Coast. Once again, this is a New Orleans–focused memory in 2009, one that varied as respondents' residences moved further down the Coast.

Rooftop Rescues

It was almost apocalyptic. Families squatting on top of islands in the sea, waving white flags of surrender to Mother Nature. Viewers of the Katrina aftermath could not shake the image of these stranded people perched on top of their roofs, frantically waving to circling helicopters, drawing attention to their S.O.S. pleas. The rescues filled the twenty-four-hour news cycle, as Coast Guard helicopters lowered basket after basket to take survivors to dry land. The repeated visual stuck in their memories and was chosen by viewers as the most memorable image when surveyed in 2005 and again four years later. In fact, in 2009, it remained the most iconic image of Katrina by an increase of 10 percent.

Figure 2. Trapped residents were rescued from their rooftops in the days after Hurricane Katrina. Over time, this motif of images has held as the most memorable from the disaster. Credit: USN/Pugh image provided by IllinoisPhoto.com

The nail-biting rescues stuck not only because they were made for TV, but because the images were repeated over and over and over again. A different victim, a different chopper, a different rooftop, but a successful rescue each time was the simple script viewers could easily program into memory. It was the visual the media offered viewers most, first aired in prime time once the levees failed, and then recalled on each anniversary, milestone, and setback of Katrina. Whether viewers were from the Gulf Coast or across the nation, they chose these rooftop rescues as the iconic visual of Hurricane Katrina.

Repetition aside, rooftop rescue scenes contained heroes and victims; a cathartic experience where all is well in the end that encapsulated the entire meaning of the event in one compelling visual.[4] This kind of human drama fits into the themes of former tragedies, "the myth of the working class

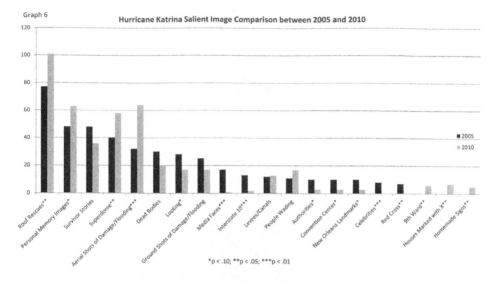

Graph 6

Hurricane Katrina Salient Image Comparison between 2005 and 2010

*p < .10; **p < .05; ***p < .01

hero sacrificing self for the victims," a classic imagery found in September 11 and Oklahoma City bombing coverage.[5] For viewers, to watch society's ordinary heroes save victims brings about hope rather than despair.[6]

In the Katrina case, the heroes-victims image could also be viewed as a reinforcer of negative stereotypes of American class struggles. In this case, heroes, overwhelmingly white, were coming to the rescue of disheveled victims—overwhelmingly African American. Six weeks after the storm, while people were still in the middle of the mud and the muck, the comments from survey respondents were very raw. Respondents made candid comments on their interpretation of the imagery. "Those people should have left," one survey respondent wrote, and another: "All the blacks in New Orleans on roofs, in the water, looting . . . we need to change our welfare system."[7] A third wrote: "All of the black people that were too stubborn to leave piling in the Superdome. '*Dumb.*' It means they want to die."[8]

Four years later, the comments concerning those left behind were less targeted and more thoughtful, the emotion of the event less fresh. It appeared the nation did have some form of a catharsis. Racial feelings toward stranded African Americans had been vetted through the debates surrounding the event by local figures, such as Mayor Ray Nagin, resulting in a nuanced response to the image of the stranded African American.[9] Some viewers felt sorry for the stranded residents, questioning what conditions prevented them from leaving. One survey respondent "felt concern and fear for the people that were stranded there and still in their homes."

While viewers' feelings about Katrina's most iconic images may have morphed with more contextual reporting four years later, the images recalled as iconic were consistent. Eight of the ten original 2005 iconic categories remained as chosen images by respondents in the 2009 survey. As with the enduring rooftop rescues images, the remaining seven images are the visuals that the public has continued to see in the media over the years since the event.[10]

Looting

Stranded residents stormed the Tchoupitoulas Walmart, a random clothing store, a pharmacy here, a convenience store there, and continued the apocalyptic drama of the Katrina visual narrative. Collectively, images of looting New Orleanians, while not the most iconic Katrina image, carried the most emotional response from viewers. In a city predominantly African American before the storm, as with the disaster's rooftop rescues, viewers voiced opinions immediately after Katrina that were in no shape color-blind. "Three black guys looting a clothing store that were laughing . . . why would you want to steal clothes in this time of tragedy," one surveyed viewer wrote.[11] Another added: "You have city under water and people stuck on rooftops and these people are stealing DVD's."[12] The scenes of looting on Poydras Street, one respondent wrote, looked like Mardi Gras reveling, devoid of all decency. "There's no hope for humankind," the respondent continued, "as long as these animals are allowed to flourish."[13]

By 2009, viewers retreated from describing Katrina's looters as "animals" but were no less apologetic about their disdain for the desperate acts. Calling the looters selfish and idiotic for senseless looting, one local viewer felt "sick that in a time of crisis, this is how the community acts." In desperate times, looting a store for beer only reinforced stereotypes about the carefree, *laissez le bon temps roulez* perception of New Orleanians, another respondent noted. Disaster was an excuse to throw a party, and a reckless, havoc-wreaking one at that.

Like the rooftop rescue visuals, looting visuals were played and replayed on a loop. Unlike the many rooftop rescue visuals, however, there was just a handful of actual looting scenes recorded. The same videos of the same three or four looting events were shown continuously by all national news outlets and a few local outlets.[14] By repeating looting clips, particularly on top of the hour recaps of the unfolding crisis, the media perpetuated the notion that an American city had descended into chaos. Even while with time the looting scenes were put in context, racial tensions stemming from the scenes could not be escaped. White viewers surveyed, who were least affected by Katrina, were most likely to suggest that looting was a dominant iconic visual. It supports the finding that the more removed an observer is from viewing a crisis, the more the media shapes their interpretation of the imagery of the event.

It helps to look at the treatment of African Americans and whites in the visuals of Katrina to understand where the emotions originate. In a tragedy of such proportions, there was no doubt that the visuals were going to be negative and compelling. Yet, in studying television news use of Katrina visuals, African Americans were always cast in a negative light.[15] In a state and city that boasts numerous African American officials, including the mayor and commander of the Joint Task Force Katrina, there were opportunities to show them in official capacities or as professionals. Instead, African Americans in leadership were replaced with press conference visuals of white officials in charge (as discussed in chapter 5). Whether these white officials were doing an effective job or not, if one placed the television set on mute, a white official at a podium evoked impressions of order and control, while a vast aerial of mostly African American New Orleanians outside the Superdome conveyed disorder.

Negative visual portrayals of African Americans in the Katrina disaster mattered. Scholars have found that in times of disaster viewers look to the media to cope, understand the crisis and the victims' circumstances, and to know how to respond.[16] With Katrina, when the dominant visuals contained mostly victims, the visuals affected how the rest of the world viewed these victims. With words like "dumb," "idiot," and "animals" used to describe what were mostly African American victims, when victims are shown in the media in only a negative context, the response is also negative.[17] Katrina did trigger an outpouring of cash and other donations on the part of the average American. Yet, the general perception remains in New Orleans among its leaders and people that negative stereotypes about African Americans, played out in the storm's visuals, contributed to a slow federal response and release of reconstruction dollars. The sight of a handful of African American looters being part of the chaos sent a signal that the victims were not worthy of the nation's long-term help. It reinforced the notion of the region's popular culture as well, not just of African American New Orleanians, but of the South's "swamp people." Those victims who appear not to act in a "civilized" fashion are not deserving of society's help in desperate times.

Proximity and Interpreting the Image

The interpretation of visuals is highly complex and in fact what makes iconicity. The media can present an image, but it is how the public interprets that image that gives it meaning far beyond framing, composition, and color. As we have seen with looting, interpretation of images has consequences. It sways a viewer to act in a crisis or to look away. However, the media's shaping of interpretation is not the only force in play. The viewer's "preexisting schema, previous knowledge and experience" contests the media's visual encoding of events.[18] No image can be viewed separately from an individual's life experience and exposure to cultures, societies, and history. Becoming iconic "is an evolutionary process taking place over time in the minds of individuals who are part of a socially, biologically, and culturally influential world."[19] Individual factors can affect interpretation and therefore iconicity by linking private memories or experiences to an already media-reinforced image.[20] The personal connection to an event can redefine how a viewer interprets images, and in Katrina, it meant two things. First, viewers interpreted media-fed images along personal lines, and second, they presented their own personal imagery as iconic visuals of this disaster.

Because of the closeness of the surveyed viewers to the Katrina disaster, some chose personal icons—images that you or I did not see—or images that we could not specifically identify, but they could, as being iconic of the event. Some specified "my house" or "my neighborhood" in flooding aerial footage that looked to most of us like an unrecognizable disaster zone.[21] We found that a person's closeness to an event can, in some cases, override the effects of repetition and prominence found with media-selected images. If a viewer was a Biloxi resident or a New Orleanian, they were more likely to redefine iconicity, bypassing the media's visual agenda setting. This was not for lack of exposure to media images of the event, but iconic was not universalized; it became personalized as the crisis had hit home.

Most of us view disaster from a distance. For example, the horrors of the 2004 Christmastime Indonesian tsunami and the 2011 Norway bombing and killing rampage could only be experienced through multimedia reports and images. With Hurricane Katrina, the respondents who took our survey six weeks after the storm lived close to the disaster, "in my backyard" close. Twenty-two percent of respondents were actually displaced by the storm, evacuating to Baton Rouge from New Orleans universities and surrounding areas. While outsiders saw muddy water and rooftops, our respondents saw their street signs. While outsiders saw the roof blown off the Superdome, our respondents recognized the malls where they shopped, their high schools, and even the corner store where they got weekend ice-cream treats from grandparents. The repetitious media-fed images could not mediate the personal connections respondents had to these images.[22] It was the contextual details that fleshed out Katrina's visuals and informed what they remembered and how they interpreted them.

Four years later, 85 percent of respondents lived in Louisiana; however, only three people surveyed said that they were displaced by Katrina. Those who made up the bulk of the second survey lived in the areas surrounding the impact zone and, while still on the periphery, carried fewer ties to the destroyed areas. This number is reflected in those who chose personalized iconic images. Personal images decreased from 10.3 percent six weeks after the storm to 4.5 percent, or almost by half, four years later. Personal image choices, "my creek," "my friend's dad," were still chosen by this group; however, it is possible that individual memories had faded and been replaced by images that had been shown in the media consistently over the years. The 2009 survey participants did experience the short-term and long-term recovery effects of the storm, though they were not as physically, economically, and emotionally affected as the group four years earlier.[23]

Faded Images Give Way to New Ones

As you will recall from previous chapters, the antics of some "celebrity" journalists received significant attention. In fact, Fox News Channel's Shepard Smith and Geraldo Rivera and CNN's Anderson Cooper were actually chosen by people as part of their most memorable images in the six weeks after the event. Four years later, however, those images had faded.

Not only have individual faces been lost with time, but individual stories. Take, for example, an on-camera interview with an elderly man who tearfully described his inability to save his wife as the waters swept her out of his hands. In 2005, 3 percent of our surveyed viewers recalled this interview and listed it as iconic. In 2009, only one viewer thought it was iconic. Instead viewers remembered more universal details from the search and rescue footage of Katrina. People holding signs that said "SOS," "Help," and "I am an American" as they waited for rescue emerged as an even stronger category. So did journalist Chris Slaughter's category suggestion—the houses marked with Xs. The individual faces and stories were lost and were replaced by collective images that had greater meaning for a larger audience. "I am an American" is universal.

Many visuals selected as iconic in 2009 echoed the narratives in the media and have come to symbolize the mistakes of government and the preexisting economic inequalities.[24] The rise of the images of the levees and canals from ranking number twelve as an iconic image to number eight mirrored the rise in national discourse on the levee failures as the true source of the flooding of New Orleans. Repairing and reinforcing the levees continues to be an issue New Orleans struggles with today, as returned residents are threatened every hurricane season. By 2009, the New Orleans Ninth Ward was also on viewers' lists. For respondents who were not residents of the city's metropolitan area to name the notorious district meant that post-Katrina analysis had filtered in to image interpretation. The Ninth Ward devastation became the crowning image for the economic inequities and the failures of government at all levels.[25] In the opposite direction, the Red Cross and its good work, a memorable image from 2005, faded from memory, without being recalled in iconography in 2009. Yet while images faded, feelings did not. The visuals of Katrina made respondents in 2005 and in 2009 feel sad, and a sense of loss summed up their reactions to viewing this disaster.

Oil-Soaked Images of Disaster

From the very beginning of the oil spill, an effort to keep visuals out of sight of the public was orchestrated. As discussed in chapter 4, on May 1, 2010, eleven days after the Deepwater Horizon oil rig exploded, the Coast Guard had still only released a single, fuzzy photograph of oil leaking a mile beneath the surface.[26] You'll recall it took two months for a reporter to discover that more visuals were available—BP just would not allow the White House or the Coast Guard to release the existing video. Once the pictures were released, media outlets realized BP's estimates of the amount of oil spewing into the Gulf, taken at face value, were wrong. The visual gatekeeping efforts by BP kept not only news outlets in the dark about the depth of this disaster, but scientists also weren't allowed to understand and thus help analyze the situation.

Once the pelican pictures appeared, the trust placed in the authorities was long eroded and the public outcry was as fierce and sustained as the gushing Macondo Well. The environmental groups had their mascot, and the visuals were difficult to watch. It was an "I told you so" moment for environmental groups. The gusher represented the enormous, out-of-control nature of the tragedy and big business, and the pelicans represented the most innocent of victims. This is what viewers recognized and recalled most.

The mood of the nation also needs to be considered regarding the oil spill's visuals and their meanings. At the time of explosion and throughout the sustained disaster, the country was experiencing a recession with unemployment approaching 10 percent. Wall Street excesses and failures were being blamed for what turned out to be a global economic downturn and subsequent slow recovery. The climate was extremely anti–big business, and BP, with its massive profits, became an exemplar of that view. While providing a visual of the underwater gusher should have portrayed BP as a responsible corporation when it came to accountability for the disaster, the visual had the opposite effect for a country tired of corporate laxness and waste.

Other media observers, particularly local ones, considered the BP daily oil gusher feed as a smoke screen, diverting the press's attention away from the oil seeping into the marshes. BP enjoyed control over physical access to the underwater gusher and was aware, some wrote, that access to the marshes was difficult. Several anecdotal stories of Coast Guard and BP workers keeping media boats out of certain areas testify to this visual gatekeeping. BP, observers said, had banked on a public relations strategy where *not* seeing was believing. In the initial coverage of the Deepwater Horizon oil disaster, a corporate public relations tactic through the use of one fixating visual, the underwater gusher, distracted viewers from considering the other consequences of this disaster.

As Katrina reached its fourth anniversary, we found Gulf Coast viewers of the oil spill expressing similar views on the second event's iconic images. The Katrina solidarity that brought the region together showed up in interpretations of images from the oil spill. Respondents with direct ties to the region felt outraged and violated. Given the difficulty of actually getting to the site of the disaster and because the harm was being done on the bottom of the ocean and not in the middle of an American city, there were fewer categories of images recalled by the respondents. For Hurricane Katrina, there were twenty-five categories of iconic images viewers recalled both in 2005 and in 2009, with an "other" category remaining quite large and diverse. For the oil spill, there were only ten visual categories, including "other." The press had given the viewers fewer visual choices and it showed in our survey. Likewise, viewers generated less personal iconography given their proximity to the disaster, although they were residents of the region.

Figure 3. The pictures of birds coated in thick oil became symbolic of the consequences of the BP oil disaster. Credit: USCG image provided by IllinoisPhoto.com

Almost half of our surveyed viewers (47.3 percent) named the oil-soaked animals as their number-one most memorable image from the oil spill coverage. But it was more specific than that. Just over 23 percent of those respondents specifically named the pelicans in their answers. Others named "animals," "birds," "ducks," "turtles," and "sea gulls." This is by far the largest category of images—almost half of all respondents remembered a themed-set of images that invoked outrage and sympathy. A dead bird drenched in oil, a pelican unable to take flight off the water with the weight of the slick on its feathers, its natural color turned to muck, only its eyes revealing its distress. These were a few of the terms viewers used to describe the iconic imagery of the Gulf's pelicans during this disaster. Viewers were no less sympathetic for the species affected, ranging in emotional response from "sad," "upset," and "frustrating" to "heartbroken" and "sick."

Figure 4. On April 20, 2010, the Deepwater Horizon drilling rig exploded in the Gulf of Mexico, killing eleven workers and causing the worst environmental disaster in U.S. history. Credit: USCG image provided by IllinoisPhoto.com

A distant second behind the iconic images of the oiled animals was the live, underwater gusher chosen by 17 percent of our surveyed viewers. Shown live by news outlets, this image, as discussed, was not put forth by journalists, but was one managed and supplied by BP. BP had access to the bottom of the ocean; journalists did not. Journalists relied on the company to supply this video to them. With the absence of a development on land, it was often the only new video of the day throughout this prolonged crisis.

The third most iconic category of images was the Deepwater Horizon rig on fire—pictures taken from helicopters in the beginning hours of the crisis. The fourth and sixth most recalled categories included specific referrals to oil on the surface of the Gulf (7.2 percent) and oil on land (5 percent), in reference to seepage on marshes and beaches.

The fifth most memorable category of images chosen by recipients was a graphic of the spill. BP supplied the gusher video; the press then created aerial maps of the Gulf Coast showing the "possible" spread of oil across the region. While only chosen as an iconic visual of the oil spill at just over 5 percent, it shows the efforts of news outlets to create a memorable, informational visual in the absence of choices and control.

As with Katrina, because surveyed viewers lived close to the disaster, personalized iconic images were recalled, but with less frequency. One viewer described the image a friend took of a turtle drenched in oil near the coast of Venice, downriver from New Orleans. Another spoke of personal pictures her father took at Pensacola Beach, Florida, of the oil globs that washed ashore, turning the pristine beach into an eyesore as far as the shoreline extended. Others found iconic imagery shared in an oceanography class and on Facebook with eyewitness pictures of destruction to marine flora and fauna.

The fact that personalized visuals of a disaster emerge demonstrates that proximity allows for images to compete with the media or corporations like BP when it comes to iconography. Likewise, interpretations of images are also more personal than how the media frames the images when viewers are close to the subject matter. The emotion that images evoke also corresponds with how viewers respond to the crisis. Viewers' anger at the responsible parties and belief that the event was preventable placed pressure on entities like BP to begin a public and regional campaign through a series of advertisements showing its commitment to the Gulf and its people. One viewer said, "BP took their time to fix their mistake while thousands of animals and wetlands were dying" and fisheries and fishermen remained in debt, unable to feed their families. Watching hours of oil gushing from the Gulf's sea floor made other viewers question the slow response of both BP and the government. It echoed feelings residents held after Katrina about the loss of New Orleans or their favorite local spot. For one viewer the "vacations, seafood in Louisiana, and our coast would be affected for at least the next 10 years to come."

When the Deepwater Horizon oil rig exploded in the Gulf of Mexico in April of 2010, no one realized the event would turn into a lengthy, sustained crisis event, lasting almost three months and spewing more than 200 million gallons of crude oil into the offshore waters. Given the duration of this crisis compared to Katrina, the visuals of the disaster changed over time. Yet, the images remained predictable and conventional just like oil disasters of the past. A fiery oil rig gave way to an aerial view of the travelling oil slick. Then an oil-covered beach or marshland visual would emerge, followed by an underwater "gusher cam," timelining the efforts to cap the source of the problem. Finally, we are left with the destruction of marine life, the image of the helpless, near-death pelicans.

However, what was recalled of a disaster by viewers is only a snapshot of a wider visual narrative the media carries in a crisis. A content analysis of

news coverage reflects a more diverse portrayal of the oil spill's visual narrative as it morphed over time and changed over the event's three-month
duration.[27]

Week One Oil Visuals

The day of the explosion, managers from BP and Transocean (rig owners)
were celebrating seven years on the Deepwater Horizon oil rig without a
safety violation.[28] The companies were also making history by drilling
approximately five thousand feet into the earth's surface. The rig exploded
at 9:45 that evening, making it too late for the 10:00 news and thus rel-
egating it to an "overnight" news story. What we found in our content
analysis is that the national outlets would not pick up the story again until
almost two days later when the loss of life and endurance of the story were
recognized.[29]

   CBS Evening News was the first national network to lead with the Deepwater Horizon oil rig fire, giving the story more prominence than even the
Baton Rouge television stations, despite the fact that one of the eleven who
died was a twenty-eight-year-old man from Baton Rouge. This continued
even on the day of his memorial service and is in line with previous research
that suggests national news outlets devote the first week of coverage in
memorial of the loss of human life, or the looming death toll of the event.[30]

   While national stations told the human interest story, local news stations focused on the visual images of the oil story happening at each
moment: the Deepwater Horizon rig on fire, aerial views of the oil on the
surface, response boats and the skimmers on the Gulf. When local news
outlets supplied this video to cable partner networks, national viewers
caught a glimpse of this diverse local visual narrative. National media visuals focused on overarching disaster consequences such as the toll on all species, human and animal alike, as the globs of oil reached the shoreline of
the region's marshes and beaches. With a national audience to serve, stories
featured the potential losses to the environment, the restaurant industry,
and recreation and vacation attractions. Locally, the visuals focused on
solutions, the miles of oil-containing boom and cleanup and containment
vessels at sea working to save the coastline.[31] With a responsibility and
mantra to serve its community, local media focused its visual narrative on
remedies rather than consequences. The visuals were representative of how
the local tourism and fishing industries were going to be saved.

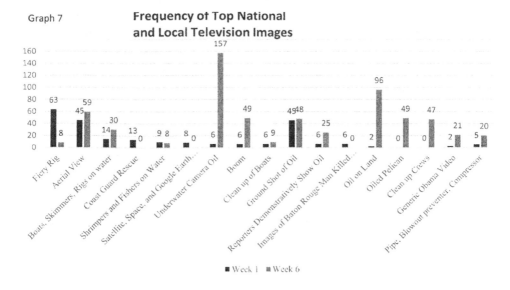

Graph 7

Frequency of Top National and Local Television Images

The local and national coverage differed at first, with the exception of CBS. The relationship between local and national appears to be a plausible explanation. In New Orleans, the highest-rated station is the CBS affiliate WWL-TV. Both the network and the local affiliate seemed to understand the enormity of the disaster early. Because WWL is a strong number one in the market, perhaps it gave the station a measure of authority to express to its national network the importance of this story. The symbiotic relationship between networks and their affiliates affects what viewers see at both media levels and is uniquely cultivated in times of crisis.[32]

Week Six Oil Visuals

As the story progressed into the sixth week, so too did the visual narrative. No longer did local stations focus on the Horizon on fire and aerial views of the disaster but shifted to visuals of cleanup: booms and skimmers on the Gulf. Again, local stations continued to stress images of recovery efforts while national stations continued to emphasize the size of the environmental disaster. National stations shifted their oil images to underwater camera views, visuals of the oil on the shorelines and, of course, the oiled pelicans. When the oiled pelican visual emerged, network reporters took advantage of this conventional "money shot" and would repeat the same images, giving viewers a dose of the pelicans at the top of their news story, during the news report, and often at the end as the parting shot.[33]

By week six, national networks led their entire newscasts with the oil disaster story and local stations did not (that is, until the dynamic visual of the oiled pelican appeared). Each week represented a different facet of the coverage—a logical progression from the breaking news event of the oil rig fire to the sustained thematic coverage of the event as the underwater gusher travelled to the Gulf's shores and became a polluting spill. The images aired during the first and sixth week of the oil spill alerted viewers to what visuals were important during key periods of this disaster—the cause at the beginning and the consequences over time. At first the images centered on the breaking news of a disaster; however, by the sixth week, the cleanup phase had begun and the theme shifted to recovery, mostly for the local news outlets.[34]

Media Put Forward Their Own Visual Narrative

A disaster that has happened before at a different time and in a different location results in predictable media visuals. In an oil spill, a logical progression of conventional imagery is expected. Thirty years earlier, the Exxon Valdez had given the media somewhat of a template to follow; ribbons of oil in the water would appear first, then oil-covered land, and finally oil-covered wildlife. The visual narrative unfolded just as expected, once again making the nonroutine coverage of tragedy routine. The pictures of the oil-soaked pelicans did not appear in the media until May 31, almost six weeks into the event, yet the visuals were only a matter of time and almost a given.

The visuals of the first week of the oil disaster represent media attempting to convey to the public the loss of life, the enormity of the disaster, and the difficulties in reporting on it. The visuals of week six capture the consequences of the spill and attempts to contain it. The images that the survey respondents recalled corresponded with the actual media content: the fiery rig, oil on land and in the water, struggling pelicans. Yet the human victims, the oil rig workers, were not part of what they remembered. The stories showing boats in dock, empty fishing nets and restaurants—all part of the victim narrative—were not the visuals the viewers remembered. Stories on victims comprised less than 3 percent of the actual media content sampled. In turn, victim visuals were almost nonexistent in the oil disaster survey when compared to what people remembered about Katrina, thus reflecting what the media fed them. Animal victims were present in the coverage, yet human victims were not.

We knew from the very beginning that the diversity of images would be limited. Although it was a prolonged crisis event, opportunities to show and tell the story were limited and sporadic. It was a geographically vast story with consequences occurring forty miles offshore and along the shorelines of four states. The story was also a complex, scientific one which was difficult to explain in words, let alone visuals. For example, chemical dispersants used to break up surface oil was and remains a significant part of the story. However, video of dispersants was nowhere to be found in the coverage we analyzed. Reporters and audiences had a vague idea of the purpose of dispersants, but no idea of what they looked like.

Despite the restraints on media access to the oil disaster, both the local and national media did manage to serve their individual audiences through the use of visuals. The national media's focus on visuals demonstrating the disaster's consequences is an example of the underlying narrative of the region as victim of yet another external mismanagement. However, local media, as expected, looked at it differently. They chose to create a "can-do" nonvictim narrative of the region, which we call "community spirit," given its preference for images of locals trying to remedy the situation through resilient, collective efforts.

Envisioning the Gulf Through Crisis

The similarities in the visuals of Hurricane Katrina and the BP oil disaster lay in the social themes that were the skeletons in the closets of the crises. Social disparities were common themes in news coverage and in the respondents' chosen images. Ultimately, socioeconomic inequities were at the heart of both tragedies. The poverty of the Ninth Ward rose to the surface in Katrina and the greed of BP gushed onto the bottom of the Gulf.

What makes the iconography of the dual Gulf Coast disasters different from what we know of the visual portrayal of crises in the past is that no one *single* image dominated the viewers' memories of the events over time. This is quite a contrast to the singular iconic photo we often associate with historic events such as the raising of the flag at Iwo Jima. For Katrina and the oil spill, the visuals of victims (human for Katrina, animal for the spill) dominated; there were hundreds if not thousands of stranded people on rooftops and marine creatures, all of whom had to be rescued. There were hundreds of people with signs asking for help. There were hundreds of aerial shots of flooded neighborhoods and ripples of oil looming offshore. The damage and destruction visuals taken from the ground and from helicopters for both disasters include a large spectrum of images that represent the vastness of the disasters. Simply put, it wasn't just one image that was chosen, but categories of images. This dramatic turn away from single shots, perhaps brought about by digital technology, represents a shift in the definition of iconic, and poses a challenge for scholars investigating visuals in our collective consciousness.[35] In no way has iconic imagery lost its potency; in some ways with pervasive and immediate exposure, the power of visuals has grown.

The iconography of these two crises are in fact quite fluid in that one event evokes feelings of the other and vice versa. For scholars of visual images, we argue that perhaps for a region that is in constant crisis mode one disaster is representative of another, harkens back to the other, and evokes shared emotions. Katrina and the oil spill have become fused in their visual interpretations, and this was clear for residents of the region who offered such insight in survey responses. One surveyed viewer, upset that another disaster had hit the region, wrote that the visuals affected the "people who were just getting over Katrina, making them relive the pain in joblessness and suffering."

CONCLUSION

When everyday people talk about Katrina or the Deepwater Horizon disaster, both crises are often discussed as "Louisiana disasters." But the scopes of the tragedies are far-reaching on land and at sea. Stories of manmade and natural disasters and recovery are narratives that are told over and over again not only in our society but around the world. The media tell these stories first. The power of news producers to shape the framing and interpretation of major events determines the immediate response and future outcomes of crises. Katrina and the oil spill were crises that were different from most, because they occurred back-to-back in the local journalists' backyard. The journalists didn't have to parachute in to cover the story. They lived it. This book is not just about the unprecedented events of Katrina or the Deepwater Horizon explosion but the lessons that journalists and consumers can learn about communication during crises.

Sense of Community

History shows that there is a special connection between tragic events and local media. A mutual relationship emerges when local media assume hegemony over other competing sources of information, and users who may have strayed in loyalty come running home for information.[1] The relationship during disaster seems driven more by the users' needs at the time than the local news sources' advantage on news content in their home turf. Communities immediately turn to local news organizations, first for information, and second for context as they seek to rebuild and recover from a crisis. In the past, researchers have labeled media users in a crisis as passive, but a behavior change occurred during Katrina. Hurricane Katrina evacuees in all phases of the disaster actively sought out local media news coverage. New Orleans *Times-Picayune* journalists who roamed the city found sources begging them for updates or to tell their stories. At one point during the aftermath when evacuated *Times-Picayune* reporters visited the River Center in Baton Rouge, displaced residents scrambled to get the few copies of the paper the reporters walked in with, despite the numerous television screens around the center showing national news.

Compared to unpredictable disasters such as the oil spill, hurricanes can be prepared for, people having been forewarned. The media operated in a "management role" before the storm and became a conduit for local officials to issue warnings, alert the public to emergency services, and transmit updates.[2] It was in the "impact" and "recovery" phases when media transformed users from passive to active consumers of information.[3] This is the "linkage" or "social utility" role of the media.[4] Local media were actively sought out as a lifeline, a source of connection when the power went out, or all that was left was a battery-operated or car radio.

What sustained this community connection five years later during the oil disaster was that locality. Local media users had continued the relationship not necessarily because they felt that local news sources were any more accurate than national ones, but because they witnessed their local news sources in the same position as they were. They performed admirably under severe conditions, allowing the users to get what they needed. With the oil spill, users looked to the journalists to once again lead them through a tough time. The challenges were different. There was physical distance and the enormity of the disaster, as well as ignorance. In fact, business interests relied on these barriers to give them time to craft their own narrative. There weren't any flooded neighborhoods at the epicenter of the crisis; there weren't people who needed to be rescued. The unfolding drama was hidden beneath the surface of the ocean, and the complex physical location coupled with the complex scientific story lessened the dependency on mass media. Cleanup crews were told not to talk to reporters and journalists, and fishers were banned from the coastal waters and marshes. It was much more controlled and because of this the truth often remained on the bottom. Even then, local users tuned in not because they needed officials to give them updates; they were looking for something else. They needed a sense of community, a reassurance that they were in this together and would get through this together—again. While the nature of the oil spill called for less dependency on news coverage, local media still became an outlet for authorities and those affected to tell their stories of survival and recovery. Marty Haag, former senior vice president for news for Belo Corporation, parent company of a New Orleans television station, stated about this relationship, "There is an immediate feeling that these are people who live in my area. They are seen almost as family."[5]

For Katrina victims who saw disheveled local journalists roaming around the city or on an affiliate station's reports, there was a sense that these communicators were in fact "family." Local Gulf Coast media were also able to shake the stigma that local news is short on in-depth coverage and weak on investigative news.[6] In the surveys conducted with evacuees, local news reports were considered far superior in information and scope and more reliable than national news sources in the aftermath of Katrina. It took just one disaster to transform how local users perceived and interacted with their local media, and more than five years after this natural disaster, this trend, although expanded to other media, persisted.

In both crises, those who suffered used media as a "coping mechanism" for emotional support. Users described that the local media made them seem less disconnected and in solidarity with an unseen community, whether to vent frustration or to seek out companionship. The recovery phase many years later still has not ended, and what started as an active relationship for "social utility" and "linkage" between local media and displaced local users has continued to this very day. While local users may continue to incorporate national news sources into their daily media use routine, and are doing so online more than in 2005, the social use for local media has continued years later. The new relationship has completely changed the way local news outlets along the Gulf Coast region view local audiences and their interaction with their news outlets. From local newspapers to radio stations, they have made drastic changes to their online and traditional formats to feature citizen input and voices in their coverage. They also provide more space for their audiences to engage in dialog and to share information where news and feedback are actively encouraged. No longer do we see a disconnect between local media and their users; there is an active effort on the part of the local media and a desire by local users to continue to interact long beyond the "impact phase."

Local, "Restructured"

A new definition of "impact phase" may be coming. As we were writing this book, word came from the parent company of the New Orleans *Times-Picayune*, Advance Publications, of a restructuring of the paper. The daily, which had been printed every day (with the exception of three days during Katrina)[7] for 175 years, would now print three times a week. It would be relying primarily on its online presence, the evolved outgrowth of

Hurricane Katrina necessities, to report the news 24-7. Advance has also announced similar changes at its three Alabama papers, the *Birmingham News*, the Mobile *Press-Register*, and the *Huntsville Times*. Perhaps this is a sign of the digital maturation times. But the consequences could be devastating. New Orleans remains in recovery, still dealing with the loss of some 140,000 residents.[8] The school system is an experiment in progress. The murder rate continues to be one of the highest per capita for an American city. The politics continues to produce colorful characters. The thought of a downscaling of news information at this time is nothing short of scary. And what if another crisis hits the Gulf Coast? The fear, for these three former journalists and social science researchers who study the importance of media in a crisis, becomes breathtaking. The *Times-Picayune*, which had suffered and served its city so well, had been unable to ride the Pulitzer success of Katrina. Reporters and news management know that if a crisis is covered well, not only do the accolades come in, but so do the offers from larger news markets. Some decided to leave New Orleans, but many stayed only to find out that many of them would now be cut. Political communication professor and author Robert Mann posted this on his Facebook page the day of the announcement:

> Among the many, very sad aspects of the slow death of a great American newspaper—one that held together a city during its worst moments—is the fact that the loyalty of the staff to the paper and the devotion to their city was rewarded by learning of their fate on the pages of *The New York Times*. The leadership did not have the decency to tell editors and reporters face to face that their paper is being dismantled and they are about to lose their jobs. No way to honor the loyalty of staff that gave its all to that paper and to the city of New Orleans.

While it is not the focus of this book to concentrate entirely on New Orleans, we believe what is happening in the New Orleans media market will be a test case of the industry going forward. New Orleans is the major metropolis of the Gulf Coast region. It is also now, in light of the developments, the largest metropolitan area for this type of major downsizing to take place. Only 36 percent of New Orleans's approximately 343,000 residents have Internet access.[9] This digital divide is a local problem that reared its ugly head during Katrina. The huge discrepancy between the haves and the have-nots in New Orleans continues to be ignored. It took the perfect storm for authorities to admit the long-neglected underclass only as they were plucking many from their rooftops. The possible lack of access to information in the new media landscape that is now New Orleans—post-Katrina, post-daily—could very well lead to loss of life. The concern is a legitimate one. Katrina showed us that the poor, sick, elderly, and marginalized are left behind, without an advocate. They found this in their local news outlets. The paper was a lifeline for so many, including the news workers who took that duty seriously and did not abandon their city and in fact persevered with relentlessness and resiliency. While those who work in mass media knew changes to formats were coming, we were surprised to see that not even a news market that had proven its worth to the public could escape the industry tide.

The reductions to the *Times-Picayune* started a conversation across the nation about the value of local news in a disaster and for sustaining recovery. It was a conversation that included the two cents of the world's third richest billionaire, Warren Buffet.[10] Evan Christopher, a prominent New Orleans musician and founding member of Nola Art House Music, wrote an open letter to the Berkshire Hathaway owner in his column for NolaVie. com. Christopher was looking for solidarity from Buffet,[11] who was once a newspaper boy, and who had recently stepped in to save his own hometown newspaper, the *Omaha World-Herald*, in November 2011.[12]

Christopher wrote:

Regarding that purchase, you said, "In towns and cities where there is a strong sense of community, there is no more important institution than the local paper."

I know you share the world's admiration for our city's strong sense of community, and I am hoping that you already have your eye on this situation. When you were here almost exactly one year ago speaking to small business entrepreneurs, you called us a city with spunk and recognized a wealth of talent and energy. Certainly, our newspaper's Pulitzer Prize–winning staff, who never stopped reporting when the federal levees failed, despite power outages and flooded offices, exemplify that well. Indeed, our *Times-Picayune*, which has been around for more than 150 years, like our music culture that has been part of the city's lifeblood for more than a century before that, are integral facets of the culture that bind us.

. . . Our mayor, Mitch Landrieu, once a paperboy in his youth like you, is expecting "ferocious and very aggressive attempts to communicate to the ownership how important this paper is to the city of New Orleans." In this spirit, if it is possible for you to come down, we would very much like to arrange a meeting with prominent members of our community who share an ambition to maintain daily print news service.

. . . This support is evidence that many of us believe our paper to be indispensable not only because of its watchdog role, but as a public service and beacon for our city's rich cultural life.[13]

Buffet responded with an economic argument in support of the local paper, which he considered the heart of local news. He started his billion-dollar firm with the five thousand dollars he earned delivering local newspapers, and understood the importance of it as a driving force in keeping local economies vibrant, particularly those vulnerable to disaster. Buffet placed the headquarters of his empire in Omaha and in 2011, the year he bought the *World-Herald*, Omaha, along with the rest of the Midwest, posted national records for tornadoes and storm activity.[14] A total of 1,691 tornadoes ripped the Midwest in 2011, breaking records in the month of April in number and damage estimates.[15] In June 2011, a wedge tornado sent fans of a college World Series baseball game scampering out of an Omaha stadium.[16] Omaha is also home to the most expensive tornado disaster in U.S. history in May 1975, destroying over four thousand buildings and costing as high as a billion dollars, by some estimates.[17] All across the nation, the economic viability of major cities is threatened each year by seasonal natural disasters and unexpected human errors. Buffet's hometown, like those on the Gulf, has a functional role for a vigilant local media to prepare citizens for the annual threats, and to steer the community toward rebuilding and recovery. For Buffet, who made his fortune by investing in industries and icons he believes withstand trends and the test of time, the importance of his local newspaper made sense in dollars and cents. When purchasing his region's newspaper Buffet told stakeholders, "I'm not comfortable without an honest-to-God newspaper in my hand."[18] Describing local news as the "primary source of information for the community," Buffet said of his decision to spend roughly $150 million to buy the paper that a vibrant local economy and culture require a newspaper. In support of the *Times-Picayune*, Buffet told Christopher that "either a publication is a newspaper or a periodical, and I think three days a week crossed the line . . . I believe the *Times-Pic* has high penetration. Therefore, I'm puzzled as to why the economics don't work on a seven-day basis."[19]

Sentimentality aside, Buffet's argument that the role of the local press for maintaining and fostering a local culture where an economic recovery and expansion can thrive is one that is often missed. This is the same argument Christopher and business leaders in New Orleans hoped to high-light in describing the loss of niche reporters in New Orleans who captured and shared with the world the essence of the city and the region. There is no place better for the region to sell the news that it is open again for busi-ness than through its local media. Local media are important for sustained long-term social and economic recovery after disaster, as Buffet wrote in his show of solidarity with the region.

The *Times-Picayune* isn't the only shrinking local news entity on the Gulf Coast. Alabama newspapers owned by Advance Publications lost four hun-dred news workers in the layoffs. Local television is also being challenged along the Mississippi Gulf Coast. The longtime ABC affiliate, WLOX, has started carrying CBS on its digital subchannel. The longtime Fox affili-ate, WXXV, does the same with NBC. That means some cable and satellite subscribers on the coast lost two New Orleans stations, WWL and WDSU. WLOX is said to have hired only one more person in the move and is sim-ply simulcasting local news. WXXV hasn't done local news for *years*, but claimed it will hire a news staff of eighteen to handle the load for both sta-tions.[20] The people making the decisions about cuts across the region are perhaps not too familiar with the Gulf Coast. One of the effects of stereo-typing is that it often has an insidious and unseen influence on people and their decisions. The Gulf Coast media that sacrificed so much and endured so much to save others now find they must save themselves. How unfortu-nate to say that perhaps the most influential media products coming out of Louisiana right now are pop culture reality shows.

The main takeaway from this book is the importance of local news to communities. This finding throughout all of our studies on Katrina and the oil disaster is inescapable. Local news drives preparation, endurance, resil-ience, and recovery. It provides a collective voice. If the main voice of a com-munity is not silenced, but asked to whisper, too many will not hear, others will not speak.

Before CNN's Anderson Cooper arrived to report to the world on the aftermath of the 7.0 magnitude earthquake that hit Haiti in 2010, Haiti's popular local radio networks had begun a relay of information whereby Hai-tians began digging themselves out of the rubble, long before international relief groups got their acts together. The Noula project (We Are Here) is a Web-based system for mapping local needs and sources of assistance cre-ated after the earthquake. The director of Noula, Kurt Jean Charles, said of the local media effort: "We wanted to show that we could take some respon-sibility to change things at our own level, at a Haitian level. The more we can take responsibility for our situation, the more we can communicate and negotiate with the aid world."[21]

Then in Japan in 2011, as word of the triple threat—the earthquake, tsunami, and nuclear reactor meltdown—captured global attention, the initial news feeds of anchors shaking at their desks, letting viewers know to "remain calm" and follow protocol, shocked onlookers. The role that local Japanese media played in preventing public panic contrasted significantly with international reports covering the troubling effects should the reactors overheat at the Fukushima nuclear power plant.[22]

Time and time again, internationally and in the U.S., we have seen where disaster and crises call for the need of local media, both in the heat of the crisis and then to rally a community through the recovery process. When Ted and Kate Stefani were forced to evacuate their Colorado Springs home in June 2012, along with thirty-six thousand other residents, Ted, an army surgeon, paid close attention to local reports. He evacuated his family first, and then at the precise moment packed up a few precious belongings and dashed out of the neighborhood as the flames came over the mountain behind his home. Thousands of families then waited for word on the fate of their homes in the state's worst recorded wildfire. It was the iconic image of this disaster, first taken by the *Denver Post* and then reprinted on the front page of the *New York Times* and shown on CNN and national networks, that brought the needed closure for the Stefanis, victims of this disaster. In an interview on KMGH-TV Denver's 7, which was reaired on affiliates and on cable stations, Ted recalled his reaction to first seeing the iconic image of the summer wildfires on the *Denver Post*'s website. He immediately recognized his neighborhood, their "house a bonfire."[23] Ted told the local station: "It was just total shock to see our house pretty much in a fireball, but I think that was also therapeutic too because we knew over the last couple days where there's a lot of families that don't know the outcome of their home, we knew from pretty much the get-go that we had lost the house."[24]

It was not the only image the *Denver Post* offered residents. On its website, the DenverPost.com, the paper told residents if they recognized their homes in the pictures, to notify the paper and they could receive a copy of the image via e-mail. One such image that led the slide show embodied the importance of local media in spurring the recovery of a community after a disaster. The photo is of a homeowner surveying the charred rubble that was now his home, with hands on his head distressed, standing behind two makeshift signs—"We love Courtney Drive" and "We will return."[25] Images like these, spread among local media but which did not make it into national images of this record-breaking disaster, are why residents like the Stefanis told their local TV station that they will rebuild their lives there, bit by bit.

Looking Back in Order to Look Ahead

The media lessons from these two events significantly add to the small body of literature on disaster news. The tenets of journalism are clear, but some are extremely influential in a crisis. While each disaster is a unique event, there are takeaways from Katrina and the spill that can inform communication as a whole from the mass media to audiences and vice versa.

Accuracy—Sources of Information. Facts must be transmitted in a timely, well-thought-out, well-sourced manner. Life-changing decisions are made based on the messages you are sending out. Since disasters are usually nonroutine, journalists are not assigned such phenomena as a news beat. It is considered breaking news, and all comers are thrown at the scene. There are obstacles to successful information transmission that we explored. For example, during the Deepwater Horizon oil disaster, scientists became frustrated when journalists interviewed the first name on a university list that had a Ph.D. and failed to understand the layers of a story topic. A good crisis plan calls for news outlets to identify the best sources *before* the tragedy. While both crises were unprecedented, these types of crises hitting the Gulf Coast were not entirely unexpected.

Specialized Journalism—More Than Lagniappe. Both Katrina and the oil disaster have taught us that being a "jack-of-all-trades" doesn't always serve the community. Specialized training allows the press to do its duty as the fourth estate and ask questions that often mistake-makers are not expecting you to ask. BP was relying on journalists' ignorance concerning the amount of oil gushing into the Gulf. BP was relying on the slow process of scientific inquiry. If an area is prone to crises such as storms or house industries such as oil, gas, and chemical, crisis plans should include training for those who will be asking the questions if an accident or disaster happens—questions of causes, blame, solutions, and consequences. We make the argument here for the ongoing need for specialized journalism that can address more complex topics and issues.

Storytelling with Context—Community-Focused. Every neighborhood, every city has its own story to tell—a collective web of history, politics, economics, and culture that gives the story a deep richness. Developing the sense of community with every story is especially important for the community in crisis. Local journalists should not give up on the stories in their backyard because of lack of resources or because a larger network comes to town. The man-on-the-street voices are the voices journalists should serve.

Call to Action—Civic Journalism. Every story has 360 degrees' worth of angles and never enough news crews to cover them. Relying on those who lived in the Ninth Ward or on the Deepwater Horizon rig to tell their stories and giving them multiple forums to do so is a necessity. However, the standard remains; all facts, figures, and sound bites must be checked for accuracy. Civic journalism and "call to action" news is an effective way to get a news audience involved, however, it is prudent to remember that the audience has not been trained in fact-checking, ethics, and objectivity. Litigious and credibility issues can arise when media organizations just copy over content viewers/readers/users send. The last thing news outlets need in a crisis is a question of credibility.

Call to Action—Advocacy Journalism. Journalists as advocates? The argument we want to make is that in times of crisis, which include entrenched and systematic wrongs or injustices, how can journalists not be? The editorial space has traditionally been the place to which news outlets relegate opinions, but Katrina and the oil spill blurred this line. When rampant crime, educational and socioeconomic discrepancies, and corruption are routine and left unchecked, it makes living through and recovering from the nonroutine—tragedies and disasters—that much more difficult. Journalists must do their jobs as watchdogs of and conduits for the nonelite before, during, and after the crises.

Crisis and Trauma Training. Journalists need to know how traumatic events could possibly affect them. The first story assignment of a novice reporter is often an overnight murder or a multifatality car accident. Images of death and destruction affect both new and seasoned reporters. Training in journalism schools or newsrooms of the effects and warning signs of trauma would lay a foundation for coping. It would also begin an understanding that would allow the journalist to connect with victims on more educated and empathetic levels. Since Katrina, many of the region's journalists have experienced disaster fatigue. When interviewed in 2006 many were committed to the role they played in reporting on the recovery. By 2008, more glamorous and certainly less stressful opportunities arose, luring many of the journalists we interviewed to posts with the *New York Times*, the *Houston Chronicle*, the *Huffington Post*, *ABC News*, and larger TV network markets across the country. Whenever news breaks from the Gulf, many of these journalists are asked to once again cover the region or provide opinion pieces for their new audiences. It is clear that, despite their departure from one of the biggest stories of their careers and personal lives, it is still hard to shake the trauma of Katrina, and the pressure and guilt of seemingly abandoning a community that relies on the news to rebuild their lives.

And finally, in light of the information about downsizing and restructuring, we felt compelled to add another media lesson that before seemed a given:

Access to Information—A Crisis Necessity. More people have Internet access via smartphones than home Web access. Crisis information transmission via all platforms must be explored by news organizations—through an app, Twitter, Facebook pages, even a direct text via an individual or a community organization. Such strategies need to be utilized as part of news crisis plans. One hundred forty characters are sufficient when you think about vital, lifesaving information. With fewer local journalists to cover more news, streamlining constant updates across media is the beginning of finding a way to manage the news from the crisis. The disaster itself will increase media coverage and make information readily accessible for most users, be it victims or observers. But the boots on the ground will now be fewer—the journalistic immersion next time may not be present. Local communities may have to wait for journalists to parachute in and play catch-up when there is no time to do so.

This book has attempted to be all inclusive, to tell the stories of the journalists, victims, readers and viewers, sources and scientists, and the visuals and text of the news content. Every picture, every word has the opportunity to change the meaning and understanding of a disaster. Regarding the oil spill, the nation and viewers around the world will always remember the Gulf's beaches with tar balls and clean-up crews, oil-filled booms, the Horizon rig on fire, oil spewing from the bottom of the ocean floor, shrimp boats stalled in dock, and oil slicks on the ocean's surface. It took the media's broadcasting of this iconic series of photos of the oil-soaked pelicans to turn the tide of coverage to one critical of the public and private response. Media lessons of tragedy are a complex web of intertwined stakeholders and news product—each contributing to the overall narrative. Disasters are not episodic events but ongoing stories that continue to emit important, evolving information, information that can be used as context with the facing of a new tragedy or the recovery from an old one. The media are forever linked with every tragedy. It is an inescapable link now fostered by digital landscapes.

Therefore the responsibility of that disaster narrative, visual and textual, must be recognized by every journalist.

The Gulf Coast will continue to recover but there is no guarantee that the region has seen the last natural or man-made mishap. Many along the Gulf Coast look forward to June 1 as the beginning of summer, but dread it as the beginning of hurricane season as well. Katrina and the oil disaster are not the alpha and the omega of the Gulf Coast. They are crucial events in the development and perception of the area—events that will be part of the story journalists will tell of the region for decades to come.

APPENDIX 1
Studying the News of Two Disasters: A Timeline

2005

—August–September: Survey of 250 displaced Gulf Coast residents on media use before, during, and after Katrina.

—September: Interviews with 10 Gulf Coast journalists in the days after the storm.

—October: Survey of 466 Louisiana State University students (most displaced) on the most memorable visual images of Katrina.

2006

—September: Taped interviews with 30 Gulf Coast print, radio, television, and online journalists on covering the Katrina disaster.

—October: Content analysis of 647 *Times-Picayune* and Biloxi *Sun Herald* news stories from 2004 and 2006.

—September–December: Content analysis of sampled hours of 7 days of CNN, Fox News, WWL-TV, and WBRZ-TV Katrina news coverage for television framing of the disaster.

2007

—March: Content analysis of negative and positive coverage of Katrina by Fox News, CNN, WWL-TV, and WBRZ-TV.

2009

—Summer–Fall: Interviews with 24 journalists, scientists, and government emergency officials concerning effective hurricane communication. One of two studies funded under the title "HIPIP—Hurricanes, Institutional Procedures, and Information Processing: Engagement with Decision-Makers and Coast Residents." Grant awarded by the Mississippi–Alabama Sea Grant Consortium.

—October–November: Telephone survey of 519 Gulf Coast residents concerning storm knowledge and preparedness (HIPIP study).

2010

—August: Survey of 458 Louisiana State University students on the most memorable visual images of Katrina on the five-year anniversary.

—September–November: Survey of 252 Louisiana State University students on the most memorable visual images of the Deepwater Horizon oil disaster.

—April–December: Two content analyses on local and national television coverage of the oil disaster analyzing visuals, sourcing, and framing.

—June–July: Interviews with more than 40 Gulf Coast journalists on covering the Deepwater Horizon disaster.

—June–July: Interviews with 9 Gulf Coast scientists who were expert sources in the Deepwater Horizon disaster news coverage.

2011

—April: Tweets collected during the month of the one-year anniversary of the Deepwater Horizon disaster.

—June–July: Follow-up interviews with Gulf Coast journalists and scientists on the oil disaster anniversary.

—December: Additional interviews with social scientists (historian and pop culture researcher) and a Katrina Red Cross worker.

APPENDIX 2
Annotated Bibliography of Studies Contributing to This Book

Bemker LaPoe, Victoria, and Andrea Miller. "Local vs. National Coverage: How Journalists Covered the Largest U.S. Marine Oil Disaster as Industry Resources Decline." Presented to the Internet, Media and Politics division at the Southern Political Science Association conference, New Orleans, LA, January 2012.

More than forty interviews were conducted in a New Orleans newsroom as what would be the largest marine oil disaster in U.S. history was taking place offshore. Local journalists were clearly frustrated by their managers' zeal for ratings and their lack of resources to cover the story. National networks parachuted into the local journalists' backyard—arriving late to the scene yet with more access to stories. This study compares the local journalists' interviews with top-cited scientists on the oil disaster to ascertain if both groups felt this disaster was covered accurately and fairly. The overall goal of this study is to analyze how local news organizations are covering stories in light of market-driven economic models when staff is being downsized and digital technology is evolving.

Bemker LaPoe, Victoria, and Andrea Miller. "Oil Soaked Images of Disaster: Identifying the National vs. Local Television Visuals." Presented to the Visual Communication division at the Association for Education in Journalism and Mass Communication Conference, St. Louis, MO, August 2011.

This study identifies the television visual imagery of the Deepwater Horizon oil disaster across national and local news outlets as it unfolded over time. The study compared a content analysis of the visuals from week one of the disaster to week six. The visuals of the first week represent media trying to come to terms with the loss of life, the enormity of the disaster, and the difficulties in covering it. The visuals of week six represent consequences and containment. National versus local differences in visual coverage are discussed in terms of their individual missions and responsibilities to their public.

Dahmen, Nicole, and Andrea Miller. "Four Years Later: A Longitudinal Study of Emerging Visual Icons of Hurricane Katrina." *Visual Communication Quarterly* 9 (2012): 4–19.

Using content analysis and survey data (memorable images, 2005 and 2010), this study took a longitudinal approach to understanding the most memorable images of Hurricane Katrina in order to determine iconicity. We conclude that widespread digital technology has complicated the formation of a visual collective consciousness and the scholarly study of iconic images. Thus, we propose a redefinition of iconicity.

Edwards, Renee, Andrea Miller, David Brown, and Stephanie Houston Grey. "Hurricanes, Institutional Procedures, and Information Processing (HIPIP): Engagement with Decision-Makers and Coast Residents." http://www.lsu.edu/hipip/.

This project, funded by the Mississippi–Alabama Sea Grant Consortium (MASGC) Coastal Storms Program, contained two studies designed to create more effective hurricane communication among forecasters, government officials, media representatives, and ultimately the public. The studies consisted of in-depth interviews with stakeholders and a survey of Gulf Coast residents. Funded in 2009–2010, the project resulted in the following academic papers that contributed to this book:

Miller, Andrea, David Brown, Stephanie Houston Grey, and Renee Edwards. "Crisis Knowledge and Preparedness Four Years After Hurricane Katrina: Comparing Gulf Coast Populations According to Race." Presented at the Association for Education in Journalism and Mass Communication Conference, Denver, CO, August 2010.

The study's purpose was to gauge the hurricane knowledge and preparedness of Gulf Coast residents four years after Hurricane Katrina, with particular interest in racial differences. Five hundred nineteen residents were surveyed in fall 2009. Findings showed that African Americans have less hurricane knowledge than whites, and that mistrust of government and the media may be obstacles to information. Additionally, there was a positive correlation between residents' awareness of a statewide preparedness campaign and having a storm plan in place.

Edwards, Renee, Andrea Miller, Stephanie Houston Grey, and David Brown. "Hurricanes and Decision-Making: The Role of Emotion, Knowledge, and Past Experience." Presented at the annual meeting of the National Communication Association, San Diego, CA, April 2010.

Residents in coastal regions must make three types of decisions regarding hurricanes: planning, evacuation, and relocation. This study examined emotion, knowledge, and past experience as factors influencing those decisions with a telephone survey to coastal residents (n = 519). Results revealed that anxiety and a previous experience with evacuating predicted the most outcomes. Confidence in hurricane protection systems, knowledge of storms, and knowledge of state programs were also related to the decisions. Place attachment was not correlated with any outcome.

Miller, Andrea. "Memorable Images of the Deepwater Horizon Oil Disaster." Unpublished research, Louisiana State University, 2010.

This survey asked participants to name their most memorable image of the oil disaster (n = 252). The same questions that were asked of students concerning Hurricane Katrina (2005 and 2010) were also asked in the context of the oil spill: most memorable image, where it was viewed, and how it made them feel. Not surprisingly, the most memorable image noted was that of the oiled pelicans, followed by the rig on fire.

Miller, Andrea, and Shearon Roberts. "Visual Agenda-Setting and Proximity after Hurricane Katrina: A Study of Those Closest to the Event." *Visual Communication Quarterly* 17 (2010): 31–46.

This study identifies the most memorable media images of Hurricane Katrina chosen by those closest to the event. Four hundred sixty-six Louisiana State University students were surveyed six weeks after Katrina. Most participants chose the conventional, compelling, and repetitious imagery the media provided; thus visual agenda-setting was reflected in their choices. However, those affected chose personal images. Proximity appeared to mediate visuals and limit agenda-setting. This study also considered emotions, gender, and ethnicity.

Miller, Andrea, and Victoria Bemker LaPoe. "Sourcing in National vs. Local Television News Coverage of the Deepwater Horizon Oil Spill: A Study of Experts, Victims, Roles and Race." Paper presented for the Electronic News division at the Association for Education in Journalism and Mass Communication Conference, St. Louis, MO, August 2011.

The purpose of this study was to identify the sources used by national and local television news outlets in the Deepwater Horizon oil disaster coverage and how those sources contributed to the frames and functions of the media in crisis. The study consisted of a content analysis of the sourcing from weeks one and six of the disaster. Findings show national press did a better job of serving the management role, but also operated in a responsibility frame and relied heavily on political analysts. Local outlets relied more on state officials and scientists. National versus local differences in sourcing (experts, victims, race) and frames are discussed in terms of their individual missions and responsibilities to their public during a crisis situation.

Roberts, Shearon. "Media Use and Hurricane Katrina." Unpublished research, Louisiana State University, 2005.

Data for this study was obtained through surveys filled out by displaced residents during the months of October and November, approximately two months after the disaster. Two hundred and fifty respondents completed this survey on media use before, during, and in the aftermath of the storm and rated the performance of national media and local media coverage of the crisis. Residents included displaced students, professionals, and rescued victims staying at a FEMA trailer site in Baker, Louisiana. Results showed that when faced with competing news sources, displaced residents sought out their own displaced media more than national news media. They, however, shared similar attitudes and opinions about the performance of both national and local news coverage of the disaster.

Roberts, Shearon. "Gulf Coast Journalists and Hurricane Katrina: Mounting Challenges to the Work Routine." Master's thesis, Louisiana State University, 2007.

This mixed-methodology study included a quantitative content analysis of newspaper archives of 2004 and 2006 coverage by the *Times-Picayune* and the Biloxi *Sun Herald*. It also included qualitative in-depth interviews conducted in 2005 and 2006 from thirty Gulf Coast journalists who covered the Katrina disaster. Portions of the interviews were used in Shearon Roberts, *Gulf Coast Journalists and Hurricane Katrina: The Story Behind the Stories*, a documentary film, 2006.

APPENDIX 3
Additional Disaster-Related Research by the Authors

Abel, Scott, Andrea Miller, and Vince Filak. "TV Coverage of Breaking News in First Hours of Tragedy." In *Media in an American Crisis: Studies of September 11, 2001*, edited by Elinor Kelley Grusin and Sandra Utt, 105–116. Lanham: University Press of America, Inc., 2005.

Bemker LaPoe, Victoria. "The Penetrating Agenda of Norms and Routines: Tweeting the First Anniversary of the Deepwater Horizon Oil Disaster." Unpublished research, Louisiana State University, 2012.

Dabbous, Yasmine, and Andrea Miller. "Same Disasters, Different Stories: How Three Arab Newspapers Framed the Asian Tsunami and Hurricane Katrina." Presented at the annual meeting of the International Communication Association, Singapore, June 2010.

Edwards, Renee, Andrea Miller, Christopher Mapp, and Michael Rold. "Communication and Information Processing by Coastal Residents Concerning Hurricanes." Presented at the annual meeting of the Southern States Communication Association, Memphis, TN, April 2010.

LaPoe, Ben, and Andrea Miller. "Supervising Public Opinion: Voices Diffusing Disaster Coverage of the Dalian Oil Spill in China." Presented at the Internet, Technology & Media Division of the Southern Political Science Association Annual Convention, New Orleans, LA, January 2011.

Miller, Andrea. "Me News: What Draws Attention to Breaking News?" Research Summary Posted on the Newslab Website, 2004. http://newslab.org/research/breakingnews.htm.

———. "Television News Coverage of Tragedy: Live, Breaking & Ethics." *The Community College Journalist* 32 (2005): 33–34.

———. "Watching Viewers Watch TV: Processing Live, Breaking, and Emotional Television News in a Naturalistic Setting." *Journalism & Mass Communication Quarterly* 83(2006): 511–529.

Miller, Andrea, and Robert Goidel. "News Organizations and Information Gathering During a Natural Disaster: Lessons from Hurricane Katrina." *Journal of Contingencies and Crisis Management* 17 (2009): 266–273.

Miller, Andrea, and Glenn Leshner. "How Viewers Process Live, Breaking, and Emotional Television News." *Media Psychology* 10 (2007): 1–18.

————. "Tragedy & Ratings: Searching for the Influence of Economic Factors on a Television Market's Breaking News Coverage." Presented at the Broadcast Education Association Conference, Las Vegas, NV, April 2002.

Miller, Andrea, and Shearon Roberts. "Local vs. National Television News Coverage of Hurricane Katrina: Comparing Roles, Frames, and Affect." Unpublished research, October 2007.

————. "Race in National Versus Local News Coverage of Hurricane Katrina: A Study of Sources, Victims, and Negative Video." Presented at the Association for Education in Journalism and Mass Communication Convention, Chicago, IL, August 2008.

Roberts, Shearon. "Gulf Coast Journalists and Hurricane Katrina: Mounting Challenge to the Work Routine." Presented at the Newspaper/Mass Communication Division of the Association for Education in Journalism and Mass Communication Conference, Washington, D.C., August 2007.

————. "Haiti's Counter-Hegemonic Media: Media Roles and Framing Post-2010 Earthquake." Unpublished research, Tulane University, 2012.

————. "Split Personalities: Journalists as Victims." In *Covering Disaster: Lessons from Coverage of Katrina and Rita*, edited by Ralph Izard and Jay Perkins. Piscataway, NJ: Transaction Publishers, 2010.

————. "We Are All Haitians: Framing Haitian Solidarity and Its 'Missing-in-Action' Government in U.S. Media Coverage of the 2010 Earthquake." Presented at the Haiti: Disaster Development Panel of the Latin American Graduate Organization Graduate Student Conference, Tulane University, October 2010.

NOTES

Introduction

1. Sheldon Fox interview, July 2010.

2. See the National Hurricane Center, "Tropical Cyclone Report Hurricane Katrina," August 2005, and Richard D. Knabb, Jamie R. Rhome, and Daniel P. Brown, "National Hurricane Center," December 2005, accessed June 20, 2012. http://www.nhc.noaa.gov/pdf/TCR-AL122005_Katrina.pdf.

3. Bob Mann interview, December 6, 2011.

4. Danny Shipka interview, December 5, 2011.

5. Ibid.

6. Louisiana Film Tax Incentives Help Create "Hollywood South," accessed June 20, 2012. http://www.fbtfilm.com/hollywood-south.aspx.

7. Dave Walker, "HBO's Treme Finally Gets New Orleans Right," *Times-Picayune*, accessed June 20, 2012. http://www.nola.com/treme-hbo/index.ssf/2010/04/treme_is_probably_as_good_as_i.html.

8. Froma Harrop, "Feds Should Take Over Louisiana," *Columbus Dispatch*, June 18, 2010, accessed June 20, 2012. http://www.dispatch.com/content/stories/editorials/2010/06/18/feds-should-take-over-louisiana.html.

9. "Four-in-Ten Question Rebuilding New Orleans in Present Location," Pew Research Center, accessed June 20, 2010. http://www.people-press.org/2005/09/12/four-in-ten-question-rebuilding-new-orleans-in-present-location/.

10. Robert Dowie interview, December 6, 2011.

Chapter 1

1. Marla Perez-Lugo, "Media Uses in Disaster Situations: A New Focus on the Impact Phase," *Sociological Inquiry* 74 (2004): 210–225; Chris Piotrowski and Terry Armstrong, "Mass Media Preferences in Disaster: A Study of Hurricane Danny," *Social Behavior and Personality* 26 (1998): 341–346.

2. Shearon Roberts, "Media Use and Hurricane Katrina," unpublished research, 2005, Louisiana State University. This study surveyed 250 New Orleans area residents on their media use before, during, and after Hurricane Katrina during September 2005. We were given exclusive access to the FEMA trailer site in Baker, Louisiana, for evacuated students

at LSU, and we snowballed displaced residents scattered across the Gulf during that month.

3. Craig M. Allen, *News Is People: The Rise of Local TV News and the Fall of News from New York* (Ames, IA: Iowa State University Press, 2001); Franklin Gilliam Jr. and Shanto Iyengar, "Prime Suspects: The Influence of Local Television News on the Viewing Public," *American Journal of Political Science* 44 (2000): 560–573; Diane Nicodemus, "Mobilizing Information: Local News and the Formation of a Viable Political Community," *Political Communication* 21 (2004): 161–176; Lou Prato, "In Local TV News We Trust, But Why?" *American Journalism Review* (November 1998): 68.

4. These students were surveyed at the LSU dorms they were temporarily housed in and in the special section courses they took.

5. For a few, the survey had to be read aloud and the answers written down by the researcher.

6. Those "caught in the storm" were fifty-one respondents in the post-Katrina survey.

7. Marla Perez-Lugo, "Media Uses in Disaster Situations."

8. See example of information relay in the 2010 Haitian earthquake in Imogen Wall and Sharon Reader, "Citizen Initiatives in Haiti," *Forced Migration Review* 38 (2011): 4–6.

9. Shearon Roberts, *Gulf Coast Journalists and Hurricane Katrina: The Story behind the Stories*, documentary film, 2006; Dave Walker, "On the Air," Radio, New Orleans *Times-Picayune*, November 11, 2006.

10. Chris Piotrowski and Terry Armstrong, "Mass Media Preferences in Disaster"; Marla Perez-Lugo, "Media Uses in Disaster Situations."

11. Imogen Wall and Sharon Reader, "Citizen Initiatives in Haiti," 4–6.

12. Renee Edwards, Andrea Miller, David Brown, and Stephanie Grey, "Hurricanes, Institutional Procedures, and Information Processing (HIPIP): Engagement with Decision-Makers and Coastal Residents." Funding for two studies (2009–2010, survey and in-depth interviews) from the Mississippi–Alabama Sea Grant Consortium. http://www .lsu.edu/hipip/index.html.

13. Shearon Roberts, "Media Use and Hurricane Katrina."

14. Marla Perez-Lugo, "Media Uses in Disaster Situations."

15. Renee Edwards, Andrea Miller, David Brown, and Stephanie Grey, "Hurricanes, Institutional Procedures, and Information Processing (HIPIP): Engagement with Decision-Makers and Coastal Residents."

16. Shearon Roberts, "Gulf Coast Journalists and Hurricane Katrina: Mounting Challenges to the Work Routine" (master's thesis, Louisiana State University, 2007); interview with David Meeks in September 2006 at the *Times-Picayune* building in New Orleans.

17. Renee Edwards, Andrea Miller, David Brown, and Stephanie Grey, "Hurricanes, Institutional Procedures, and Information Processing (HIPIP): Engagement with Decision-Makers and Coastal Residents."

18. Ibid.

19. Ibid.

20. Ibid.

21. Ibid.

22. Ibid.

23. Kirby Goidel and Ashley Kirzinger, "The View from the Coast: A Survey of 924 Coastal Residents on the 2010 Gulf Oil Spill" (unpublished research, Reilly Center for Media & Public Affairs, Louisiana State University, 2010). Survey sponsored by the Reilly Center for Media & Public Affairs, The Manship School of Mass Communication, and LSU. Survey executed by LSU and Manship's Public Policy Research Lab.

Chapter 2

1. Chris Rose quoted Peter Kovacs during a 2006 speech recorded for Shearon Roberts, *Gulf Coast Journalists and Hurricane Katrina: The Story behind the Stories*, documentary film, 2006.

2. Chris Rose speech at the 2006 Associated Press Managing Editors Conference in New Orleans, recorded for Shearon Roberts, *Gulf Coast Journalists and Hurricane Katrina*.

3. Ibid.

4. Ibid.

5. Logan Banks interview conducted in September 2006 for Shearon Roberts, *Gulf Coast Journalists and Hurricane Katrina*.

6. Lucy Bustamante interview, September 2006.

7. Logan Banks interview, September 2006.

8. Jim Amos interview, September 2006.

9. Daniel A. Berkowitz, "Telling What-A-Story News through Myth and Ritual: The Middle East as Wild West," in *Media Anthropology*, ed. Eric W. Rothenbuhler and Mihai Coman (Thousand Oaks, CA: Sage Publications, 2005), 210–220; Daniel A. Berkowitz, "Non-Routine News and Newswork: Exploring a What-A-Story," *Journal of Communication* 42 (1992): 82–94.

10. Gaye Tuchman, *Making News: A Study in the Construction of Reality* (New York: Free Press, 1978).

11. Michael Schudson, *The Sociology of News* (New York: W.W. Norton & Company, 2003).

12. Herbert Gans, *Deciding What's News: A Study of CBS Evening News, NBC Nightly News, Newsweek and Time* (New York, NY: Pantheon Books, 1979).

13. John McManus, *Market-Driven Journalism: Let the Citizen Beware?* (Thousand Oaks, CA: Sage Publications, 1994).

14. Ibid.

15. Ray Nagin interview with Garland Robinette transcribed from personal copy of recording.

16. Monica Pierre interview, September 2006.

17. Mark Glaser, "NOLA.com Blogs and Forums Help Save Lives after Katrina," *The Online Journalism Review*, September 13, 2005, accessed October 10, 2010. http://www.ojr.org/ojr/stories/050913glaser.

18. Ibid.

19. Ibid.

20. Ibid.

21. Ibid.

22. Kevin Held interview, September 2006.

23. Ibid.

24. John Donley interview, September 2006.

25. Trymaine Lee interview, September 2006.

26. Interviews were conducted in 2005 and 2006 at the *Times-Picayune* building, Entercom station, and WWL-TV station in New Orleans, as well as at the journalists' speaking engagements in New Orleans and Baton Rouge.

27. Staff Reports, "N.O. Man Arrested After Chase. He Asked Cops to Shoot Him, Police Say," *Times-Picayune*, August 9, 2006, B1; Daryl Lang, "Katrina Photographer McCusker Fined, Placed on Probation," *PDNonline*, December 13, 2007, accessed March 8, 2008. http://www.pdnonline.com/pdn/newswire/article_display.jsp?vnc_content_id=1003685185; Adeline Goss, Britt Harwood, Peter McElroy, and Colin Baker, "Profile: Katrina Photojournalist John McCusker," Voices of New Orleans, Audio Broadcast, PRX.org, May 12, 2006, accessed September 13, 2006. http://publicradioexchange.org/pieces/12547-katrina-photojournalist-john-mccusker.

28. Chris Rose speech at the 2006 Associated Press Managing Editors Conference in New Orleans, recorded for Shearon Roberts, *Gulf Coast Journalists and Hurricane Katrina*.

29. Trymaine Lee interview, September 2006.

30. Ibid.

31. Monica Pierre interview, September 2006.

32. Ibid.

33. Gordon Russell interview, September 2006.

34. David Meeks interview, September 2006.

35. Lucy Bustamante interview, September 2006.

36. David Meeks interview, September 2006.

37. Gordon Russell interview, September 2006.

38. John McConnell interview, September 2006.

39. Ibid.

40. Jim Amos interview, September 2006.

41. Belo Corporation, "News Release: Belo to Create Separate Television and Newspaper Businesses," Belo.com, October 1, 2007, accessed August 27, 2010. http://www.belo.com/pressRelease.x2?release=20071001-1279.html.

42. Radio Television Digital News Association, "News Release: RTDNA/Hofstra Survey Finds One-Man-Band Usage up Modestly," RTDNA.org, May 14, 2010, accessed May 16, 2010. http://www.rtdna.org/pages/posts/rtdna-hofstra-survey-finds-one-man-band-usage-up-modestly946.php; Radio Television Digital News Association, "News Release: RTDNA/Hofstra Survey: Number of Minority Journalists Down in 2009; Story Mixed

for Female Journalists Modestly," RTDNA.org, September 22, 2010, accessed October 11, 2010. http://mobile.rtdna.org/pages/posts/rtdnahofstra-survey-number-of-minority -journalists-down-in-2009-story-mixed-for-female-journalists1083.php.

43. John McCollam, "Up and Down on the Bayou: A Snapshot of the Times-Picayune 5 Years after Katrina," *Columbia Journalism Review*, July 1, 2010, accessed September 13, 2010. http://www.cjr.org/behind_the_news/timespicayune_five_years_later.php.

44. Chris Rose, "Rose's Reflections: How Far We've Come?" Fox8Live.com, August, 2010, accessed September 26, 2010. http://www.fox8live.com/content/entertainment/chris_rose/ story/Roses-Reflections-How-far-weve-come/hRGWYK8Ojoueqbz_5vYNBg.cspx.

45. Ibid.

46. Victoria LaPoe, confidential interview with journalists, July 2010.

47. Ibid.

48. Ibid.

49. Frank Donze interview, September 2006.

50. Confidential interview, July 2010.

51. Commission on Civil Disorders, "The Role of the Mass Media in Reporting of News about Minorities," in *Killing the Messenger: 100 Years of Media Criticism*, ed. Tom Goldstein (New York: Columbia University Press, 2007), 253–278.

52. Lucy Lampila interview, July 2010.

53. Bob Thomas interview, July 2010.

54. David Folkenflik, "In Gulf Spill Area, Reporters Face Security Hurdles," NPR.com, July 12, 2010, accessed September 12, 2010. http://www.npr.org/templates/story/story .php?storyId=128419985; Heather Horn, "Are Journalists Being Kept from Oil Spill?," *The Atlantic Wire*, June 10, 2010, accessed September 13, 2010. http://www.theatlanticwire .com/opinions/view/opinion/Are-Journalists-Being-Kept-From-the-Oil-Spill-3934; *The Huffington Post*, "BP, Coast Guard Officers Block Journalists from Filming Oil-Covered Beach," Huffingtonpost.com, May 19, 2010, accessed September 12, 2010. http://www .huffingtonpost.com/2010/05/19/bp-coast-guard-officers-b_n_581779.html.

55. Jeremy W. Peters, "BP and Officials Block Some Coverage of Gulf Oil Spill," *New York Times*, June 9, 2010, accessed September 11, 2010. http://www.nytimes .com/2010/06/10/us/10access.html.

56. Ibid.

57. *Louisiana Bucket Brigade*, "Citizen Journalists Needed for Oil Spill Crisis Map," LAbucketbrigade.org, March 3, 2010, accessed September 13, 2010. http://www .labucketbrigade.org/article.php?id=579.

58. Confidential interview, July 2010.

59. Sheldon Fox interview, July 2010.

60. Confidential interview, July 2010.

61. Confidential interview, July 2010.

62. Confidential interview, July 2010.

63. Confidential interview, July 2010.

64. Sheldon Fox interview, July 2010.

65. Confidential interview, July 2010.

66. Kathy Anderson interview, September 2006.

Chapter 3

1. The authors tracked this themselves.

2. Jacquetta White, "*Times-Picayune* Citizens' Group Aims to Stop Publication Changes at Newspaper," *Times-Picayune*, June 5, 2012, accessed June 22, 2012. http://www.nola .com/business/index.ssf/2012/06/times-picayune_citizens_group.html.

3. "*Times-Picayune* Citizens' Group Speaks Out on Proposed Changes to the *Times-Picayune*." accessed June 22, 2012.http://gnoinc.org/news/publications/press-release/ times-picayune-citizens-group-speaks-out-on-proposed-changes-to-the-times-picayune/.

4. David Carr, "New Orleans Paper Said to Face Deep Cuts and May Cut Back Publication," *New York Times*, May 23, 2012, accessed June 22, 2012. http://mediadecoder .blogs.nytimes.com/2012/05/23/new-orleans-paper-said-to-face-deep-cuts-and-may -cut-back-on-publication/?hp.

5. Michelle Krupa, "Mayor Mitch Landrieu Vows to Help *Times-Picayune* 'Grow and Not Diminish,'" *Times-Picayune*, May 24, 2012, accessed June 22, 2012. http://www.nola .com/politics/index.ssf/2012/05/mayor_mitch_landrieu_vows_to_h.html.

6. Jaquetta White, "Rally in Support of the *Times-Picayune* Draws Hundreds of Readers," *Times-Picayune*, June 5, 2012, accessed June 22, 2012. http://www.nola.com/ business/index.ssf/2012/06/rally_in_support_of_the_times-.html.

7. Lolis Eric Elie, "Demise of New Orleans Daily Limits Access in the Information Age," Urban Conservancy, June 9, 2012, accessed June 22, 2012. http://www.urbanconservancy. org/news/demise-of-new-orleans-daily-limits-access-in-the-information-age.

8. David Carr, "New Orleans Paper Said to Face Deep Cuts and May Cut Back Publication."

9. Marla Perez-Lugo, "Media Uses in Disaster Situations: A New Focus on the Impact Phase," *Sociological Inquiry* 74 (2004): 210–225.

10. Tania Dall, "Save the *Times-Picayune* Movement Takes Off," WWL-TV, June 4, 2012, accessed June 22, 2012. http://www.wwltv.com/news/Citizens-group-of-business-leaders -activists-forms-to-try-to-save-Times-Picayune-157035525.html.

11. Steve Myers, "Advance Publications Lays Off 600 People at *Times-Picayune*, Alabama Papers," Poynter, June 12, 2012, accessed June 22, 2012. http://www.poynter .org/latest-news/mediawire/176888/employee-meetings-scheduled-today-at-advance -papers-in-new-orleans-alabama-times-picayune-birmingham-news-mobile-press -register-huntsville-times/.

12. Michael Schudson, *Discovering the News: A Social History of American Newspapers* (New York: Basic Books, 1978).

13. Yehudith Auerbach and Yaeli Bloch-Elkon, "Media Framing and Foreign Policy: The Elite Press vis-à-vis US Policy in Bosnia, 1992–95," *Journal of Peace Research* 42 (2005): 83–89.

14. Dietram A. Scheufele, "Agenda-Setting, Priming, and Framing Revisited: Another Look at Cognitive Effects of Political Communication," *Mass Communication & Society* 3 (2000): 297–217.

15. Robert M. Entman, "Framing: Toward Clarification of a Fractured Paradigm," *Journal of Communication* 43 (1993): 51–59.

16. Heather E. Bullock, Karen F. Wyche, and Wendy R. Williams, "Media Images of the Poor," *Journal of Social Issues* 57 (2001): 229–247.

17. Auerbach and Bloch-Elkon, 2005; Paul D'Angelo, "News Framing as a Multiparadigmatic Research Program: A Response to Entman," *Journal of Communication* 52 (2002): 870–889.

18. Shanto Iyengar, *Is Anyone Responsible?* (Chicago: University of Chicago Press, 1991).

19. Ibid.

20. Ibid.

21. Lori Dorfman, Lawrence Wallack, and Katie Woodruff, "More than a Message: Framing Public Health Advocacy to Change Corporate Practices," *Health Education & Behavior* 32 (2005): 320–336.

22. Iyengar, *Is Anyone Responsible?*

23. Steven Jones, D. Charles Whitney, Sharon Mazzarella, and Lana Rakow, "Geographic and Source Biases in Network Television News 1982–1984," *Journal of Broadcasting & Electronic Media* 33 (1989): 159–174; Lee Ross, "The Intuitive Psychologist and His Shortcomings: Distortions in the Attribution Process," in *Advances in Experimental Psychology*, ed. L. Berkowitz (New York, NY: American Press, 1977).

24. Holli Semetko and Patti Valkenburg, "Framing European Politics: A Content Analysis of Press and Television," *Journal of Communication* 50 (2000): 93–109.

25. Katherine Fry, *Constructing the Heartland: Television News and Natural Disaster* (Cresskill, NJ: Hampton Press, 2003).

26. Vincent Price and David Tewksbury, "Measuring the Third Person Effect of News: The Impact of Question Order, Contrast and Knowledge," *International Journal of Public Opinion Research* 8 (1996): 120–141; Salma Ghanem, "Filling in the Tapestry: The Second Level of Agenda Setting," in *Communication and Democracy: Exploring the Intellectual Frontiers in Agenda-Setting Theory*, ed. M. D. McCombs, D. L. Shaw, and D. Weaver (Mahwah, NJ: Lawrence Erlbaum Associates, 1997), 12.

27. Salma Ghanem, "Filling in the Tapestry," 3–14.

28. Jeff Jarvis, a media critic and associate professor and director of the interactive journalism program at the City University of New York, told National Public Radio that network television "was given a government mandate to have this apparently neutral voice to serve all of the people, to become, you know, one-size-fits-all," in a segment titled "Should Objectivity Still Be Standard in News?," November 16, 2010, accessed February 3, 2012. http://www.npr.org/2010/11/16/131361367/should-objectivity-still-be-the-standard-in-news.

29. Victoria LaPoe, confidential interview with journalists, July 2010.

30. James O'Byrne interview for HIPIP, summer 2009.

31. Chris Slaughter interview for HIPIP, summer 2009.

32. Peter Kovacs interview, summer 2011.

33. Lisa de Moraes, "The TV Column: In Covering Japan Tragedy, Broadcast TV Flexes its Ratings Muscle," March 17, 2011, accessed January 20, 2012. http://www .washingtonpost.com/lifestyle/style/the-tv-column-in-covering-japan-tragedy -broadcast-tv-flexes-its-ratings-muscle/2011/03/17/ABogJ6m_story.html.

34. Allison Romano, "Weathering the Storm; TV News Operations Face Enormous Obstacles in Delivering Critical News," *Broadcasting & Cable*, September 5, 2005, 4.

35. Ibid.; Jessica Hamblen, "The Effects of Media Coverage of Terrorist Attacks on Viewers (Fact Sheet)" (White River Junction, VT: National Center for PTSD, 2003); Pew Research Center, "American Psyche Reeling from Terror Attacks," Pew Research Center, September 19, 2001, accessed April 20, 2007. http://people-press.org/reports/print .php3?ReportID=3.

36. Doris Graber, *Media Power in Politics* (Chicago: CQ Press, 1984).

37. Chris Piotrowski and Terry Armstrong, "Mass Media Preferences in Disaster: A Study of Hurricane Danny," *Social Behavior and Personality* 26 (1998): 341–346.

38. Marla Perez-Lugo, "Media Uses in Disaster Situations," 210–225.

39. Ibid., 212.

40. Ibid.

41. Ibid.

42. Karen A. Cerulo and Janet M. Ruane, "Coming Together: New Taxonomies for the Analysis of Social Relations," *Social Inquiry* 68 (1998): 398–425; Karen A. Cerulo, Janet Ruane, and Mary Chayko, "Technological Ties that Bind: Media-Generated Primary Groups," *Communication Research* 19 (1992): 109–129.

43. Mike Hoss interview, September 2006.

44. Michael B. Salwen, "News of Hurricane Andrew: The Agenda of Sources and the Sources Agendas," *Journalism and Mass Communication Quarterly* 72 (1995): 826–840.

45. Katherine Fry, *Constructing the Heartland*, 83.

46. We performed a content analysis on one hour of prime-time programming across four television news outlets (two local, two national) for an eight-day period beginning with August 29, 2005, the day Hurricane Katrina hit the New Orleans area. The local stations included WWL-TV of New Orleans and WBRZ-TV of Baton Rouge in partnership with WGNO-TV of New Orleans. The national television sample included CNN and Fox News. Four fifteen-minute blocks were randomly sampled from the four-hour, 6 p.m. to 10 p.m. prime-time news block and coded for episodic and thematic framing, natural disaster functions of the press, and tone of the coverage, as well as other frames that included race, socioeconomic status, and attribution of responsibility.

47. Andrea Miller and Shearon Roberts, "Visual Agenda-Setting & Proximity After Hurricane Katrina: A Study of Those Closest to the Event," *Visual Communication Quarterly* 17 (2005): 31–46.

48. Shearon Roberts, "Gulf Coast Journalists and Hurricane Katrina: Mounting Challenges to the Work Routine" (master's thesis, Louisiana State University, 2007).

49. Additionally, a majority of our sample took place after the storm hit. Perez-Lugo argues that assumption of the management role takes place before disasters strike. Therefore, we were sampling the time period when recovery would be most prevalent.

50. Shearon Roberts, *Gulf Coast Journalists and Hurricane Katrina: The Story behind the Stories*, documentary film, 2006.

51. Joe Bob Hester and Rhonda Gibson, "The Relationship between Tone of TV News Coverage and Public Opinion for a Controversial Issue," *Electronic News: A Journal of Applied Research & Ideas* 1 (2007): 89–102.

52. Shearon Roberts, "Gulf Coast Journalists and Hurricane Katrina," 27–28.

Chapter 4

1. George W. Bush, *Decision Points* (New York, NY: Crown Publishers, 2010), 326. The excerpt was included in transcript of the *Today* clip airing on November 10, 2010, of pretaped *Matt Lauer Reports* special.

2. The pretaped *Matt Lauer Reports* special aired on NBC on November 8 from 8–9 p.m.

3. Amy Goodman, "Kanye West: 'Bush Doesn't Care About Black People,'" accessed February 1, 2012. http://www.democracynow.org/2005/9/5/kanye_west_bush_doesnt_care_ about.

4. Ibid.

5. Ibid.

6. Excerpt taken from transcript of pretaped *Matt Lauer Reports* special aired on NBC on November 8, 2010, from 8–9 p.m. Interview preceded the release of the president's book by Crown Publishers on November 9, 2010, accessed February 1, 2012. http://watching-tv.ew.com/2010/11/02/george-bush-kanye-west-lauer-today/.

7. In November 2010, Kanye West told Matt Lauer for the *Today* show that he regretted criticizing the president. West said: "I would tell George Bush in my moment of frustration, I didn't have the grounds to call him a racist. I believe that in a situation of high emotion like that we as human beings don't always choose the right words." The president told Matt Lauer the following day he accepted West's apology. "I'm not a hater," Bush said. "I don't hate Kanye West. I was talking about an environment in which people were willing to say things that hurt. Nobody wants to be called a racist if in your heart you believe in equality of races." Kanye quotes: *Today*'s Lauer on Kanye interview, accessed February 1, 2012. http://video.today.msnbc.msn.com/today/40128321#40128321. Bush quotes: John Springer, "Bush Reacts to Apology from Kanye West," Today.com, 2010, accessed February 1, 2012. http://today.msnbc.msn.com/id/40108402/ns/today-today_news/t/bush-reacts-apology-kanye-west/#.T9paTWBuFXU.

8. Amy Goodman, "George Bush Doesn't Care About Black People."

9. Interview conducted with Jim Amos in September 2006 for research for Shearon Roberts, "Gulf Coast Journalists and Hurricane Katrina: Mounting Challenges to the Work Routine" (master's thesis, Louisiana State University, 2007).

10. *Times-Picayune*, "An Open Letter to the President, Nola.com," September 2005, accessed February 12, 2012. http://www.nola.com/katrina/pages/090405/a15.pdf.

11. CNN.com, "New Orleans Paper Rips Federal Response," September 4, 2005, accessed February 1, 2012. http://articles.cnn.com/2005-09-04/us/katrina .blame_1_michael-chertoff-response-director-michael-brown?_s=PM:US.

12. Interview transcribed from personal copy as part of Shearon Roberts, *Gulf Coast Journalists and Hurricane Katrina: The Story behind the Stories*, documentary film, 2006.

13. CNN, "Mayor to Feds: 'Get Off Your Asses,'" September 2, 2005, accessed June 4, 2012. http://articles.cnn.com/2005-09-02/us/nagin. transcript_1_public-school-bus-drivers-new-orleans-nagin-major-deal?_s=PM:US.

14. Shearon Roberts, *Gulf Coast Journalists and Hurricane Katrina: The Story behind the Stories*.

15. Ibid.

16. WWL-TV transcript of Ray Nagin's 2010 "chocolate city speech," accessed February 1, 2012. http://www.wwltv.com/news/local/Full-video-of-Nagins-chocolate-city-speech -92368619.

17. *Times-Picayune* and Biloxi *Sun Herald* articles selected were used in a content analysis study for Shearon Roberts, "Gulf Coast Journalists and Hurricane Katrina: Mounting Challenges to the Work Routine." The content analysis included a random selection of two weeks of news coverage for both papers in 2004, and then two weeks in 2006 providing some 672 front-page articles. The author was given access to the *Times-Picayune* archives to conduct this study in November 2006.

18. Adina Postelnicu, "Some Call Speech a Snub From Bush: No Mississippi Mention in State of the Union," *Sun Herald*, February 5, 2006, A5.

19. Bill Walsh, "Federal Report Predicted Cataclysm: White House Had Research Before Katrina Hit Land," *Times-Picayune*, January 24, 2006, 1.

20. Ibid.

21. James Varney, "Bush Gets Taste of Etouffee, Katrina Relief Talk: President to Mark Anniversary," *Times-Picayune*, August 29, 2006, 13.

22. Ibid.

23. Ricky Mathews, "President Rolls Up His Sleeves Over Lunch in Biloxi," *Sun Herald*, August 29, 2006, C2.

24. Ibid.

25. Shearon Roberts, "Gulf Coast Journalists and Hurricane Katrina: Mounting Challenges to the Work Routine."

26. Ibid.

27. Ibid.

28. Kay Lyons, "Bravo for Calm Response," *Times-Picayune*, September 20, 2004, 4.

29. Stephanie Grace, "Mayor Makes It Clear He's Ready to Rumble," *Times-Picayune*, December 28, 2004, 5.

30. Gordon Russell, Frank Donze, and Michelle Krupa, "It's Nagin: 'It's Time for Us to Be One New Orleans,'" *Times-Picayune*, May 21, 2006, 1.

31. Gordon Russell and Frank Donze, "Nagin Says City Making Progress: Mayor Cites Trash Pickups, Water Pressure, Crime Fighting," *Times-Picayune*, September, 13, 2006, 1.

32. Shearon Roberts, "Gulf Coast Journalists and Hurricane Katrina: Mounting Challenges to the Work Routine."

33. *New York Times* reporter Charles Blow, MSNBC's *Hardball with Chris Matthews*, June 1, 2010.

34. Dr. Frank Rohwer interview, May 27, 2011.

35. Lucy Lampila interview, July 2010.

36. Julie Anderson interview, June 16, 2011.

37. Brian Ross, Matthew Mosk, and Avni Patel, "BP and Feds Withheld Videos Showing Massive Scope of Oil Spill," ABCNews, June 3, 2010, para. 2–3, accessed June 20, 2012. http://abcnews.go.com/Blotter/bp-feds-withheld-videos-showing-massive-scope-oil/story?id=10819367.

38. *Times-Picayune* editorial, "What BP knew early in the Deepwater Horizon disaster: An editorial," January 31, 2012, accessed June 20, 2012. http://www.nola.com/opinions/index.ssf/2012/01/what_bp_knew_early_in_the_deep.html.

39. Andrea Miller and Victoria LaPoe, "Oil-Soaked Images of Disaster: Identifying the National vs. Local Television Visuals of the Deepwater Horizon Oil Spill." Presentation at the Association for Education in Journalism and Mass Communication, St. Louis, MO, August 2011.

40. *New York Times* reporter Charles Blow on MSNBC's *Hardball with Chris Matthews*, June 1, 2010.

41. Andrea Miller and Victoria LaPoe, "Oil-Soaked Images of Disaster."

42. Victoria LaPoe confidential interview with journalist at WAFB, May 15, 2010.

43. Robert Entman, *Projections of Power: Framing News, Public Opinion, and U.S. Foreign Policy* (Chicago: University of Chicago Press, 2004).

44. Michael B. Salwen, "News of Hurricane Andrew: The Agenda of Sources and the Sources Agendas," *Journalism and Mass Communication Quarterly* 72 (1995): 826–840.

45. Holli A. Semetko and Patti M. Valkenburg, "Framing European Politics: A Content Analysis of Press and Television News," *Journal of Communication* 50 (2000): 93–109.

46. "BP Oil Disaster Largely Blamed on Cement Failure: Poor Management Decisions Cited in Report," CBCNews, September 14, 2011, accessed June 20, 2012. http://www.cbc.ca/news/business/story/2011/09/14/bp-offshore-oil-spill-report.html.

47. John Rudolf, "BP Spill Fight Looms With Feds, Despite Settlement Of Private Claims," *Huffington Post*, April 19, 2012, accessed June 20, 2012. http://www.huffingtonpost.com/2012/04/19/bp-settles-private-spill-lawsuit_n_1437993.html.

48. Ibid.

49. Suzanne Goldenberg, "BP Engineer's Arrest May Force Company to Reveal Internal Estimates on Gulf Spill," *The Guardian*, April 25, 2012, accessed June 20, 2012. http://www.guardian.co.uk/environment/2012/apr/25/bp-engineer-arrest-internal-estimates.

50. Ibid.

51. "BP Oil Disaster Largely Blamed on Cement Failure: Poor Management Decisions Cited in Report," CBCNews.

Chapter 5

1. Dan Berkowitz, "TV News Sources and News Channels: A Study in Agenda Building," *Journalism Quarterly* (Summer 1987): 508–513; Dan Berkowitz and Douglas Beach, "News Sources and News Context: The Effect of Routine News, Conflict and Proximity," *Journalism Quarterly* (Spring 1993): 4–12; Dan Berkowitz and James V. TerKeurst, "Community as Interpretive Community: Rethinking the Journalist-Source Relationship," *Journal of Communication* (Summer 1999): 125–136.

2. *Times-Picayune*, "Breaking News from the Times-Picayune and Nola.com: Hurricane Katrina, the Storm Arrives," August 29, 2005, weblog, 99.

3. Ibid.

4. Ibid.

5. Ibid.

6. Ibid.

7. Interview conducted with Mike Hoss in September 2006 for research for Shearon Roberts, "Gulf Coast Journalists and Hurricane Katrina: Mounting Challenges to the Work Routine" (master's thesis, Louisiana State University, 2007).

8. Interview conducted with Ernesto Schweikert in September 2006 for Shearon Roberts, "Gulf Coast Journalists and Hurricane Katrina: Mounting Challenges to the Work Routine."

9. Dan Berkowitz, "TV News Sources and News Channels."

10. Ibid. Therefore, sources were coded as belonging to governmental, corporate, nonprofit, law enforcement, and educational institutions, to name a few.

11. The articles were retrieved using the *Times-Picayune*'s archive system and through Nexis-Lexis for the Biloxi *Sun Herald*. Two coders were trained extensively to identify types of sources. During the pretest period, the coders and the trainer discussed questions, and a pretest included 10 percent of the sample (N = 67), with intercoder reliability of 83 percent, using Holsti's formula that measures percentages. A second test took place to improve reliability to 92 percent.

12. Source affiliations that fell under the nonroutine designation included "unaffiliated U.S. citizen," "foreign citizen," and the "other" option. The unaffiliated citizen attained a higher mean score in 2006 ($\underline{M}$ = 2.45; $\underline{SD}$ = .142) than in 2004 ($\underline{M}$ = 2.05; $\underline{SD}$ = .118) and was significant at p = .044. A significant increase in the unaffiliated citizen, $t_{(196)}$ = -2.024, $p < .05$, supports an increase in nonroutine sources.

13. Additionally, the agency types which were considered nonroutine included "nongovernmental/nonprofit," "educational," "civic," "other," and "none," as in belonging to no agency at all. Sources belonging to agencies that were in the "none" category, meaning they did not belong to any agency, increased at a mean difference of .50 and also significant at $t_{(198)}$ = -2.546, $p < .05$.

14. The source status categories that were nonroutine included "worker/employee/member," "position not specified," "victim," "eyewitness," "common man/man on the street," and "other." Here the "common man/man on the street" category had the most noteworthy increase from ($\underline{M}$ = 1.91; $\underline{SD}$ = .127) in 2004 to ($\underline{M}$ = 2.40; $\underline{SD}$ = .152). This mean increase in the common man as a source was significant at the .05 level, $t_{(169)}$ = .-2.237, p < .05.

15. Nonroutine sources were almost identically highest in the human interest and conflict frames. However, a chi-square test for association showed positive relationships between the human interest technique and nonroutine source categories. The three most significant nonroutine sources were unaffiliated citizens, persons belonging to no agency, and persons identified as the common man. Using Kendall's tau c, the unaffiliated citizen held a significantly strong association to the human interest framing technique, $x^{2(35)}$ = .142, p < .001. Persons belonging to no agency had a positive association with the human interest technique with significance at $x^{2(35)}$ = .137, p < .001. Persons who were identified as the common man were significantly associated with stories using the human interest frame at $x^{2(35)}$ = .147, p < .05. Although the human interest technique was not the only frame to carry the highest number of nonroutine sources, its relationship to nonroutine sources was highly significant.

16. Interview conducted with David Meeks in September 2006 for research for Shearon Roberts, "Gulf Coast Journalists and Hurricane Katrina: Mounting Challenges to the Work Routine."

17. "Law and Disorder: After Katrina," accessed June 4, 2012. http://www.propublica.org/nola/.

18. "Law and Disorder," accessed June 4, 2012. http://media.nola.com/law_and_disorder/other/NOPD-Katrina-Incidents2.pdf.

19. Gordon Russell, "Defillo Negligent in Glover Case: One Charge Against NOPD," *Times-Picayune*, July 9, 2011, A1.

20. Ron Thibodeaux and Gordon Russell, "7th Day of Hell: A Week of Horror Ends With More Evacuations and Uncertainty," *Times-Picayune*, September 5, 2005, A1.

21. Interview conducted with Gordon Russell in September 2006 for research for Shearon Roberts, "Gulf Coast Journalists and Hurricane Katrina: Mounting Challenges to the Work Routine."

22. James Varney, "Four Officers Suspended, Acting Police Chief Says Looting Is Focus of One Investigation: 'Deserters' May Have Been Working in Other Precincts," *Times-Picayune*, September 30, 2005, Hurricane Katrina: Special Coverage.

23. James Varney, "N.O. Cops Reported to Take Cadillacs From Dealership Foti Investigating Looting," *Times-Picayune*, September 29, 2005, Hurricane Katrina: Special Coverage.

24. James Varney and Michael Perlstein, "Compass Resigns: Abrupt Departure Comes as NOPD Katrina Response Is Questioned," *Times-Picayune*, September 28, 2005, A1.

25. Brendan McCarthy and Laura Maggi, "After Years of Legal Twists and Turns the Violent Encounter on the Danziger Bridge Finally Goes to Trial: Federal Prosecutors Allege Civil Rights Abuses," *Times-Picayune*, June 19, 2011, A1.

26. Laura Maggi, "7 N.O. Cops Indicted in Killings on Bridge: Shooting Deaths Came 6 Days After Katrina Police Chief Cautions Against Rush to Judgment," *Times-Picayune*, December 29, 2006, 1.

27. "Law and Disorder After Katrina, New Orleans Police Shot Frequently and Asked Few Questions Body of Evidence," accessed June 4, 2012. www.propublica.org/article/body-of-evidence.

28. Laura Maggi, "N.O. Cops Accused in Grisly Storm Story: Charred Body Found in Stolen Car, Survivor Says," *Times-Picayune*, March 28, 2009, 1.

29. Ibid.

30. Victoria LaPoe and Andrea Miller, "Sourcing in National vs. Local Television News Coverage of the Deepwater Horizon Oil Spill: A Study of Experts, Victims, Roles and Race." Presentation at the Association for Education in Journalism and Mass Communication, St. Louis, MO, August 2011.

A content analysis was conducted for the first week (April 21–28, 2010) and sixth week (May 31–June 8, 2010) of the Deepwater Horizon oil spill weekday primetime television coverage. This included the evening newscasts of ABC, CBS, NBC, MSNBC, CNN, Fox News Channel, and two local Louisiana affiliates—WBRZ and WAFB. The Baton Rouge affiliates were an appropriate part of the sample because they are located in the state's capital where the governmental decisions are made and where many of the scientific sources are headquartered (flagship university). The network newscasts were coded for the 5:30 p.m. central time half hour, while the local affiliates were coded for the 6 p.m. half hour of news. The cable newscasts were coded for the first thirty minutes of the 6 p.m. hour of news.

31. To give texture to the content of the sources, we interviewed seven scientists for this book for the first time during the spill and a second time a year after the spill. The scientists were heavily relied upon by the media as sources during and after the spill locally, nationally, and internationally.

32. Dr. Robert Thomas interview, June 14, 2011.

33. Ibid.

34. Victoria LaPoe confidential interview with journalist, July 2010.

35. Dr. Julie Anderson (assistant professor and fisheries specialist, LSU AgCenter and Louisiana Sea Grant) explained to the author, on June 16, 2011, that the dispersant Corexit, while the same dispersant used after the Valdez, was not the same toxicity level.

36. *CBS Evening News*, "Gulf Oil Spill: How BP's Dispersants May Contaminate Seafood for Years," June 4, 2012, accessed June 20, 2012. http://www.cbsnews.com/8301-505123_162-44040932/gulf-oil-spill-how-bps-dispersants-may-contaminate-seafood-for-years/.

37. Dr. Chris D'Elia interview, June 10, 2011.

38. Dr. Julie Anderson interview, June 16, 2011.

39. Ibid.

40. Dr. Lucina Lampila interview, June 17, 2011.

41. Dr. Ed Overton interview, May 27, 2011.

42. Dr. Robert Thomas interview, June 14, 2011.

43. Dr. Ed Overton interview, May 27, 2011.

44. Dr. Robert Thomas interview, June 14, 2011.

45. "I'd give them the same grade [C or D] because they are now completely ignoring it. You just don't hear much about follow-up." Dr. Frank Rowher interview, May 27, 2011.

46. Dr. Robert Thomas interview, June 14, 2011.

47. Dr. Ed Overton interview, May 27, 2011.

48. Ibid.

49. Peter Kovacs interview, June 7, 2011.

50. The scientists interviewed in 2010 and 2011 after the Deepwater Horizon disaster are some of the most quoted oil scientists. Being interviewed for an hour plus on two occasions for this book, the scientists spoke in terms that an everyday person could understand; it was clear why they were quoted so often. Ed Overton spent more than an hour of his time, as he sat in his LSU coastal environment office drinking orange juice with shelves behind him filled with science books. Frank Rowher is a straightforward, award-winning research professor. Julie Anderson, an LSU newbie who moved here from Delaware right before the gusher, is a leading crab expert.

51. Dr. Frank Rowher interview, May 27, 2011.

52. Dr. Robert Thomas interview, June 14, 2011.

53. Dr. Frank Rowher interview, May 27, 2011.

54. Dr. Chris D'Elia interview, June 10, 2011.

55. Peter Kovacs interview, June 7, 2011.

56. Dr. Robert Thomas interview, June 14, 2011.

57. Amy Wold, "Studies: Gulf Oil Affecting La. Fish," accessed April 9, 2012. http://theadvocate.com/news/982969-64/studies-gulf-oil-affecting-la.#.Tohucvb3eGk.mailto.

58. "The FDA Thinks It's Totally Cool For Us To Eat Seafood 10,000 Times Over The Contamination Limit," accessed June 4, 2012. http://www.businessinsider.com/seafood-10000-times-more-carcinogens2011-12#ixzz1rZpziMF9.

Chapter 6

1. Chris Slaughter personal conversation with author, April 2010.

2. The crux of the survey was four open-ended questions asking the respondents to describe the most memorable visual image of Katrina or the disaster, where they saw it, why they thought it was so memorable, and what the image meant to them.

3. The survey consisted of a mixed methodological approach and, for Katrina, was executed longitudinally. The crux was an open-ended qualitative survey asking respondents to choose the most memorable image from Hurricane Katrina. However, quantitative content analysis and statistical analysis were used to answer the research questions concerning possible relationships between image choice and the degree to which participants were affected. The same survey was administered to a purposive sample of students at a Gulf Coast university six weeks after the storm (Time 1, pen and

paper, October 2005, N = 466) and four years after Katrina (Time 2, pen and paper, fall 2009, N = 221). For Times 1 and 2, twenty-five image categories were created. For Time 2, the university and the surrounding city were the locus of many of the evacuees. The students surveyed in the Time 1 were enrolled in large general education classes and all were freshmen. For Time 2, many of the freshmen who lived through Katrina were now upperclassmen, making them the ideal cohort to study enduring images over time. The same twenty-six-item survey instrument was also used to study oil disaster visuals and was distributed via an online survey in September and October of 2010 (N = 252). Only ten categories were created for this disaster. This sample was made up students enrolled in mass communication classes who received extra credit for their participation.

4. Andrea Miller and Shearon Roberts, "Visual Agenda-Setting & Proximity after Hurricane Katrina: A Study of Those Closest to the Event," *Visual Communication Quarterly* 17 (2010): 31–46. Nicole Dahmen and Andrea Miller, "Redefining Iconicity: A Five-Year Study of Visual Themes of Hurricane Katrina," *Visual Communication Quarterly* 19 (2012): 4–19.

5. Carolyn Kitch, "'Mourning in America': Ritual, Redemption and Recovery in News Narrative After September 11," *Journalism Studies* 4 (2003): 213–224. She found similar conventional imagery in the September 11 coverage. Edward Linenthal, *Preserving Memory: The Struggle to Create America's Holocaust Museum* (New York: Columbia University Press, 2001). He found this also when studying the Oklahoma City bombing.

6. Carolyn Kitch, "'Mourning in America.'"

7. Andrea Miller and Shearon Roberts, "Visual Agenda-Setting & Proximity after Hurricane Katrina."

8. Ibid.

9. Nicole Dahmen and Andrea Miller, "Redefining Iconicity: A Five-Year Study of Visual Themes of Hurricane Katrina."

10. Ibid.

11. Andrea Miller and Shearon Roberts, "Visual Agenda-Setting & Proximity after Hurricane Katrina."

12. Ibid.

13. Ibid.

14. Ibid.

15. Ibid.

16. Marla Perez-Lugo, "Media Uses in Disaster Situations: A New Focus on the Impact Phase," *Sociological Inquiry* 74 (2004): 222–223.

17. Andrea Miller and Shearon Roberts, "Visual Agenda-Setting & Proximity after Hurricane Katrina."

18. Meg Spratt, April Peterson, and Taso Lagos, "Of Photographs and Flags: Uses and Perceptions of an Iconic Image Before and After September 11, 2001," *Popular Communication* 3 (2005): 117–136. The authors argue that it is in the response: "reactions to such [iconic images] are highly personalized and depend on preexisting schema, previous knowledge, and experience" (119).

19. David Perlmutter and Nicole Dahmen, "(In)Visible Evidence: Pictorially-Enhanced Disbelief in the 1969 Apollo Moon Landing," *Visual Communication* 7 (2008): 229–251.

20. Nicole Dahmen and Andrea Miller, "Redefining Iconicity," 7–8; David Perlmutter and Nicole Dahmen, "(In)Visible Evidence."

21. Andrea Miller and Shearon Roberts, "Visual Agenda-Setting & Proximity after Hurricane Katrina."

22. Ibid.

23. Nicole Dahmen and Andrea Miller, "Redefining Iconicity."

24. Ibid.

25. Ibid.

26. Brian Ross, Matthew Mosk, and Avni Patel, "BP and Feds Withheld Videos Showing Massive Scope of Oil Spill," ABCNews, June 3, 2010, para. 2–3, accessed June 20, 2012. http://abcnews.go.com/Blotter/bp-feds-withheld-videos-showing-massive-scope-oil/story?id=10819367.

27. Andrea Miller and Victoria LaPoe, "Oil-Soaked Images of Disaster: Identifying the National vs. Local Television Visuals of the Deepwater Horizon Oil Spill." Presentation at the Association for Education in Journalism and Mass Communication, St. Louis, MO, August 2011.

Two weeks (first and sixth) of prime-time television coverage were studied. This included the evening newscasts of ABC, CBS, NBC, MSNBC, CNN, Fox News Channel, and the local Baton Rouge affiliates—WBRZ and WAFB. The network newscasts were coded for the 5:30 p.m. central time half hour, while the local affiliates were coded for the 6 p.m. half hour of news. The cable newscasts were coded for the first thirty minutes of the 6 p.m. hour of news.

The first and sixth weeks of the newscast were chosen for this study because both included key visual moments within the overall oil disaster coverage. The first week of the newscast contained the fiery image of the explosion of the Deepwater Horizon and during the sixth week the image of the oiled pelican emerged. The newscasts included in this study were weekday newscasts April 21 through April 28 and May 31 through June 8. This totaled thirty-six hours of national news and twelve hours of local news.

28. Russell Gold, Ben Casselman, and Guy Chazan, "Leaking Oil Well Lacked Safeguard Device," *Wall Street Journal*, April 28, 2012, accessed June 22, 2012. http://calmap.gisc.berkeley.edu/dwh_doc_link/News_Articles/wall_street_journal_BP_article.pdf.

29. Andrea Miller and Victoria LaPoe, "Oil-Soaked Images of Disaster."

30. Carolyn Kitch, "'Mourning in America.'"

31. Ibid.

32. Ibid.

33. Ibid.

34. Ibid.

35. Nicole Dahmen and Andrea Miller, "Redefining Iconicity."

Conclusion

1. Kimberly Massey, "Analyzing the Uses and Gratifications Concept of Audience Activity with a Qualitative Approach: Media Encounters during the 1998 Loma Prieta Earthquake Disaster," *Journal of Broadcasting & Electronic Media* 39 (1995): 328–350.

2. Chris Piotrowski and Terry Armstrong, "Mass Media Preferences in Disaster: A Study of Hurricane Danny," *Social Behavior and Personality* 26 (1998): 341–346.

3. Marla Perez-Lugo, "Media Uses in Disaster Situations: A New Focus on the Impact Phase," *Sociological Inquiry* 74 (2004): 212.

4. Ibid.

5. Lou Prato, "In Local TV News We Trust, But Why?," *American Journalism Review* (November 1998): 68.

6. Karen Slattery and Ernest Hakanen, "Sensationalism Versus Public Affairs Content of Local TV News: Pennsylvania Revisited," *Journal of Broadcasting & Electronic Media* 38 (1994): 205–217; Tom Rosensteil, Carl Gottlieb, and Lee Ann Brady, "Local TV News Project 1998: What Works, What Flops, and Why," Pew Research Center's Project for Excellence in Journalism, accessed July 2, 2012. http://www.journalism.org/node/377.

7. Although the paper did not run off the presses, the pdfs of the entire newspaper were available online for August 30, August 31, and September 1, 2005.

8. Greater New Orleans Community Data Center, "Hurricane Katrina Recovery," accessed June 20, 2012. http://www.gnocdc.org/Factsforfeatures/HurricaneKatrina Recovery/index.html.

9. Melissa Block, "Times-Picayune Paper Slashes Staff by 200 People," *Times-Picayune*, June 13, 2012, accessed June 20, 2012. http://www.npr.org/2012/06/13/154959095/times-picayune-paper-slashes-600-people-from-staff.

10. Forbes, "The World's Billionaires List, 2012," Forbes.com, accessed June 5, 2012. http://www.forbes.com/billionaires/list/.

11. Evan Christopher, "Riffing On the Tradition: Open Letter to Mr. Warren Buffett re The Times-Picayune," NolaVie.com, May, 25, 2012, accessed June 1, 2012. http://nolavie.com/2012/05/riffing-on-the-tradition-open-letter-to-mr-warren-buffett-re-the-times-picayune-81243.html.

12. Omaha.com, "Buffet to Buy the World Herald," *Omaha World-Herald*, November 30, 2011, accessed June 1, 2012. http://www.omaha.com/article/20111130/NEWS01/111139986.

13. Evan Christopher, "Riffing On the Tradition: Open Letter to Mr. Warren Buffett re The Times-Picayune," NolaVie.com.

14. Federal Emergency Management Authority, "Nebraska Disaster History," FEMA, accessed July 1, 2012. http://www.fema.gov/news/disasters_state.fema?id=31.

15. National Oceanic and Atmospheric Administration, "2011 Tornado Information," NOAA, March 20, 2012, accessed June 1, 2012. http://www.noaanews.noaa.gov/2011_tornado_information.html.

16. T. J. Winick, "Dozens of Tornadoes Plague Midwest," WPVI-TV, June 21, 2011, accessed June 1, 2012. http://abclocal.go.com/wpvi/story?section=news/national_world&id=8203863.

17. Federal Emergency Management Authority, "Nebraska Disaster History," FEMA.

18. Omaha.com, "Buffet to Buy the World Herald," *Omaha World-Herald*.

19. Evan Christopher, "Riffing On the Tradition: Thank You, Mr. Buffett," NolaVie.com, June 1, 2012, accessed June 2, 2012. http://nolavie.com/2012/06/riffing-on-the-tradition -thank-you-mr-buffett-80488.html.

20. Ibid.

21. Imogen Wall and Sharon Reader, "Citizen Initiatives in Haiti," *Forced Migration Review* 38 (2011): 4–6.

22. Philip Brasor, "Media Mix: Local Broadcasters Remain Calm During the Quake Crisis," *Japan Times*, March 20, 2011, accessed June 1, 2012. http://www.japantimes.co.jp/ text/fd20110320pb.html#.T_UuxmBuFXU.

23. Jim Spellman, "Stefani Family Loses Home in Wildfire," KMGH-TV, June 28, 2012, accessed July 1, 2012. KMGH-TV, channel 7, is the ABC-affiliated television station in Denver, Colorado. http://www.ksdk.com/news/world/article/326131/28/ Colorado-family-loses-home-in-wildfire.

24. Ibid.

25. DenverPost.com, "Photos: Waldo Canyon Fire—Residents Return to Mountain Shadows," Denverpost.com, July 1, 2012, accessed July 2, 2012. http://photos.denverpost .com/mediacenter/2012/07/photos-waldo-canyon-fire-residents-return-to-mountain -shadows/38849/#name%20here.

INDEX

ABC News, 29, 58, 72, 90, 95, 154; affiliates, 22, 53, 151

Alabama, 7, 18, 28, 65, 67, 68, 148, 151

Allen, Thad, 57

Amos, Jim, 38, 52, 54, 84, 89

Anderson, Julie, 95, 117, 119, 120, 124

Anderson, Kathy, 63, 64

Arredondo, Carl, 30, 33

Banks, Logan, 37, 38, 41

Baton Rouge, 5, 7, 16, 17, 18, 20, 22, 25, 26, 29, 41, 133, 140; media outlets, 37–39, 51, 122; River Center, 7, 19–20, 26, 145

Belo Corporation, 29, 38, 53, 56, 146

Bethany World Prayer Center, 20

Biloxi *Sun Herald*, 37, 42, 89, 90, 91, 92, 100, 104

Blanco, Kathleen, 5, 91, 97

BP (British Petroleum), 115, 140; media relations, 55, 57–58, 60–61, 136, 138–39; public campaign, 3, 5, 61, 70, 135–36; spill response, 58, 95–96, 98

Brown, Michael, 86

Buffet, Warren, 149, 150

Bush, George W., 82, 83, 84, 85, 89, 90, 94, 96

Bustamante, Lucy, 37, 44, 46, 50

CBS News, 29, 41, 56, 58, 116, 140; affiliates, 53, 71, 126, 141, 151

Cell phone, 15, 21, 27, 29, 43

Civic journalism, 9, 66, 154

Clear Channel New Orleans, 39, 40, 48, 88

CNN, 40, 72; anchors, 77, 119, 134; coverage, 57–58

Coast Guard, 57, 58, 60, 61, 95, 98, 105, 115, 128, 135, 136

Coastal wetlands, 62, 139, 146

Cohen, David, 27, 73

Communications blackout, 10, 15, 16, 20, 22, 25, 26, 27, 29, 34, 74, 100

Community: and local media, 31, 40, 65–68, 73–75, 80, 85–86, 92; sense of, 45–49, 145–47

Compass, Eddie, 45, 112

Cooper, Anderson, 15, 23, 49, 57, 58, 119, 121, 134, 151

Cowen, Scott, 65, 66

Crisis communication, 33, 145, 148, 153; plan, 33, 72, 155; training, 47, 121, 153, 154

Dahmen, Nicole, 6

Dallas, 17, 28, 38, 53

Deepwater Horizon Disaster, 3, 89, 94, 95, 98, 114, 115, 116, 120, 123, 135, 136, 139, 145, 153; access for journalists, 11, 55, 56, 57, 58, 59, 60, 61, 64, 95, 96, 136, 138, 143, 146; blowout, 34, 120; clean up, 12, 62, 70, 97, 140, 142, 146, 155; crisis, 139; fire, 115, 138, 139, 140, 141, 142, 155; frames, 57, 61, 70, 115, 116, 118; gusher, 6, 9, 10, 12, 61, 71, 94, 95, 96, 116, 135, 136, 138, 142, 143; prevention, 4, 98, 139; sourcing, 58, 99, 114, 115, 116, 117, 118, 119, 124; spill, 34, 53, 55–59, 61, 63–64, 115–17, 123, 126, 135–38, 140, 142, 143, 153; visuals, 95, 96, 99, 115, 137, 138, 139, 141, 142

Defillo, Marlon, 45, 110, 111

D'Elia, Chris, 117, 122, 123
Demographics: Deepwater Horizon, 7, 115,
    143; Katrina evacuees/victims, 10, 15,
    16, 17, 18, 19, 20, 22, 24, 25, 30, 32, 44, 45,
    130, 143; Katrina media use, 20, 21, 22,
    23, 24, 25, 26, 27, 28, 29, 34, 53, 145, 147
Disaster news coverage, 8, 12, 13, 80;
    communication, 8, 10, 21, 24, 29, 33,
    34, 39, 72, 145, 152, 153; frames, 11, 12,
    57, 68, 69, 70, 71, 75, 76, 79, 80, 111,
    114, 115, 130, 131, 132, 133, 145; local,
    18, 24, 25, 29, 31, 32, 52, 57–59, 67, 72,
    73, 74, 75, 118, 119, 149, 150, 151, 152;
    national, 8, 9, 11, 21, 24, 25, 29, 32, 51,
    52, 57, 58, 59, 72, 73, 118, 119; 24-hour,
    41, 52, 56, 104, 128, 148
Dispersants, 7, 116, 117, 123
Donley, John, 42
Donze, Frank, 58
Dowie, Rob, 7
Duke, David, 4

Elie, Lolis, 66, 67
Entercom, 39, 48, 51, 88
Evacuees. See Demographics
Exxon Valdez, 94, 116, 142

Facebook, 15, 41, 125, 126, 139, 148, 155
FDA, 123
FEMA, 20, 46, 86, 90, 128
Flooding, 13, 18, 22, 25, 37, 40, 45, 47, 54,
    77, 101, 102, 103, 104, 105, 114, 127, 133
Florida, 4, 7, 18, 22, 139
Fox News, 23, 25, 41, 71, 72, 134
Framing: effects, 69, 70, 75, 76, 77, 133,
    145; episodic, 69, 70, 75, 76, 78, 155;
    media frames, 11, 12, 57, 61, 68, 71, 76,
    77, 79, 81, 92, 94, 98, 115, 116, 130, 131,
    132, 133, 139; thematic, 69, 70, 75, 76,
    78, 92, 142
Franchi, Christy, 101
French Quarter, 3, 101

Gaddy, Peggy, 36
Glover, Henry, 109, 110, 113, 114
Government Response: blame, 9, 85, 86,
    90, 92, 94, 95, 97, 98, 99; Deepwater
    Horizon, 12, 94, 95, 96, 97, 98, 119, 139;
    Katrina, 12, 40, 71, 84, 85, 86, 87, 90,
    109, 132
Gulf Coast. See Narratives

Haag, Marty, 146
Haiti earthquake, 22, 26, 151
Hammack, Don, 104
Held, Kevin, 41
Hoss, Mike, 48, 74, 77, 104, 105
Houston, 17, 20, 64, 100
Hurricanes: Andrew, 3, 4; category, 4, 33;
    Katrina, 13, 16, 22, 29, 37, 40, 50, 53,
    55, 75, 77, 81, 90, 91, 108, 114, 136, 143,
    148; knowledge, 10, 33, 34, 72; Rita,
    51, 92

Iconic, 13, 125, 127, 128, 129, 131, 132, 133,
    134, 135, 138, 139, 143, 144
Internet: digital divide, 25, 29, 148; impact
    during disaster, 15, 21, 28, 29, 30, 40,
    41, 42, 60, 73, 155; use, 15, 19, 20, 21, 22,
    28, 29, 30, 31, 41, 42, 148

Jindal, Bobby, 5, 97
Journalism: accuracy, 9, 10, 61, 68, 84,
    100, 104, 106, 119, 146, 153, 154;
    audience, 9, 11, 42, 45, 46, 52, 56,
    69, 71, 74, 75, 77, 78, 80, 81, 115, 122,
    143, 154, 155; broadcast, 48, 54, 71,
    76, 120; fourth estate, 8, 67; local
    reporters, 11, 42, 43, 48, 52; norms
    and routines, 30, 31, 39, 40, 43, 47,
    52, 55, 61, 69, 76; objectivity, 11, 68,
    154; parachute journalists, 13, 51, 52,
    57, 58, 63, 71, 80, 145, 155; predicted
    future, 8, 50, 51, 52, 54, 156. See also
    Print; Radio

Katrina: during/impact phase, 21, 24, 28, 29, 72, 73, 80, 100, 101, 146, 147; evacuation, 17, 18, 19, 20, 21, 22, 23, 24, 25, 26, 27, 28; frames, 11, 12, 75, 76, 130, 131, 132, 133; pre-, 2, 15, 16; post-, 2, 15, 17, 22, 24, 33, 43, 44, 46, 48, 49, 50, 52, 64, 91, 108, 109, 112, 114, 135, 149; sourcing, 99, 100, 101, 104, 105, 106, 108, 109, 114, 124; visuals, 128, 129, 132, 135
KGLA, 105
Knowledge gap, 32
Kovacs, Peter, 36, 71, 120, 122

Lampila, Lucina, 94, 118, 121
Landrieu, Mitch, 66, 93, 149
Lauer, Matt, 82, 83, 84
Lee, Trymaine, 42, 43, 45, 46, 47, 48
Long, Huey, 4, 5
Looting, 44, 75, 87, 102, 103, 111, 112, 130, 131, 132
Louisiana: community, 28, 54, 58, 61, 66, 77; reality shows, 5, 14, 151; stereotypes, 3, 4, 5, 6, 7, 131, 132, 151
Louisiana State University, 19, 22, 34, 37, 59, 94, 116, 117, 118, 121, 123, 124, 127
Loyola, 59, 97, 116, 118

Magandy, Kate, 42, 104
Mann, Bob, 4, 5, 6, 7, 148
Manship School of Mass Communication, 37, 127
Mathews, Ricky, 67, 68, 91
McCann, Keenon, 109
McConnell, John, 51
McCusker, John, 45, 46
McManus, John, 39
McQuaid, John, 42
Media use trends, 10, 20, 21, 22, 23, 24, 25, 26, 27, 28, 29, 35, 39, 41
Meeks, David, 30, 49, 50, 104, 108
Milling, Anne, 66

Mississippi, 3, 6, 7, 17, 18, 22, 28, 80, 89, 91, 92, 107, 133, 151
Mississippi River, 18, 85, 113
Mix, Kurt, 98

Nagin, Ray, 39, 84, 85, 86, 88, 89, 91, 92, 93, 101, 105, 112, 130
Narratives: Gulf Coast, 4, 6, 8, 9, 11, 12; Katrina, 19–20, 109, 113, 122, 131; Oil Spill, 95–96, 98, 116, 118–20, 126
National Association of Television Program Executives, 53
National Guard, 44, 45, 64, 88, 97, 105
National Hurricane Center, 41
NBC News, 22, 29, 58, 59, 82, 83, 151
New media: consumption, 23, 29, 30, 53, 149; possible effects, 40, 54, 73, 144, 148, 149; technological advancements, 15, 16, 19, 25, 29, 30, 31, 40, 74; use, 29, 39, 40, 52, 53, 54, 126
New Orleans, 4, 6; police department, 104, 109, 110–13; population, 45, 53; Superdome, 20, 23, 40, 44, 51, 56, 76, 85, 86, 88, 130, 132, 133
Ninth Ward, 33, 44, 100, 101, 103, 135, 143, 154
NOLA.com, 15, 40, 41, 42, 43, 71, 73, 100

Obama, Barack, 9, 12, 89, 94, 95, 96, 97, 98, 115
O'Byrne, James, 40, 41, 71, 73
Oil, 3, 6, 7, 9, 10, 138, 139, 140, 141, 142, 143, 144, 153, 155
Oiled pelican, 95, 135, 136, 137, 141, 142, 155
Orlando, 22
Overton, Ed, 118, 119, 120, 121, 123

Phelps, Ashton, Jr., 38
Pierre, Monica, 40, 48, 49, 50, 88
Print, 40, 50, 54, 65, 76, 120, 147

Race, 11, 33, 75, 83
Radio, 20–22, 25, 26, 28, 33, 43, 48, 51, 53, 65, 73, 84, 87, 88, 101, 102, 104, 105, 145, 151
Red Cross, 7, 88, 135
Refugees, 45, 68
Rivera, Geraldo, 23, 71, 134
Roberts, Robin, 80
Roberts, Sally-Ann, 80
Robinette, Garland, 39, 40, 51, 84, 87, 92
Rooftop rescue, 27, 103, 128, 129, 131
Rose, Chris, 36, 37, 42, 44, 47, 54, 55
Rowher, Frank, 94, 120, 121, 122
RTDNA, 53
Russell, Gordon, 49, 51, 79, 93, 106, 111, 112

Save the Picayune, 65, 66, 68, 80
Schleifstein, Mark, 42
Schudson, Michael, 39
Schweikert, Ernesto, 105, 106
Science communication, 72, 116, 117, 120, 121
Science knowledge, 35, 60, 114, 116, 117, 118, 121, 122, 124
Shipka, Danny, 5, 6
Slaughter, Chris, 30, 31, 40, 71, 72, 73, 126, 127, 134
Socioeconomic status, 25, 69, 75, 143, 148, 149
Sources: "man on the street," 12, 100, 106, 108, 114, 115, 124, 154; official, 12, 99, 100, 104, 105, 106, 108, 112, 114, 124; scientists, 12, 59, 60, 97, 114, 116, 118, 119, 120, 121, 122; unofficial, 100, 101, 106, 108, 113, 114
Storytelling, 6, 9, 12, 124, 127, 143, 146, 153, 156

Television: depictions, 5; use, 18, 22–23
Texas, 4, 7, 10, 17, 28
Texting, 15, 21, 22, 29, 30, 43, 60, 155

Thibodeaux, Ron, 110, 111, 112
Thomas, Bob, 59, 97, 116, 118, 119, 120, 122
Times-Picayune, 37, 40, 54; changes, 65–68, 147–48; coverage, 42–44, 84–85, 89–94, 96, 100–105, 108–10, 112, 120, 122; staff, 38, 50–52, 63–64, 79
Tiner, Stan, 89
Tsunami, in Fukushima, Japan, 152
Tuchman, Gaye, 39
Tulane University, 65, 116
Twitter, 15, 41, 125, 126, 155

Underwater video of oil leak, 60, 95, 139, 141

Victims, 4, 6, 8, 11, 35, 69, 127, 130, 142, 143
Visuals: Deepwater Horizon Disaster, 137, 138, 141; interpreting images, 130; Katrina, 128, 129

Wagner-Bolger, Phyllis, 101
Walker, Dave, 6
Walsh, Bill, 90
WAPT-TV, 22
WBRZ, 29
WDSU, 22, 151
WESH, 22
West, Kanye, 82, 83, 84, 94
West Bank, 18, 37, 105
WGNO, 29
"What a story," 39
Wildlife, 34, 35, 60, 62, 63, 97, 99, 117, 123, 124, 137, 139
WLOX, 151
WWL-TV, 27, 29, 30, 33, 37, 40, 41, 44, 48, 50, 53, 56, 65, 66, 68, 71, 72, 73, 74, 77, 80, 104, 126, 127, 141
WXXV, 151

Yahoo, 29, 31, 41, 65

CPSIA information can be obtained at www.ICGtesting.com
Printed in the USA
BVOW08*1042171215

429351BV00003B/12/P